Life of the Party

Life of the Party

THE REMARKABLE STORY OF HOW
BROWNIE WISE BUILT, AND LOST,
A TUPPERWARE PARTY EMPIRE

PREVIOUSLY PUBLISHED AS *TUPPERWARE UNSEALED*

Bob Kealing

CROWN
ARCHETYPE
NEW YORK

Photos on pages ii, 4, 9, 19, 21, 36, 58, 63, 79, 85, 91, 94, 100, 102, 108,
122, 124, 143, 163, 168, 245: Smithsonian Institution. Page xvi: Orange
County Regional Historical Center. Page 247: John and Sharroll Waugh.

Originally published in hardcover as *Tupperware Unsealed* by
the University Press of Florida, 2008.

Library of Congress Cataloging-in-Publication Data
Names: Kealing, Bob, author.
Title: Life of the party: the remarkable story of how Brownie Wise built,
and lost, a Tupperware party empire / Bob Kealing.
Other titles: Tupperware unsealed
Description: New York: Crown Archetype, 2016. | Originally published
in 2008 by University Press of Florida as: Tupperware unsealed.
Identifiers: LCCN 2015048495 | ISBN 9781101903650 (hardback)
Subjects: LCSH: Tupperware Corporation—History. | Tupperware Home
Parties—History. | Wise, Brownie. | Tupper, Earl Silas. |
BISAC: BIOGRAPHY & AUTOBIOGRAPHY / Women.
Classification: LCC HD9662.C664 T865 2016 |
DDC 338.7/668497092273—dc23
LC record available: http://lccn.loc.gov/2015048495

ISBN 978-1-101-90365-0
eBook ISBN 978-1-101-90366-7

Printed in the United States of America

Jacket design by Elena Giavaldi
Front jacket photograph: Brownie Wise Papers, Archives Center, National
Museum of American History, Smithsonian Institution

1 3 5 7 9 10 8 6 4 2

First Revised Edition

In memory of
JAMES L. KEALING
and
DONNA ROSS

It may be the most brilliant marketing scheme ever devised, for it is based less on sales pitch than on friendship.

—Morley Safer, *60 Minutes*

Believe me, there can be no better thing in your life than the ability to wish, sincerely, to improve the world about you.

—Brownie Wise, *Best Wishes, Brownie Wise*

Contents

Life of the Party

Prologue

For Brownie Wise, January 29, 1958, began unremarkably; it was just another of the sunny central Florida mornings to which she had long become accustomed. As the day's heat started to set in, she pulled away from her fashionable lakeside home and navigated her trademark pink convertible on its usual route—Kings Highway, Neptune Road, and finally Orange Blossom Trail—toward the Tupperware headquarters she had helped to build. Now the head of the company's Home Party Division, the forty-four-year-old, divorced single mother with an eye for fashion and flair had come up with the definitive method to sell Earl Tupper's revolutionary product and then guided his company's explosive growth.

Since Wise had perfected her approach—selling Tupperware through home parties that showcased a feminine, social, soft-sell approach—the world of direct selling had never been the same. From Hilo to Bangor, Battle Creek to Sante Fe, Americans were buying the money-saving pastel products in record numbers. By 1958, Tupperware boasted more than ten thousand dealers and $10 million in annual sales (which would be more than $80 million today).

"Build the people," Wise preached, "and they'll build the business."

Many dealers idolized Wise as a kind of fairy godmother who spoke of wishing, not as whimsy or as psychobabble, but as a road map to success. In return, the dealers held

Tupperware parties with sick children or ailing parents in the other room, pushing themselves to their physical limit in hopes of reveling in her presence and praise. These devoted dealers, in turn, inspired Wise to wake early each morning and grind out new ways to motivate the sales force to push their numbers higher.

Now arriving at Tupperware's headquarters, Wise pulled into her parking space and prepared herself for another day. Leaving her convertible behind, she walked up to the front doors, and then back to her office, saying bright hellos to staff she met on the way. The chorus of responses she received left no doubt who Brownie Wise was, and who was in charge. However, beneath her assured countenance lay the stress of a tense standoff she'd been in with her boss—one that had put her career at risk. But she would have plenty of time to worry about that later. Right now, she had Tupperware to sell.

Earl Tupper, on the other hand, never made grand entrances. Instead, Tupperware's eccentric Yankee inventor seemed to blow in and out of central Florida like afternoon thunderstorms sparked by a July sea breeze. He didn't care much for the razzle-dazzle of Brownie Wise's Home Party Division, the company's sales arm that had helped him rake in millions. Nor did he enjoy the high-octane dealer pep rally known as the annual Tupperware Jubilee. The only picture Tupperware photographer Jack McCollum remembered taking of Tupper was of him sliding in the company's back door. The cloak-and-dagger stuff, everyone knew, was just his way.

So when the phone had rung at the homes of top Tupperware executives Hamer Wilson and Gary McDonald on an otherwise unremarkable Monday morning, they had been surprised to hear Tupper announce that he was in town—and that they should meet him the next morning, January 29, 1958, at the Angebilt Hotel in downtown Orlando. Must be good news, McDonald had thought; maybe Tupper had a new idea or, better yet, a secret invention that he wanted to share with them. He had no inkling of the bomb his boss was about to drop.

Tupper had left behind gale warnings and heavy snows in the Northeast for balmy, chamber-of-commerce weather in the outdoorsman's paradise that was central Florida in those days. On a cloudless January morning like this one, a fisherman could run a Carolina-rigged finesse worm along the Kissimmee grass in Lake Tohopekaliga—Toho for short—and with any luck snag one of the best bass in the state. On some of the plentiful rangelands near Tupperware's Orange Blossom Trail headquarters, cowboys could ride by the compass for miles without seeing an inch of paved road.

To the east, along the sweeping expanse of sand, swamp, and sunning alligators, bedeviled navy scientists on the fledgling Space Coast had been frustrated yet again in their attempts to send a tiny earth satellite into space. This time the Martin Vanguard rocket had developed mechanical faults. A month earlier, another version had barely cleared the launchpad when it burst into a million fiery bits. The explosion, reflected in the sunglasses of spectators, made for a classic photo in *Life* magazine.

Neither the Space Race nor relaxing in the Florida sunshine were on Earl Tupper's mind, however, as he arrived at the Angebilt, a familiar sight in Orlando's diminutive skyline. Built in 1923 for $1 million, Joseph Fenner Ange's eleven-story creation was about the only building Orlandoans could call a skyscraper. Its massive, wrought iron–framed canopy with scrolled brackets made for an impressive front entrance to one of the city's few grand hotels. In its heyday in the 1920s and 1930s, the Angebilt had attracted international guests visiting North America's cockfighting capital. Now, WLOF blasted 250 watts of top-40 radio from its mezzanine, ensuring that the number one hit that week, "At the Hop" by Danny and the Juniors, could be heard all the way down to Kissimmee. For Tupper, though, the Angebilt simply provided a neutral spot to meet with two of his most important deputies.

The Angebilt Hotel in downtown Orlando, site of the fateful January 1958 meeting of Earl Tupper, Hamer Wilson, and Gary McDonald.

Still in his late twenties, redheaded wunderkind Gary McDonald already had more than a decade of sales know-how under his belt. He'd worked his way up selling mops and cleaning products to suburban housewives. By 1958 he was an up-and-coming executive at one of the most celebrated direct-selling companies in America. He knew how to whip up a crowd, recruit loyal dealers, and find new ways to recognize their success.

Sales counselor Hamer Wilson was older and had a wider array of real-world business experience. He had spent most of his three years with Tupperware on the road building relationships with those crucial to the company's home party business: the dealers, managers, and distributors. He had a gift for remembering not just their names but also those of their spouses and children. His low-key approach, sense of humor, and genial smile had earned him considerable notice in his short time with the company.

As ordered, McDonald and Wilson made their way to their boss's hotel room, where the prematurely bald but imposing inventor greeted them. Never one for small talk that exceeded "Good morning," Tupper showed great loyalty to obedient and competent employees and a swift, iron hand to anyone who crossed him. He was direct, even to the point of being harsh. But you knew where you stood with Earl Tupper.

When Tupper convened the meeting, one key player was conspicuously absent: Brownie Wise. In her seven years as head of Tupper's Home Party Division, Wise had guided Tupperware to millions of dollars in sales and earned a reputation as a tough executive who could go head-to-head with strong-minded male underlings during the day, and then throw the perfect Tupperware party by night.

A master motivator and communicator, Wise was the yin to Earl Tupper's yang. Where he was fussy and reclusive, Wise lived to mingle with and inspire the dealer workforce. She was one of the few people who felt confident enough to speak her mind with Tupper, even going so far as to dress him down if she felt it necessary. If one of his products seemed like it would be easy to sell, her enthusiasm would be infectious.

But not all of his ideas were Wonder Bowls. When he pitched something impractical like the Wigloo, the job often fell to Wise to talk him out of it.

Decades before female tycoons Martha Stewart and Oprah Winfrey, Wise had also inspired in her Tupperware dealers a kind of religious devotion to their work. She promised them a better life, and they adored her to the point of competing to win her clothing, even if it meant dropping significant pounds to fit into an actual Brownie Wise dress. Her image as a trailblazing executive had been carefully crafted by the top Tupperware brass and then churned off their remarkable public relations assembly line. The press loved to write about the doting single mother and strong-willed chief executive who had built a home-party empire. Some of it was true; other parts, pure puffery. But it didn't matter. In just seven years, Brownie Wise had become a direct-selling legend, instrumental in making Tupperware an American revolution.

If Tupper had a big announcement to make, it made no sense to Wilson and McDonald that Wise wasn't there to react to it.

"I need to talk to you guys about something that's gonna happen and it's gonna happen today and it's gonna involve the two of you," Tupper told his executives. "I have had enough of Brownie Wise, and I'm going down there to headquarters and I'm going to tell her this is her last day."

The revelation met with stunned silence from McDonald and Wilson. "That was a bombshell," McDonald remembered. "We were shocked beyond saying anything."

Over the course of the past decade, and from a long, comfortable distance—usually over the telephone—the odd couple of Earl Tupper and Brownie Wise had managed to overcome their differences to build something far bigger than both of their formidable personalities.

Tupperware had swept across America in the 1950s like a flash fire. The Bell Tumblers, Wonder Bowls, and two-ounce Midget containers had become as common in American households as television, telephones, and hula hoops. Gatherings of suburban housewives playing games and exchanging gossip were central to the product's combustible growth and popularity, and to some, the "Tupperware Lady" in her hose, hat, heels, and gloves seemed to personify the feminine housewife ideal of the *Father Knows Best* 1950s.

In a very nonthreatening way, however, the Tupperware phenomenon was changing expectations of what women could achieve. One sale at a time, housewives were finding an economic niche all their own outside the household. Tupperware executives had the shrewd notion—untried in any organization before them—that women would power the engine of this home-selling revolution. And they did. Along the way, the company inspired people to be more successful than they ever thought possible, while encouraging them to help friends do the very same thing.

And yet, while Wise and Tupper had succeeded by asking dealers to help one another, their own relationship was marred by jealousy, hubris, and hurt feelings. Reporter Charles Fishman once called them "a pair of geniuses always on the brink." It was an apt description, for they had waged their battles in the past. This time, though, their fraught business relationship had fractured beyond repair.

"She's fired," Tupper said, the unexpected words ringing in McDonald's ears like shock waves. "And I want all evidence of her gone."

In the years that followed, Tupper would go on to reap

a fortune, while Wise would fade into obscurity with a pittance—unfairly, some would argue. But right now, Tupper was the president; Tupperware was his product; and in 1958 corporate America, he held all the power. Inconceivable as Wise's departure might have been only a few years earlier, on this January morning at the Angebilt, Earl Tupper was determined to solve his "Brownie Wise problem" once and for all.

Going It Alone

Had it not been for professional and personal setbacks early in the lives of Brownie Wise and Earl Tupper, the rise and spread of Tupperware might never have happened. Each forged a path toward the other out of the residue of failure and frustration.

For Wise, a young Detroit divorcée without much business experience, a failed marriage and a child to support fueled an endless drive to succeed, gleaned from the generations of women in her family who had gotten by without men in their lives. For Tupper, a bankrupted tree surgeon who fancied himself a modern-day Leonardo da Vinci, a trail of unsuccessful inventions only sparked his curious mind further and made his pursuit of a proprietary product more dogged.

Together, Wise's sales know-how and Tupper's innovation would create the unlikely alchemy at the heart of Tupperware's success. The pair didn't look at the world the way most people did, which was initially their curse, and ultimately their genius.

Brownie May Humphrey was born May 25, 1913, in Buford, Georgia, a small town near Atlanta, to plumber Jerome Humphrey and Rose Stroud Humphrey. They called their baby "Brownie" after her strikingly beautiful brown eyes, easily her most prominent feature.

The mores of the time called for working Southern mothers to quit their jobs once children came along, but Rose had no intention of becoming a housewife. Employed by a local hat factory, she not only went back to work as soon as she could, she immersed herself in union organizing, a job that required extensive travel and speechmaking.

At times, the work could be risky. When union workers went out on strike for better pay or working conditions, employers brought in strike breakers to cross picket lines and often endured violent clashes with union strongmen. Rose soldiered on nonetheless, but there was a price to pay back home. Within two years she and Jerome split up, leaving more pressure on Rose to support her only child.

Given her mother's busy schedule, young Brownie was often left in the care of her aunt Pearl in Atlanta for months at a time. She also spent a great deal of her childhood with her grandmother, the woman she later credited with galvanizing her self-motivating mantra—what Brownie liked to call "the gospel of gumption."

"My grandfather had died when their youngest of seven children was three and their future became her lone responsibility," Wise reflected. "Grandmother raised them all without appreciable help." By choice and fate, Brownie's mother and grandmother showed her that a woman could make it without a man in her life.

Along with her mother and grandmother, Brownie had plenty of cousins and uncles with whom she enjoyed simple pastimes, such as fishing, as a child. On Sundays, it was a special treat for her to hear the local African-American congregation sing their soul-stirring hymns. Conventional schooling, however, bored her. Instead, she read about fashion and tried to dress up like the models she saw in magazines. Brownie, a cousin remarked, "liked to primp."

In her teens, she dropped out of school to find her own way in life. She reunited with her mother, and by fourteen Brownie was giving speeches at union rallies herself. Through these speeches, she became a confident public speaker, polished her powers of persuasion, and developed empathy for the problems facing working women just before the onset of the Great Depression.

In 1931, she attended a Young Women's Christian Association camp in New Orleans for girls intent on pursuing business careers. During her stay she credited a Methodist minister from Shreveport, Reverend James Grambling, for inspiring her to keep moving forward despite perceived roadblocks.

"Each time that I have seen the sign at the end of the road," she wrote, "I have remembered the simple advice from Reverend Grambling. There were times when that highway to happiness seemed closed forever." That she looked up to and took advice from an African-American, albeit a man of God, was audacious and unconventional given the strict racial divide in the segregated South of the early 1930s.

In her late teens, Wise briefly considered a career in law, but settled on becoming a writer and illustrator. Her life change came in 1936 when at twenty-two she entered and won a contest to paint a mural at the Texas Centennial celebration in Dallas. The award brought with it a free pass for her to travel throughout the impressive array of exhibits, one of them put on by the Ford Motor Company and managed by a junior executive named Robert Whitcomb Wise.

To say Robert could charm women was an understatement,

but his appeal came with an edge. "When he was good, he was very good," his daughter Clorinda Sheridan remembered. "But when he was bad, he was pure evil." Brownie was smitten with Wise's stocky, rugged good looks and outgoing personality, and six months after they met, on December 15, 1936, she and Robert were married. The newlyweds made their home in Detroit, a mecca for any young executive looking to work his way up in the automotive industry.

Brownie Wise in Detroit, ca. 1945.

On her twenty-fifth birthday, May 25, 1938, Brownie Wise become a mother. Childbirth proved difficult, and doctors were forced to use forceps to help bring Jerry Wise into the world. The instrument took off the tip of the baby's left ear and gave him a permanent scar just above his left eyebrow. Despite the challenging labor, giving birth seemed to infuse Brownie with a new sense of wonder and responsibility.

"Having a child is like being given a second life to live—we see so much and feel so much and learn so much through their eyes and hearts," Wise wrote. "Nothing is quite so awesome as watching tiny hands reach out from the bassinet to first grasp this inexplicable mixture of life and love and want and achievement we mortals call Life. The blessing of having my own boy I shall never take for granted." Soon after, her mother Rose moved to Detroit to help Brownie with her baby.

Joyful as Jerry's birth was, however, it would be the only bright spot in what became a turbulent marriage. On his best days, Robert Wise was known by his friends as the ultimate "Good-time Charlie"; at his parties, everyone was welcome. But with his two strong-minded women and a baby at home, Robert often stayed out drinking until the good-time side of him was gone. Robert's daughter from a later marriage, Clorinda, also suspected that he lived most of his life with undiagnosed bipolar disorder, which brought about mood swings and violence. One of his most disturbing episodes involved him throwing a bottle of acid at his mother-in-law. Although he missed, the acid hit her 1939 Plymouth sedan, eating a hole through the upholstery and chassis.

Brownie knew this was no environment in which to raise her son, and less than five years into her marriage, she filed for divorce. In a child-support agreement dated September 17, 1941, the district court of Wayne County, Michigan, awarded her custody of her three-year-old son. The judge granted Robert Wise one visit per week. Before long, Robert had a new wife and a baby on the way and was increasingly bypassing his weekly visits with Jerry, until they stopped altogether.

Three months after the divorce, the Japanese bombed Pearl

Harbor, and the United States entered World War II. Brownie and Jerry Wise became like many women and children in wartime America, doing without husbands and fathers and trying to determine their next step.

Like Brownie Wise, Earl Silas Tupper wasn't long on formal education, barely graduating from Fitchburg High School in Fitchburg, Massachusetts, in 1925. Born to agrarian New Englander parents in 1907, Tupper showed a knack for invention and innovation early on, however. Ever the tinkerer, he developed means for improving work life on his family's farm, including his first known patent, a frame that made cleaning chickens easier. At ten years old, Tupper also realized that he could sell more of the family's produce by peddling it directly to customers, door-to-door. What he lacked in schooling, he compensated for in ambition, making it his goal to become a millionaire by age thirty.

In 1928, Tupper founded his first business, a landscaping and nursery enterprise called Tupper Tree Doctors, and in 1931 he married Marie Whitcomb. While his business and personal lives were taking shape, Tupper poured much of his passion into a notebook he used to sketch new ideas for inventions. Below a cartoon of another inventive genius, Thomas Jefferson, Tupper wrote: "DaVinci, Jefferson, Edison and a host of others are proof that an inventive, intuitive, enthusiastic and trained mind continues to experiment, study, search and develop along an entire line of human endeavor, conceiving developments in every field to which it turns."

Long before Tupperware, the young inventor drew up "No

Drip" ice-cream cones equipped with a gutter to catch the drippings and funnel them back into the cone. The "Dagger Comb" came with a clip to fit nicely on bathing suits. Tupper even devised a way to perform an appendectomy without leaving a scar. None of these inventions had the kind of mass appeal that could earn Earl Tupper a living, but he loved looking at how things worked and devising ways to make them work better.

The deepening Depression chipped away at people's spirits and their businesses, however, and the malaise took a toll in Tupper's hometown of Shirley, Massachusetts. People no longer had the disposable income to spend on trees and landscaping, and after a positive start, Tupper Tree Doctors went bankrupt in 1936. With his wife and young sons, Ronald and Myles, to support, Tupper decided to pursue his fortune in nearby Leominster, a town already known as America's "Pioneer Plastics City."

The year before, Tupper had been introduced to a man named Bernard Doyle, founder of DuPont's plastics manufacturing division known as Viscoloid. Accepting a job there in 1937, Tupper started small, making sixty cents an hour in the company's experiment and development department. Despite the meager wages, the experience he acquired from seasoned pros in the plastics business was invaluable. "That's when my education really began," he reflected.

After about a year, Tupper broke away from Viscoloid and founded his own industrial plastics company. To say the young entrepreneur was dedicated to the work is an understatement. According to an unpublished biographical sketch in Tupper's papers, he "would often stay at the molding machine 22 hours per day, 2–5 days at a time, breaking only to eat and to sleep on a cot next to the machine." During one stretch, he suffered a serious injury that almost cost him his sight in one eye.

With the onset of World War II in the following years, Tupper expanded his business, opening his first plant. Located in Farnumsville, Massachussets, Tupper Plastics sprawled forty-five thousand square feet and churned out parts for an array of wartime materials: jeeps, gas masks, and navy signal lamps. Three shifts of workers kept the molding machines humming away. It was a time of supply shortages, self-sacrifice, and Rosie the Riveter. As men streamed to war by the millions, American women entered the workforce out of necessity.

With Robert Wise out of the picture, Brownie, Jerry, and Rose made their home at 845 North Melborn Street in Dearborn, Michigan, the Detroit suburb best known as the home of Henry Ford. A carpenter finished the attic so that Brownie could use it as both a bedroom and a sewing room, where she and her mother made all their own clothes. Rose liked to tend the large garden they planted in the lot next door, and often turned the rhubarb crop into wine. Young Jerry hated the smell, but during the war Rose could trade it for something they didn't have, like butter, which was in short supply. Jerry passed the time in the basement, playing with the big train set he had situated on top of nine sheets of plywood.

In wartime, the family got rid of the sewing machines and turned the attic into bedrooms for airmen who needed a place to live. During the worst part of the war, their basement became a first-aid center for wounded soldiers, and the home next door, a hospital. During this time Brownie took a job as an executive secretary to the general manager at Bendix, the company manufacturing brakes and struts for the *Avenger*, a navy torpedo plane. Now on her own, Wise was stretching her wings in other ways, as well. Draftsmen were in short supply, so Wise studied drafting at Detroit City College and became proficient in mechanical drawing in a matter of weeks.

Brownie Wise in her early days as a divorced executive secretary at Bendix, ca. 1947.

In the little spare time her schedule afforded, Brownie enjoyed playing the violin and sax and listening to patriotic songs. More often than not, though, in her rare moments of rest, she could be found in her favorite chair as she indulged in a more creative passion, writing.

Brownie's thoughts on the life she aspired to lead appear in a notebook from the 1940s: "I was searching for a basic premise on which to plan my life. I was trying to piece together some of the many lessons I learned from my mother, my teachers, my ministers, old friends," Wise wrote. "I wanted to work and expected to work hard to build a successful life. Not just money—but to be a success in dealing with people, bringing Jerry up and to find an inner sense of accomplishment. I was fiercely determined to draw a blueprint for this as I had done for my home. I wanted to be a *successful human being.*"

Her correspondence didn't end with letters or personal journals. Wise also wrote an advice column in a local newspaper under the pen name Hibiscus, a favorite flower often found in the sunny reaches of Florida. With "something lovely on the radio awfully late," she wrote, "I feel a writing jag coming to life." As snowflakes "the size of silver dollars" drifted past her Melborn Street window, Hibiscus blossomed:

> The earth holds its breath when it's snowing as it is tonight— death could be no more quiet. . . . Nor more beautiful, either. Even the swish of auto tires on the streets is muted, and people pass to and fro under the warm circle of street-light without making a sound. The evergreens, especially the long needled Scotch and Austrian pines, are already coated heavily—they look as though some giant hand had picked them up, and dipped them upside down in marshmallow frosting. I love walking in the new snow, before the dirge of snow shovels sets in—a form of conceit, I suppose, if you look deeply enough into it, to want to make tracks where none have been made before.

As Hibiscus, Wise commented on wartime strife: "I have despaired at each new war bulletin and prayed to God for something better for his children; I have watched the sun go down in a riot of breathless color, and seen the moon rise over the crest of a little hill, like a benediction to a day. I have done many things lately; life is full and rich and beautiful to your Hibiscus."

In her fictional world, Wise created a devoted husband she named "Coeur" and a great palace of a home called Lovehaven. The Hibiscus letters foreshadow many of the techniques Wise would later use to inspire the Tupperware faithful by creating a kind of idealized, shared existence with her readers:

> I thought, as I swung open the door, of what a grave responsibility Coeur had placed upon us who will live in this house. A haven of love it must always be. I stood a moment in the wide reception hall, thinking of the many feet that will tread those tiles, of the friends who would come bringing us cheer and gaiety, and a corner of my heart hoped that if any came in search of encouragement or happiness they would never fail to find it.

In real life, Wise had held a torch for a South Carolina doctor named Wade C. Marshall. On a mid-July night, with Pat, her Boston bull terrier, snoring at her side, she sat down at the typewriter. "Wade Dearest, a waning moon is caught in the tops of little elms down in the lower corner of my garden now," Wise observed. "Is it the inference of the train whistle, I wonder, that brings you so close tonight? You might be sitting in that big chair over there by the window, with a pipe in your hand, for all the closeness I feel about you—and yet time and distance have taken away the certainty of what your smile is actually like."

In the same letter, Wise praised her long-distance love as someone who would never have a "satisfied" life. "You'll always be seeking the bit of life that's just around the next curve in the road, and that's how it should be," Wise observed. "You not only dream but you seek—and consequently life will be very rich for you."

Brownie might as well have been writing about herself here, and soon after, her own mix of curiosity and necessity inspired her to set out on a new path. Prevailing stereotypes about women, as well as her lack of formal education, could have tempered her ambition, but Brownie had a young son to support. "I'm going to be making a change in jobs in the first of the year," Wise reported in one of her Hibiscus columns. "And I think I feel more enthusiastic about it than I have about anything." She stood on the precipice of a life-changing career move that would make business history.

The Go-Getter

In the spring of 1947, Brownie Wise's dramatic life change arrived at the front door of her Dearborn home in the form of a Stanley Home Products sales rep who fumbled his pitch so badly that she remembered thinking, "I could do better than that." The introduction—and the seed of ambition it planted—created the historic bridge between Wise and Frank Stanley Beveridge, the man credited with being the first to use the home-party plan as his primary sales strategy.

As the sales director of the Fuller Brush Company, Beveridge's name had become synonymous with door-to-door selling in the early part of the twentieth century. Then, in 1933, fifty-four-year-old Beveridge founded Stanley Home Products, in part to create jobs for friends stuck in the throes of the Depression. The Stanley line included the Brown Beauty mop and an array of cleaners, detergents, and floor waxes—utilitarian products that appealed mainly to the American housewife. The first person to use home parties to sell Stanley products was a New Hampshire salesman who set up a card table at a customer's home and, with the resident's permission, invited other neighborhood women to come over and watch his demonstration. The simple concept brought the business to him, and it also appealed to homemakers who cherished some time away from children and chores. When Beveridge saw firsthand that the salesman's home parties were the reason for such formidable sales numbers, he went back and told his employees, "We have to change." At first, many salesmen resisted the idea of putting on parties and recruited their wives to help with that part of the business.

For Wise, a new career could not have come at a better time. The years of rationing and doing without during World War II had given way to a new American consumer culture. Across the country soldiers streamed home, settled down, and started building suburban neighborhoods and families. Rosie the Riveter, celebrated during the war, was now expected to resume her feminine role and let the men handle the heavy lifting. But in many cases, that quintessential American wartime woman had gotten a taste of what it was like to be out on her own, earning a little money and enjoying a few of the finer things it bought. In 1947, this was an apt description of the thirty-four-year-old divorcée Brownie Wise, an executive secretary now dabbling in sales.

At first, Wise saw Stanley as a way to supplement her secretarial income on evenings and weekends. In June 1947, she received her first Stanley Speaker's kit and an outline of an effective-speaking course. "The voice exercise has practical value if you use it," Stanley's director of education advised. Wise already had public speaking experience thanks to the union rallies of her teenage years, and the confidence she had gained by persuading even the toughest crowds made talking to women about how Stanley products could make their homes more spic-and-span seem easy in comparison. Results soon followed, allowing her say good-bye to her wartime Bendix job for good and focus on Stanley's demanding requirements.

Dealers like Wise were expected to fill out a daily report, including delivery-day Saturdays, that started at 8:30 each morning and ended "6 p.m. or later." During specified blocks of time, dealers were asked: "Did you go prospecting? Did you put on a party? If so, how many did you book? Did you verify your parties? Anything else for Stanley?" Beveridge told his sales force that there were only two types of salesmen: "The man who plods along and by his own force gains mediocre success, and the man who keeps every channel for new ideas open, welcomes all suggestions from his own organization and other fields, and then profits from the other fellow's experience. To which class do you belong?" Wise was no plodder; by 1948, she had risen through the ranks of the Michigan area, becoming manager of the so-called Triangle Unit.

Wise continued to learn the Frank Stanley Beveridge sales mantra and to correspond with the company's director of education, Elmer Nyberg. He wrote back on letterhead from Stanley's "Little Red School House." "If you and I learn to fill each sixty seconds of the passing minutes with purposeful work," Nyberg opined, "we will succeed beyond our dreams." Extra effort, he told her, combined with a strong personality is the key to success. Wise internalized and expanded upon many of these concepts at Tupperware, including Nyberg's five characteristics of a strong-willed person (whom he seemed to assume was a man):

He has a *Love of Humanity* = He loves people.

He has *Warmth* = He is not a "cold fish."

He is *Friendly* = He is a friend. He gives out kindness. The way to have a friend is to be one.

He has *Courage* = He stands on his own feet. He works terribly hard and he keeps his mouth shut.

He is *Genuine* = He doesn't deal in tricks. He is genuine in his dealings with people.

Nyberg also included seven ways "to make people like you."

1. Make it a habit of being interested in other people

2. Smile. A true smile comes from within. Smile with your eyes.

3. Pronounce a man's name as though it is the most important sound in the language.

4. Be a sympathetic, enthusiastic listener. Stimulate the other person to talk about himself.

5. Talk in terms of the other man's interest and he will listen to you.

6. Make the other person feel important, not as a trick but sincerely.

7. Treat every person you meet as though he is a messenger from heaven.

The company had a Stanley prayer and, as a way to develop resourcefulness, encouraged employees to use their Sundays to "reproduce at home the central thought of the morning sermon."

With the zeal of someone who had found a new religion, Brownie Wise soaked in all of these lessons and applied them to motivate her own sales force. In another practice she would amplify at Tupperware, Wise started producing a regular newsletter called the *Go-Getter.* "Anybody who works in the

Triangle Unit is going to be a Go-Getter, who gets what he goes after," Wise wrote to her team of dealers. "As a unit, we're out for first place again; as a dealer you're out for more parties, bigger weeks, fatter profits . . . or you're part of the problem."

One quote she used often in her newsletters came from J. G. Holland: "God gives every bird his food, but He does not throw it into the nest." Wise wrote to Nyberg, sharing that she felt she had hit upon a key principle to motivating her sales force: "The secret of education lies in respecting the pupil."

Wise lavished attention on big earners and high achievers and found a way to give recognition to new recruits. "Ray Arsenault and his Stanley case went to a party the other nite . . . his Michigan debut and they rang the bell with a quality party! Swell." Wise punctuated many passages with a kind of calculated corniness. "Florence's sales this week averaged almost $8.00 per person!" she gushed. "That's real, honest-to-goodness sizzlemanship."

Between the "swells" and "sizzles," Wise was beginning to harness a concept that would bring her the devotion of thousands of Americans, women especially. The profits coming in from all the evening parties, Saturday deliveries, and Monday morning sales meetings were good, but for housewives used to an invisible role behind their breadwinning husbands, the recognition was even better. Wise seemed to use an intuitive balance of praise, motivation, and discipline.

"One half of knowing what you want is knowing what you must give up before you get it." Wise told her go-getters, "40 hours a week will give you success: if you want a new fur coat, another room added to your house, a new car . . . the next step is filling a 40-hour week out on your yellow sheet, and following through." At the beginning of each week Wise would decide who was go-getting and who needed some goading. "Monday morning—9:30 here at my house," Wise instructed dealers in her newsletter. "See Grace with your fines if you're late."

Across Detroit, some members of Wise's sales force who would go on to be major players with Tupperware were also getting their start by selling Stanley, including Rose Humphrey, Florence Zewicky, Peter and Elsie Block, and Dorothy Shannon and her nephew Gary McDonald. For McDonald, the Stanley job provided a way to make money while he was still in school. He helped his aunt fill orders and delivered them to the homes of party hostesses. Afterward, Shannon would collect the money paid by party guests and then go home and count the take into two piles. One, covering the cost of acquiring the goods, would go into her business account. Shannon took what was left of the profits and deposited that into her personal account. The industrious teen McDonald saw his aunt do this week in and week out and asked if he could be a dealer. "Sure," she told him, "but you'll have to book [arrange] your own parties."

A month shy of his sixteenth birthday, Gary McDonald held his first Stanley party, in suburban Detroit. In time, McDonald saw success as a Stanley dealer, selling the complete line to homemakers all over town, who took to calling him "Mister Stanley." McDonald as a dealer and his aunt Dorothy Shannon as a manager both eventually took their place on the roster of star Stanley manager Brownie Wise. Now that they all knew how to put on successful home parties and motivate others to do the same, the stage was set for a new home-sale product to come in and transform their lives.

✳

The end of the war gave Earl Tupper an opportunity to sink his money into all sorts of surplus at fire-sale rates. However, the nagging shortage of raw materials did not subside as quickly. Plastic resins—one of the cornerstone materials Tupper needed for manufacturing—were still hard to come by or subject to a steep markup. "Sorry, there's just not enough to go around and there's nothing we can do about it," a Bakelite representative told him. "Well, in that case, what else have you got?" Tupper asked. "You must have something kicking around."

"As a matter of fact, we do," the rep conceded. What he handed Tupper was a smelly glob of greasy, rubbery, black slag. "We have tons of this stuff sitting around and we don't know what to do with it," the rep told Tupper. "You can have all of it you want."

The substance was polyethylene, a smelting waste product. During the war, both the British and the United States had used it in radar installations and as a way to protect weapons from the elements. In peacetime, companies like DuPont and Bakelite had no use for it. However, in this worthless glob of waste product, this smelly slag, Earl Tupper saw an opportunity.

Earl Silas Tupper, inventor of Tupperware.

Earl Tupper wrote to one of his early ad men, J. C. Healy, about why polyethylene had so much potential: "With the end of the war it was another young veteran that had accelerated from childhood to a fighting job. It had done its job well, but like all young vets returning from the wars it had never had civilian adult experience." Tupper saw the economic possibilities of developing polyethylene "as a civilian." But transforming it into something new and revolutionary would take a great deal of time, dedication, and know-how.

As a manufacturer of plastic products, Tupper was looking for something that would hold up better than the generally brittle plastic products. During wartime, polyethylene had shown that it did not give off odors or other chemicals harmful to food, even when exposed to highly acidic agents like lemon juice or vinegar. But in its wartime form, the dark clump would hardly appeal to homemakers. It would take months of experimentation, patience, and refinement before Tupper found his solution.

After months of sample testing, he hit on what he thought was the correct balance of temperature and pressure. Now the polyethylene could be flowed into a variety of shapes and sizes with the appropriate thickness. Unlike other, more fragile, plastics of the day, it was flexible and didn't break or chip. Tupper also devised a precise system of adding colored dyes to give his new translucent product attractive pastel tones. This was something new and different—a polished, waxy, upscale plastic that needed a name to reflect its inventor's swagger. Tupper called it "Poly-T: Material of the Future." By itself, Poly-T would still not solve the problem of how to keep food fresh longer than the shower caps and tin foil that women were using at the time to prolong the life of leftovers in the icebox.

Tupper got the idea for his next great invention from

a paint-can lid. He realized that he could take the flexible Poly-T material and manufacture covers that fit tightly on top of metal cans. But finding a way to make the lids fit on top of his narrow-lipped, flexible, Poly-T plastic bowls took more work. On June 2, 1947, Tupper filed a patent application for the "E. S. Tupper Open Mouth Container and Nonsnap type of Closure Therefor." In a series of eight now-classic drawings, Tupper outlined the noiseless and non-snapping cover that fit snugly over the top of his Poly-T food and beverage containers. The "simple hand manipulation" used to expel air as the cover was placed over the container created an airtight, spill-proof vacuum seal, even if the container was dropped on the floor. He christened his line of Poly-T products "Tupperware."

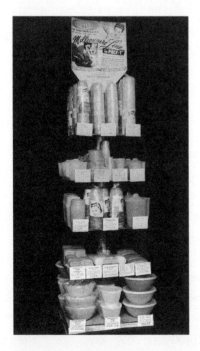

Earl Tupper's early Tupperware "Millionaire Line" languished in department stores.

In a September 8, 1947, article on Tupper and his new invention, *Time* magazine called him a "one-man boom" and raved that Tupper's "all important contribution is a process which overcomes the material's tendency to split, makes it tough enough to withstand almost anything except knife cuts and near-boiling water." Tupper had given his World War II veteran polyethylene a mettle tough enough to withstand almost any typical American household, and he had done something more. Tupper had improved the reputation of plastic in the eyes of the middle-class American consumer. *House Beautiful* called Tupperware, "Fine Art for 39 cents," and editor Elizabeth Gordon gushed that the bowls looked "as good as a piece of sculpture." Like a proud father, Earl Tupper was thrilled to see his new Poly-T bowls included in a housewares exhibit at the Museum of Modern Art in New York City.

Tupper called the original fourteen Tupperware products produced behind the big windows of his Farnumsville plant the "Millionaire Line." As a youngster, Tupper had predicted he'd be a millionaire by the age of thirty. While his teenage prediction was off by a few years, his instincts about his debut Tupperware collection were spot-on. Camel ordered three hundred thousand cigarette cases; Canada Dry Ginger Ale bought fifty thousand bowls to sell with beverages; and the Tek Corporation purchased fifty thousand of Tupper's Bell Tumblers to market alongside toothbrushes. "A Massachusetts mental institution found Tupperware an almost ideal replacement for its noisy, easily battered aluminum cups and plates." As *Time* reported, "Patients could damage Tupperware only by persistent chewing."

After the initial flood of positive publicity and brisk wholesale orders, a problem started to develop for Tupper in the marketing of his new Poly-T products. "We always try to remember," Tupper wrote, "that a product is not exactly what you make it in the factory, but it is also and more so what you make it when you sell it." He turned down offers to develop a line of flexible dog-feeding dishes for fear that "such a thing could have made our job more difficult to sell our dishes as appropriate for any table." To counter preconceived notions about plastic being cheap or flimsy, Tupperware ads implored housewives to "think of it as having taken its rightful place with other fine table furnishings . . . silver, linen, china. Tupperware is here in a most substantial way. . . . Its position is assured."

In 1948, that claim was not yet quite true. Tupperware retail sales were flat, and the issue went beyond perception. People didn't know the proper way to "lock in freshness" with Tupper's new airtight seal. Some sent the containers back, concerned that the tops didn't fit. In big department stores across America, Tupperware languished on shelves. The product itself was revolutionary; now it just needed someone equally innovative to figure out how to sell it.

In the late 1940s, people regarded the J. L. Hudson department store as the heart of downtown Detroit. Established in 1911 by Joseph Lowthian Hudson, the soaring twenty-five-story behemoth occupied the old Detroit Opera House. People came from all over the city to marvel at the massive American flag—seven stories high and weighing sixteen hundred pounds—that hung on its side. Twelve thousand employees rang up one hundred thousand sales a day, and patrons feasted on Hudson's famous Maurice salad. In the days before racial unrest exploded in downtown Detroit, a young Diana Ross was the first black busgirl in the store's basement cafeteria.

It's no wonder a place so bustling would attract the attention of an ambitious teenager like Gary McDonald. On a trip through the store one day after high school, the Wonder Bowl caught his eye. Nearby, he also spied the Bell Tumbler on sale for a dollar. But these so-called products of the future were hardly flying off the shelves. McDonald noticed that they just sat there until a store employee showed customers how to apply the Tupper seal. Then containers could be turned upside down or even dropped without the contents inside being spilled or otherwise ruined. People had to be told that the bowls and canisters were specially designed for the refrigerator or pantry shelf, to stretch the life of leftovers and the family budget. After the explanation, customers were much more enthusiastic and bought the new product. Immediately, McDonald told himself, "*That* could be a great home-demonstration product!"

McDonald was not the only member of the Stanley family starting to get excited about the potential of Tupperware. In suburban Boston, husband and wife dealers Ann and Tom Damigella also discovered the Wonder Bowl and all the things they could do with it. Ann brought the first one to their home in Melrose, an upscale bedroom community north of Boston. "Tommy," she exclaimed, "look at this! It's made of plastic!" Yet that plastic was soft to the touch and appeared to be very functional. Where most Americans would see a simple bowl or canister, Ann and Tom Damigella immediately saw an opportunity. "This is why we were fascinated," Tom Damigella reflected decades later in Tupperware's *Our World* publication, "and then, why we got so excited. You see, we realized what a great sales opportunity this new product called Tupper Plastics could be." Soon after, they started selling the product separately from their Stanley line.

In Detroit, Gary McDonald was eager to test his theory that Tupperware would thrive on the party plan. He got on the phone, called the company he found on the bottom of one of the containers, and with money he borrowed from his father, placed his first-ever order for Tupperware. His aunt did the same thing. The only problem with Tupperware was the scarcity and lack of variety. Where the Stanley line featured more than sixty items, Tupperware had just the first fourteen. McDonald knew he had to share his discovery with Wise.

At one of the regular Monday morning Stanley sales meetings, McDonald brought Tupperware to Wise's Dearborn home. She, like most other Tupperware novices, wasn't quite sure what to do with it. "Whoever heard of a bowl you could squeeze?" Wise reflected many years later. "And in the beginning, I really struggled to get that seal on right. Then I accidentally knocked the bowl off the table and it bounced. I was so surprised I called out to my mother, 'Why, this bowl actually bounces.' We ended up using that line in our promotion: 'It bounces instead of breaks!'" As Wise struggled with the seal, she finally came to the conclusion that "you had to burp it just like a baby."

While the product intrigued Wise, she was already a successful manager with Stanley, earning a decent income and providing a good home for ten-year-old Jerry. She had also built a roster of motivated dealers who helped make their branch one of Michigan's largest. She saw no reason to walk away from that success even if the new Tupperware line did seem to hold potential. It wasn't until her esteemed mentor in Stanley Home Products, Frank Stanley Beveridge, provided some inspiration—and caused even more consternation—that she decided to leave for good.

Part of Stanley's plan to educate and motivate the sales force was the idea of an annual pilgrimage to the company's home base. On Sunday, August 22, 1948, Brownie and a contingent of her Detroit West Side dealers arrived by train at Stanley's Westfield, Massachusetts, headquarters. "You come here to Westfield to learn, to get inspiration," Beveridge told the assembled throngs in his welcome address. "Those of you who bring the greatest spirit of service, of kindness and helpfulness, will take the most home." At the Monday morning breakfast kickoff rally, Stanley's regional sales manager, Hubert L. Worrell, told the Michigan group, "You're a bunch of builders and a fine group of people." They responded with a standing ovation and sang back to him, "We Think You're Wonderful."

That spirit of camaraderie carried over to Stanley's factory in Easthampton. Traveling past a big, red-lettered sign that said, WELCOME MICHIGAN AREA, Wise and her sales force toured Stanley's manufacturing operation. Five thousand feet of gravity- and power-driven belts moved the merchandise, eliminating the need for any unnecessary handling. Dealers marveled at how the new Cel-O-Sorb mops were made. "They think this little factory can supply what we can sell," said a brash young dealer named Jack Marshall. "But we'll show 'em!"

Brownie Wise had an agenda beyond brushes and mops for this pilgrimage, however; she wanted some face time with the Stanley big shots. She refused to be stagnant, and her ambitions far exceeded Detroit's West Side branch. "Remember," she once advised her dealers, "if you don't grow, someone else will." It never occurred to Wise that her growth potential could be forever stunted because of one factor that had nothing to do with her performance.

"Don't waste your time," Beveridge informed Wise.

"Management is no place for a woman." From someone she admired, those words were deflating and inflaming, especially since they reminded her of the difficult workplace climate she faced in the 1940s. After the end of the war, the *American Economic Review* noted the number of women in America's labor force dipped from 25 percent to 22 percent in 1947. By 1949 those numbers were back on the rise, but the U.S. Census Bureau noted the number of those women in management was only around 13 percent.

Still, Wise moved on, undeterred by what she considered to be one of those temporary roadblocks Reverend Grambling had advised her to find her away around all those years before.

"I remember how mad she was when she came back from Stanley Home Parties' convention in Massachusetts," Jerry Wise recalled. After the long train ride home Wise vowed to her son, "I'll show him."

A Perfect Fit

On March 8, 1949, Earl Tupper addressed the emerging role of women in the workforce through a page-long, dress-down memo to his advertising manager, J. C. Healy. Around the office, Healy had made it clear he thought women were inferior to men in the business world and belonged in more subservient secretarial ranks. Tupper's response showed an open mind about women in management, unlike Beveridge's, and foreshadowed his willingness to entrust the success of his treasured inventions to Brownie Wise.

"I'm sure all of the ladies with whom this corporation deals will be big enough to not be angered by your expressions," Tupper wrote Healy, "but I'm afraid they wouldn't be human if they neglected an opportunity to make things a little hard for you." Tupper went on to show how his visionary nature applied to more than just plastics. "Look closely at the roster of top publishers and other business firms in this country," Tupper suggested, "who with obviously good reason have seen fit to staff their top jobs with women who are giving top performance in any man's language." In the homespun, father-to-child tone typical of Tupper, he ended the memo by chiding his top ad man. "You have delivered yourself of expressions best reserved for banter amongst the office small frye [sic]."

Office politics aside, Tupper had growth on his mind in the fall of 1949. Starting in September, countries worldwide granted Tupper Seals the affirmation and patent protection their inventor craved. From Belgium to Italy, Switzerland to South Africa, countries bestowed upon Tupper Corporation the right to have what amounted to a monopoly on manufacturing Tupperware.

In the United States, Tupper had expanded his operation west, establishing a manufacturing facility and lab at a former air base in Cuero, a town that barely registered a dot on the sweeping southeast Texas landscape. The Lone Star State seemed to have clear advantages for his business: It was a warm-weather state experiencing population growth, and the unions didn't have the kind of stranglehold they enjoyed in the Northeast. Before he could make the expansion plan a reality, however, he had to solve the problem of how to sell Tupperware to the average consumer. Former Los Angeles distributor Elsie Block summed up the marketing problem: "Everybody seemed to love the products, but nobody seemed to be buying them." Tupper sought to solve that problem by publishing his first mail-order catalogue, complete with illustrations and instructions on how to put the full range of the now twenty-two Tupperware items to use. By putting Tupperware on display in a New York City showroom on Fifth Avenue, he continued his attempts to differentiate it from the cheap plastics of the past. Tupper resisted criticism from buyers who said the colors were too plain and the products too flimsy, and that it would be "impossible to hold such a flexible tumbler filled with water." As far back as 1947, Tupper had toyed with the idea of Tupperware parties and a Tupper theme song, but he failed until years later to put those proven Stanley strategies into his own playbook. His lack of marketing instinct left him in need of outside help.

Fortunately for Tupper, the foundation of all the success

that the 1950s would bring was already taking shape. Door-to-door salespeople had started to recognize Tupperware's potential to freshen their product line. It was bright, clean, and colorful, as well as innovative and easy to carry and demonstrate. Where Tupperware sat idly on department and hardware store shelves, the tactile, in-home demonstrations brought it alive to the people Tupper had largely failed to reach. Taking notice of the steady stream of mail orders from dealers such as the Damigellas and Gary McDonald, Tupper embarked on a market-research study, sending questionnaires to the highest sellers. Intended to get to the bottom of how they were able to sell so much Tupperware, his surveys also unearthed an unexpected bonus—Brownie Wise.

Back in Michigan's West Side branch, salespeople had begun using two key catchphrases at demonstrations to preach Tupperware's money-saving benefits to a growing base of enthusiastic homemakers. "Get rid of your shower caps!" they urged. "Turn your leftovers into makeovers!" However, Brownie Wise wasn't satisfied with just slogans. Instead, she encouraged her dealers to go a step further and turn sealed containers over, or throw them across the room, to prove they didn't leak.

Though still smarting from her encounter with Beveridge, Wise hadn't let her disappointment about being dismissed derail her plans. Instead, she'd overhauled her sales force's dowdy line of brooms and brushes, substituting the bouncing pastel bowls and canisters with the seals that burped.

"We started ordering the product fast because it was selling so well and recruiting was pretty easy," Gary McDonald remembered. "This was something new and magic and different." Wise purchased as much Tupperware as possible, recruited new dealers, and supplied them with product as quickly as she could get it. If she ran short on cash, Wise put people on the waiting list, and that just added to the appeal. Less than five years after World War II, people remembered what it was like to stand in line for the commodities everybody wanted, such as butter, stockings, and automobiles. The method proved so successful that Wise used it even after she had the money to stay stocked with Tupperware. "It was the strongest recruiting tool we had," McDonald said.

Signing up new dealers is the key to building any home-based selling business. As more recruits join on at the bottom, the discount offered by managers and distributors above them increases accordingly. In the end, everyone profits. Once a territory is saturated with dealers, one of its peak performers is promoted to distributor and given a new territory to develop. When that new distributorship thrives, it becomes a success story for the territory from which it came.

In her early newsletters, it's clear Wise watched over her growing team like a doting mother, pushing them to higher and higher sales and success. "Facts and Figures from the stack of orders and reports this week point to Nola and Jayne as super-duper on the 50-oz. canister," Wise reported in the August 18, 1949, newsletter. "Nola is making hey-hey this week on a fun-leave from Poly-T Parties . . . and here's news to warm the heart—Norma Kelly's husband has just gotten home from the South Pacific after a year's absence, which is by way of explaining the glow Norma gives off these days." It wouldn't be long before Wise and her West Side branch dealers rechristened their home-based, Stanley-inspired sales gatherings, "Tupperware parties."

On October 17, 1949, with a stable of nineteen dealers and the Poly-T operation taking off, Wise moved distribution out of the Melborn Street house and into a warehouse space.

"I remember filling a lot of orders in those days," Jerry Wise recalled. "Everything she touched seemed to turn to gold."

Brownie's golden touch showed up in her end-of-the-year Poly-T sales figures for 1949. From the local Poly Supply Company in Hazel Park, Wise ordered $65,741.98 worth of merchandise. Direct from the Tupper Corporation's factory in Farnumsville, Massachusetts, she rang up a whopping $86,407.15 in orders (or close to $850,000.00 today). In the winter of 1950, the home office rang up Brownie Wise and dispatched field man Victor Collamore to meet the go-getters in Detroit.

Wise and her still teenage sidekick Gary McDonald had impressed the Tupper Corporation, and the company's representative traveled halfway across the country to take them to a get-acquainted dinner at a fancy downtown Detroit restaurant. Not long after the water was poured, Collamore got right to the point. "You guys have gotta tell me," he said, "just what in the hell are you guys doing to sell the amount of Tupperware you're doing? You're selling more Tupperware than the J. L. Hudson department store by far, and that's the biggest department store in the world!" Wise and McDonald were glad to share their secrets, but by 1950, ambitious direct sellers all over the country had started their own Tupperware operations and Tupper's people knew it. Collamore was really sizing up Wise for a promotion. Less than two years after her Stanley ambitions had been crushed, Wise was poised to ascend to the highest level of Tupperware distribution.

Wise and Collamore sealed the deal at her home on Melborn Street. She would become a distributor based in Fort Lauderdale, and the entire state of Florida would be hers to populate with Tupperware dealers and branches. With almost three million residents in 1950, Florida promised to be a lucrative territory as well as a dream home. In the midst of a frigid Michigan winter, Wise broached the idea of moving south with eleven-year-old Jerry, who gushed, "Let's go!" Rose Humphrey moved down first to find a temporary place to live and space to store Tupperware stock. Brownie and Jerry would stay in Detroit until the end of the school year, tie up all the details, hand over the reins of the Michigan branch, and then head to Florida themselves. Wise was pleased that some of her star dealers decided to stake a new claim in the Sunshine State.

After fourteen years in the Motor City, one turbulent marriage and divorce, the birth of her only child, and a couple of career changes, Brownie Wise was leaving forever. Florida would be home for the remaining forty-two years of her life. Like anyone starting out in a brand-new place and trying to build a new business, she would find the coming months exhilarating and stressful. Not only was she uprooting her own family, she would need to stand on the shoulders of other dealers who'd been comfortably established in Michigan. They were pulling their kids out of school, selling their homes, leaving friends, and placing their faith in Wise. She, in turn, was placing her faith in a company and product with a minimal track record. Success would not come easy.

Life of the Party

On Saturday morning, April 29, 1950, Brownie and Jerry Wise loaded into their car for the 1,425-mile drive from Dearborn to Fort Lauderdale. While Gary McDonald had joined the Marines and headed off to Camp Pendleton, California, a month earlier, his aunt Dorothy Shannon made the trip with Brownie and Jerry, to help out with the twenty-one hours of driving. Snow fell in "January-like flakes," making for a frosty, mid-spring send-off. Wise was sad and anxious—so much was on the line. "I could never tell you how hard it was to leave," she wrote to dealers who stayed back home in Michigan.

As they made their way out of Michigan, traversing the long miles of eastern Ohio, and then continuing south through the heart of Kentucky, the elevation increased and the mood lightened. "We oohed and aahed at the sudden glimpses of beauty from the mountain curves," Wise reflected. Hidden meadows burst with springtime fragrance and the color of dogwood and mountain laurel; oleander and buttercups lined the wooden, barbed-wire fencerows. "We gradually began, somewhere between Tennessee and Georgia," she wrote, "to get the idea that life was a smooth, serenely flowing business, and that there [wasn't] really any hurry about the thing at all." Almost seven hundred miles into her new life with Jerry, Wise and her contingent stopped for the night along U.S. 27 in Cedartown, Georgia.

The next day, after a breakfast of native smoked sausage,

hot biscuits, waffles with strawberry jam, and farm-fresh eggs that Wise claimed, "you KNOW the hens laid to order just for *you*," the group covered 450 more miles into north Florida, where they intended to do some sight-seeing in America's oldest city, Saint Augustine. By horse-drawn carriage, the group traveled narrow cobblestone streets dating back to the Revolutionary War, under live oaks "dripping with Spanish moss," and past the nation's oldest house, which was once a pub for British soldiers. The group discovered and toured the Castillo de San Marcos. Situated behind earthen berms built from native coquina shell stone, the imposing fortress protected the sea route for seventeenth-century treasure ships returning to Spain. The women bathed in the glorious Florida sun, "and considered seriously the fact that life can be a b-e-a-t-i-f-u-l [*sic*] thing . . . !" Much like something Hibiscus would have written to her readers in Detroit five years before, this trip was the stuff of dreams and ambition coming true.

After a final stop at Marineland, the group raced down the coast, ending the 285-mile last leg of their journey to Fort Lauderdale at 10 p.m. At their temporary ocean-view apartment, Rose Humphrey had a surprise awaiting them: fried chicken she had prepared that afternoon. Like the Tin Can Tourists of the 1930s, Brownie Wise, along with her son, her mother, and their friends, marveled at the Atlantic Ocean's nighttime majesty, the sense of infinite possibilities in its salty breezes. It was Sunday, April 30, 1950. "Our place faced the ocean, with only a roadway between our front door and the surf," she wrote. "The white-caps lulled us to sleep."

On Monday morning, Wise swirled into motion, looking to set up her new Florida home and business. Her mother thought she'd found a good store space, but Wise decided it wasn't big enough for the business she intended to grow.

After much searching around Broward County, Wise settled on a storefront just a block away from the space Rose found, at the corner of U.S. 441 and West McKinley Street.

The first Tupperware business Brownie Wise opened in Florida, at the corner of West McKinley Street and U.S. 441 in Hollywood, 1950.

Wise shopped for a new home farther inland, where she could get a better price. Five miles west of Fort Lauderdale, she found a three-bedroom block home situated on an acre of land. "There is a little stream at the back of the property," Wise noted, "where Jerry can park himself under a patch of shade, stick his toes in the water, and lean on a fish-pole to his heart's content."

On May 4, Wise entered into a contract to buy the home and property for $15,000, more than twice the median price for a Florida home in 1950. With the prosperity that the switch to Tupperware sales had brought in the previous year, Wise was able to pay the first two-thirds in cash. Now, content with having found a home and a storefront in less than a week, Wise wrote to her friends back in Michigan, referring to herself in the third person, as was her custom: "I'm sure you'll be right if you catch a mind-eye glimpse of Wise setting out bougainvillea vines and hibiscus bushes and cabbage palms and putting elephant ears in the ground floor boxes," she mused. "Nothing could be so blue as this tropical sky . . . and the sun is like melted gold." A salesman stopped by the new store and dropped off a fifty-pound bag of Valencia oranges as a welcome gift.

On Monday, May 15, Wise opened her first Tupperware business in Florida and called it Patio Parties. The same day, she was already heading south to Miami to meet with seven or eight prospective dealers. She drew up her own manual educating recruits on Tupperware, the party plan, and the "urgent musts" of her operation. In years to come, this system would become standard issue for all would-be Tupperware Ladies. "This plan has proved itself a tremendous and profitable success in other states, and with your cooperation, we will attain the same success here," Wise wrote in the foreword. "While this policy may be flexible in some respects, any deviation from it, on your part, will result in the loss of your rights as a dealer."

The Patio Party Plan

A patio party is the organized presentation of the values of your products. It is the KEY that unlocks the door to sales, through good product demonstration and good product display. It is your means of creating a desire for the product through visual demonstration.

The congenial atmosphere of a Patio Party is relaxing. All the guests are imbued with the group spirit of the party. The social spirit of a party tends to lower sales resistance of those present, as well as increase a competitive buying spirit. The buying spirit is *contagious;* it is a proven fact that you will sell more to a group of 15 women AS A GROUP than you will sell to them individually.

This is the essence of the Patio Party Plan.

A good demonstration is a source of entertainment, information, and the purchase of useful products. It is to your interest to work toward the accomplishment of all *three* purposes.

In the course of a Patio Party, three people must gain— you, the dealer, through the sale of your products and the booking of future parties; the hostess, who in a sense is your sub-dealer, and upon whose hospitality and initiative, the success of the party plan depends; and finally the guest, who through the medium of the Patio Party plan, enjoys a sociable get-together. In addition, the guest is impressed because she is shown, to her personal benefit, definite uses for the products she purchases.

As a hostess incentive, the following plan has been patterned for Patio Parties:

1. The hostess receives gift for having a patio party.

2. The hostess receives $1.50 for each party booked at her party. It is suggested that no more than 2 parties be booked from each hostess' party.

3. The hostess receives 5% of the total amount of merchandise sold at her party, including outside orders, which should definitely be encouraged. (See the points on verification, regarding "outside orders.") A list of the hostess gifts and their credit value will be supplied by your manager. A hostess may pay a balance of up to $1.50 on

her hostess gifts, regardless of the amount accumulated in hostess credit.

A successful party always includes entertainment in the form of games, with prizes and favors. Please make good use of the game book, with which your manager will supply you. Game prizes will be supplied to you, on your order form, at a very nominal cost. Your manager can give you excellent advice on the variety of games you can use, suitable for various groups. When circumstances do not permit the playing of games, prizes should still be awarded, and they can be given for a lucky numbered card, the oldest or youngest person, the newlywed, the mother of the most children, etc. You will receive party favors free of charge, at the rate of one favor for each wholesale dollar, with your orders. They may be used as gift souvenirs, as game prizes for relay games, etc. Suggestions along this line are included in the section of training devoted to games.

One game doubled as a surefire sales technique: Wise would throw a sealed bowl filled with liquid across the room or bounce it off the terrazzo-tiled floor and not spill a drop, to convince customers the airtight seal really worked. It was soft sell—sophisticated, social, and fun. The Brownie Wise Patio Party Plan became to home selling what Earl Tupper's Poly-T was to plastics.

Back at her new home, Wise sat down at the typewriter, producing a three-page, single-spaced "round-robin" letter, bringing everyone in her old Michigan all-star crew up to date. "I AM NOW A BONA FIDE RESIDENT OF THE SOVEREIGN STATE OF FLORIDA," she announced. "My car has a native license plate, and I'm sporting a driver's license . . .

which means, in the Florida vernacular, I have, 'sand in my shoes.'" Her warmth and attention to the details of all her former dealers' lives foreshadowed the kind of one-on-one relationship she would foster, even when the number of people in her charge multiplied many times over:

> NOLA: I hear from Betty that you are turning in your case soon. . . . I hope you're going to enjoy every minute of your newfound freedom.

> MARGE: Betty wrote me about Hank's good fortune, and I'm SO glad for you!

> IRENE TYLER: Let me know how the den turned out, will you? Good luck!

> EDNA: A kiss to the angel child . . . (still haven't seen one more beautiful than she is even in Florida!). . . . Boy, do I need a permanent!

In between lighthearted quips and witty asides, the true affection Wise shared for her Michigan team shone through. She had helped nurture, coach, and cajole them to success, and in turn their performance resulted in Wise taking a big step up the ladder:

> As I unpack these beautiful things and make them part of my Florida home, please know that they are the essence of the home itself . . . they will give me cheer and encouragement every time I look at them, and I will love you and your kindness all over again.

With thank-you and good-bye now properly expressed, it was time to get down to business. "I could go on for pages and pages," Wise wound up her long letter, "but in the meantime Patio Parties must be about the business of setting their little roots down here and there in Florida, and having their little roots watered and fertilized ... and I can't do it sitting at this typewriter." And so she zealously embarked on building a new cadre of Florida dealers, with the hope of surpassing the success she'd had in Michigan.

The initial signs were encouraging. In the first two months of Patio Parties' existence, Brownie Wise ordered $14,180.13 worth of Tupperware, roughly $137,000 worth today. Most of it went to customers in South Florida, where Wise, her mother, and local dealers could operate without sniping from competitors. Wise poured herself into weekly training sessions with dealers and two-hour weekly seminars with her unit managers, and she spent Fridays on the road visiting the West Palm branch. "In the long run," she wrote, "well-trained dealers will pay for the effort spent on them; the first three or four months doesn't always show this, but after that, the results are plain. I would go on the record for the statement that one well-trained demonstrator will outclass two, and sometimes even three dealers who are handed a line of samples, given a pat on the back, a price list and sent on their way."

It would take time for new female recruits not used to public speaking, let alone selling an entirely foreign line of product, to start seeing success. Each received a cardboard box containing a big suitcase full of the Tupperware to be shown and demonstrated at home parties. In the early days, dealers could expect to shell out $35 on their sample case, putting them in a significant hole before they sold even one Wonder Bowl. And inaugural Tupperware parties weren't always successes, as the first Orlando dealer, Gwen Lord, reported back to Wise:

I am enclosing the order form from my first party (hope it is done Right) which could not exactly be called a "howling success." Owing to some plague or virus or whatever about half those invited were sick.

Despite the sometimes less-than-stellar beginnings, dealers who stuck with it soon reaped the benefits of Tupperware's growing popularity. To cap off this period of rapid success, on May 25, Wise celebrated her thirty-seventh birthday and Jerry his twelfth. To continue the family's musical tradition in their new Florida home, Grandma Rose presented a fancy electric organ to budding pianist Jerry.

However, just as quickly as Patio Parties got off the ground, problems started to roll in. One of the Michigan dealers who followed Wise to Florida, Jayne Boltz, along with her husband, Bob, had left behind an established dealership in Detroit. Their move was as hellish as the trip for Wise was joyous. The couple sold their home, moved their two young children, and invested in a second station wagon so they both could work their Tupperware Florida operation full-time. Upon their arrival, they learned that the Tampa region where they settled had already been claimed by a Tupperware dealer named James Evans in nearby St. Petersburg. He was throwing his weight around, offering better sales commissions, and, according to Wise, not properly training his dealers. Wise had known about Evans but had gotten assurances from the Tupperware rep who moved her to Florida, Victor Collamore, that he wouldn't pose a problem for the new branch she wanted to establish across the bay in Tampa.

"The burning point is that Mr. Evans has set up in Tampa, and intends to stay there," Wise wrote to Collamore, "while

I felt very secure in telling the Boltz's that the Tampa area would be theirs, and they have slanted all their plans and efforts in that direction. They have gone to a great deal of expense in running off their primary literature and distributing it." Meanwhile, Evans was also advertising in Tampa, and had established relationships with customers in the area. "Two of our other dealers from Michigan arrived in Tampa Saturday to work with the Boltz's," Wise reported, "and I'm sure you can imagine the turmoil all four of them are in at the present time. Their hands are tied." Just a month after her own arrival, the Tampa situation had gotten so bad that Brownie Wise was desperate. "To be perfectly frank, Mr. Collamore," Wise confessed, "if I had only myself to consider, I think I would be discouraged enough about this, right at this time, to drop the entire enterprise; however, there is so much at stake for other people that I can't afford to."

As May dragged into June, her former star dealers in Detroit focused their fury on Wise. Jayne and Bob Boltz weren't getting quick answers to their concerns, and, making matters more difficult, the telephone service was bad and the couple felt Wise had left them twisting in the wind. "Brownie, this may well sound like a sob story, and well it may be," the couple wrote. "How would *you* like to sit on a fence waiting, waiting, waiting for just a few words that would put us straight as to your plans and policy? All during this waiting please keep in mind that our resources are NOT increasing, but rather the contrary, are DE-creasing." The tone of the letter turned personal and bitter, reflecting the couple's desperation. "Yes—we know that no one can tell you what to do," they criticized. "We are just trying to ascertain just what you intend to do here in Tampa." Wise had already written to Collamore, describing how dire the situation was. When the letter from Jayne and Bob Boltz arrived at her store, Wise fired back, but in a measured and empathetic tone.

"I have a genuine respect for both of you," Wise wrote. "YOUR resources, YOUR condition, YOUR possibilities are also mine in a business sense. As things go for you in Tampa, so they go for me." She explained that she was trying to get clarification from Collamore and was waiting out on the same limb with them. " 'Yes—we know that no one can tell you what to do,' I'm sorry you wrote that Bob," Wise quoted. "I'll try to forget it as soon as possible . . . because I have never, sincerely, had the attitude that no one could tell me what to do."

In July, Wise proposed splitting Florida in two, east and west, with the idea of settling the feud with Evans and getting on with business. "Whatever we can do will have my wholehearted effort in forgetting the things that are past, and working toward a good future," Wise wrote Collamore. "This thing must be good for all of us—Mr. Evans, Tupperware and Brownie Wise, or it will eventually be good for none of us." As the hot summer of 1950 wore on, Brownie realized that the fight over territory would not be settled so quickly. In a letter dated August 1, 1950, Wise reported to Collamore that Evans had ordered her dealers "out of town," and said that if they insisted on staying, "he would continue to fight them in *every* way, and *any* way he could." Wise had her back to the wall, and it's clear from the tone of her letters that she might well have considered reclaiming her Michigan operation and leaving Florida behind. "It is true that I have, in a business sense, made steps that I cannot retrace," Wise told Collamore. "I know I CAN build a good business here; I'm right now in the process of doing it; but I can't go on doing it with the present handicaps. I hope I can make you understand Mr. Collamore, that all I have is at stake here."

Earl Tupper was aware of the territorial problems going on not just in Florida, but throughout the country. Very early on, Peter and Elsie Block accepted his invitation to move their powerhouse Poly-T distributorship from Detroit to California. Not long after establishing their headquarters in Pasadena, the Blocks received a phone call from a man who told them he'd been distributing Tupperware in the area for four years. "Why in the world did we come to California?" Elsie Block wrote. "We could have stayed in the east in our own back yard. This is a serious business and we staked our future on its success. Can we depend on any word coming out of Massachusetts?" If Tupper hoped to continue to expand his burgeoning force of Tupperware missionaries, he would have to find a way to get them "singing off the same song sheet."

To prevent territorial disputes, Tupper needed to find a way to harness his distributors' selling power under one centralized operation, with a formal approach to sales and distribution. He thought he had found it in Norman Squires, who ran a Long Island–based company known as Hostess Home Accessories. His family credits him with drawing up the first Hostess party plan for Stanley as early as 1938. Together, Squires and Tupper crafted rules for what would come to be known as Tupper's new Hostess Division, and soon after, Tupper hired Squires as its general sales manager.

On September 5, 1950, the Tupper Corporation put higher prices into effect and started selling direct to all of its home dealer demonstrators. Longtime distributors like the Damigellas in the Northeast, Brownie Wise in the South, and the Blocks out West were asked to "terminate and liquidate" their own companies and invited to work for the Tupper Corporation as area managers.

Tupperware would be sold exclusively through its new Hostess Division based in Long Island, New York, under the Tupper Hostess Party Plan. The area managers would take on the responsibility of appointing qualified branch managers, district managers, and unit managers. Each would receive a product discount that corresponded to their rank within each newly outlined area. This framework was much like the systems under which distributors were already operating, but it would end the territorial competition, create a rigid price and profit structure, and standardize all dealer training. Distributors who didn't sign on as Hostess Division managers could not get a supply of product.

In California, Peter and Elsie Block received a telegram from the home office in Farnumsville: "Tupperware no longer available on party plan, no further orders will be acknowledged." The Blocks and their Poly-T business had been operating well without the help of Norman Squires and Hostess, and they weren't signed on. "The business was over," Elsie Block wrote. "Peter and I were crushed beyond words." It was the Hostess way or the highway.

The Tupper Corporation now had the infrastructure in place to handle the growth of its sales side and eliminate territorial squabbles. But now all the pressure was on this new wing of the company to keep the stream of product flowing to already-thriving distributorships used to keeping their own supply in local warehouses.

Even with these new structural changes in place, Squires

knew that the people within the company would be responsible for its success, and he immediately recognized Brownie Wise as a rising star. Barely a week after his appointment as general sales manager, he had his secretary send her a letter. "He wants me to impress upon you that he is more than anxious to make your acquaintance," Squires's secretary wrote. "He feels sure that you will be figured very prominently in the plans and policy which are now being drawn up for the future." Two weeks later, Squires traveled to Florida to meet Wise and offer her praise for the "consistent progress" she had already made. Like a good soldier, Wise dissolved her Patio Parties business and closed the warehouse.

In the following weeks, Squires and the Hostess Division gave Brownie Wise and her dealers a way out of the first serious crisis of her Florida move. The "Florida East Coast Area"—encompassing Fort Myers, Miami, West Palm Beach, Orlando, Jacksonville, and ending at and including Savannah, Georgia—was now officially hers. Evans was allowed to keep operating in Tampa Bay.

Wise's vast, 650-mile stretch included a half-dozen growing, sunny, southern metropolitan areas in which she was free to place many of her old Detroit teammates and new recruits. They, in turn, had the assurance that there would be no renegade distributors once they arrived. The battle for Florida ended in a truce: Brownie Wise didn't get the entire state as promised, but—like the Christmas gift of Savannah that Sherman gave to Lincoln during the Civil War—it was an attractive consolation prize.

With a renewed vigor and focus, on November 25, 1950, Wise published the first edition of her *Go-Getter* newsletter as part of Tupper's new Hostess Division. "A warm handclasp to all of you who join me in celebrating the birth of the Florida

East Coast Area, Tupper Hostess Division," Wise began. "No other issue of our new 'Go-Getter' newsletter will give Ye Editor quite the sense of elation and anticipation that laying out this one does!" Each page had three holes already punched so dealers could put them in binders for future reference. It was the kind of manifesto Wise would use to tell people in the field exactly what she expected of them; to offer tips on presenting the best parties possible; to recognize peak performers, newbies, and those transitioning out of the program; and to deliver inspirational messages:

> We must take *advantage* of the newness—in hostess gifts, in products, in the plan . . . and while we are making way, ourselves, for the new mechanics of the business, let's expose our customers and hostesses to the enthusiasm we feel . . . selling is showmanship, and showmanship thrives on what's NEW!

The excitement was contagious. With Wise prodding them to do so, ambitious women were scouting for places to establish new Tupperware units in Florida towns like Kissimmee, Fort Pierce, and Plymouth. Over the Thanksgiving holiday, Brownie's mother, Rose, got into the act, braving wind and rain to scout out possibilities in Sanford, a historic hamlet on Lake Monroe where gangster Al Capone once spent winter vacations and Harlem Renaissance writer Zora Neale Hurston penned her first novel, *Jonah's Gourd Vine*. Humphrey liked what she saw there and made the 230-mile move north to open her own Tupperware business. In keeping with the family tradition, Humphrey would become a trailblazing and successful Tupperware powerhouse in the years to come, often ranking among the top sellers in the country.

With this hard-fought freedom and entrepreneurial spirit sweeping the East Coast Area, party sales started to roll in. At first, the factory couldn't keep up with the number of orders, and shipping delays became more and more frequent. Dealers lost money on Christmas orders for fear they wouldn't arrive on time. "I don't know, of course, what the trucking companies are promising you at that end," Wise complained to Squires, "but they're simply not coming through with deliveries as they should be down here." One unit manager resigned because he hadn't received a commission check in months.

The continual frustrations and workload started to take a physical toll on Wise. For the last two years, she'd been experiencing chronic headaches. By the middle of December 1950, they had become so excruciating she had to be hospitalized for exploratory brain surgery. Doctors thought they might find a blood clot or, worse, a tumor, and went into her brain to tie off a series of blood vessels they suspected were causing the problem. She was allowed a two-day home respite over Christmas, and then returned to the hospital to finish her treatment. In true Brownie Wise, stiff-upper-lip fashion, she never reported any of her medical issues to the home office.

It was the end of a year in which Brownie had cut herself loose from her unhappy marriage in Michigan and gambled on the promise of her new love, Tupperware. At times, making that happen took all the energy, diplomacy, and perseverance she could muster. Finally, though not quickly enough for Wise, Florida was starting to pay off. The new year, 1951, would be even more eventful, and it would take her to the kind of position Frank Stanley Beveridge told her a *woman* would never have on his watch.

Gold Rush Days

In January 1951, Brownie Wise was out of the hospital, and she noted in a letter that it was the "first time in two years [she'd] been completely clear of headaches."

Squires had notified dealers that the division's name was changing to "Hostess Associates Inc." and dropping "Tupper" off the letterhead. Wise complained she'd been inundated with a "flood" of letters from her people concerned that Hostess might be on the verge of dropping Tupperware from its line of products. Squires assured them that the name change was just a technicality, but Wise pressed: "Will you please reassure me about this in a letter, mentioning that I have called it to your attention because of the dealers' questions to me?"

By February, Squires had responded as Wise had requested, which relieved some of her nagging insecurity about the Hostess Division. She told Squires that his letters had "driven away the sense of being 'lost' in the tropical hinterlands." Still, the "needle that bit the deepest" for Wise was learning after the fact that an area managers' meeting had been held in Worcester, Massachusetts, and she had not been invited. There were also problems with end-of-the-year commissions that Wise was forced to cover out of her own pocket. "Frankly," she wrote, "I don't consider this fair at all Mr. Squires." Confusion over shipments forced all of her dealers in Fort Lauderdale and Hollywood either to drive twenty-five miles to the Miami airport or to pay more freight to have the shipments redirected. Worse still, the customers who paid to take a chance on this new product started questioning if it would ever come. For Wise, that was more than just bad business, it was an outrage.

As the weeks wore on, the situation worsened for Wise and the stable of twenty dealers who received their Tupperware directly from her. One of them, Abbie Brant, had moved from Miami to Fort Pierce hoping to establish a unit there, but with the shipping, supply, and ordering problems, she ended up back in Miami. Dealers in Miami were starting to drop off, too, discouraged by the lack of support and consistency. In a March 16, 1951, letter to Squires, Brownie was all business: "I have little reason to do a good job of taking the company's side when my own affairs are as loosely attended to as they are, and I can't continue with my present stand if these conditions don't improve."

Wise couldn't get display cases for her new dealers, and they had to use "make-up" cases far beneath her rigid professional standards. For a month, she'd been waiting for letterhead bearing the new Hostess name and had received nothing. When Wise tried to call Squires to convey the urgency of the matter, the operator told her Squires was not free to talk and then advised that he wasn't in at all. After such a promising start, it seemed as if Wise and her dealers were back in the dire straits they had experienced before Squires and Hostess came on board. For a woman so devoted that she carried a piece of Tupperware with her twenty-four hours a day, this would not do. "Most important of all—Will you see that I get some sample cases to work with?" Wise implored Squires. "Or if I'm not going to get them, let me know, so I won't use up any more time, money, and effort on a futile cause."

Exasperated, Wise decided on another phone call, only this

time she decided to bypass Squires and Long Island and take her concerns straight to the top.

On March 27, 1951, the latest spring freeze on record hit eastern Massachusetts like an Arctic blast. The lingering winter in Farnumsville, however, was about to get some searing south Florida heat via the long-distance telephone line.

Later that day, the unassuming operator at the Tupper Corporation picked up the phone and met with a woman's screaming voice on the other end: "I *demand* to speak to Tupper!"

The call was put through immediately, and he picked up.

"This is Brownie Wise! In Miami!" Wise shouted.

"I know who you are," Tupper replied.

Brownie was fed up with the fouled-up orders, and she was going to let Earl Tupper have it.

"I wonder if you know how serious a problem this is?" she lectured.

Respect was paramount to Tupper, and that kind of insolent talk could very well get an employee fired on the spot. Then again, Brownie Wise was not his employee per se. She was more of an independent contractor building a business from which they were both benefiting. Despite the problems, Wise was selling more Tupperware per week than "anyone, anywhere," which explains why Tupper moved quickly to make sure her orders were straightened out, and then called her back that very day to let her know he was handling it.

Tupper had bigger problems on his hands, however. Barely eight months into its existence, the Hostess Division was collapsing, and he suspected Norman Squires of stealing money. Scholar Alison Clarke reported that Tupper later sued Squires for running off with "$200,000 in invested monies." Squires strongly disagreed, contending that Tupper had used the knowledge he had brought to the corporation and then "unlawfully dismissed him." The messy divorce between Tupper and his Hostess Division left Tupper looking once more to redirect the sales end of his business. Brownie Wise's screaming voice was one he needed.

When Tupper called back, he asked Wise how she was managing to move so much Tupperware, and would she come to meet with him? "I'm busy," Wise replied, fuming. If Tupper wanted to meet, she told him, "You'll have to come to me."

It was the first interaction between two titanic personalities who, in the next seven years, would guide Tupperware to spectacular sales success. "Their relationship was set right there," the writer Charles Fishman observed. The back-and-forth continued. If Tupper wanted to meet, Wise told him, he would have to invite everyone else who had experience building their party-plan businesses before Hostess got involved. Tupper agreed, inviting the likes of Ann and Tom Damigella, Russ Bassett from Connecticut, and a few of the other successful home-party people.

On Monday, April 2, 1951, Wise met Earl Tupper for the first time, during a two-day sales conference at the Garden City Hotel on Long Island. His Hostess area managers sat at the meeting table, filling Tupper in on how they were making American housewives coast to coast fall in love with Tupperware. The party plan, they told him, was the future of his product—not retail, not showroom—and only through skilled home demonstrations could it have its full impact on would-be buyers.

On the surface, it seemed like they were asking Earl Tupper to take a monumental risk—to put Tupperware, the pinnacle of his life's work, solely in the hands of a sales network comprised almost entirely of female business novices like Brownie Wise. In truth, many of them had already earned their stripes through Stanley, and they had both the smarts to see Tupperware's potential and the guts to stake their futures on it. They stood committed despite the seven months of hell they had endured riding the Hostess Division roller coaster. "I learned long ago," Wise said, "that a kite rises against, not with, the wind."

Overnight, as Tupper thought about what the group was proposing, he was taken by its persuasiveness, especially Brownie's, and on April 3, he called Wise in her hotel room. "You talk a lot and everybody listens," he told her.

It was a calculated gamble, and Earl Tupper was signing on. On Tuesday, April 3, 1951, Tupper formed the Tupperware Home Parties Division (THP) and offered Wise the position of general sales manager. Within a few months, the Hostess Division remnants would be absorbed into THP, and the association with Squires would be largely ignored in the annals of Tupperware history. Tupper was giving Brownie Wise the opportunity to eliminate the infuriating stumbling blocks she had faced under Squires, and to reach the brass ring that Beveridge said she would never attain at Stanley.

Wise's promotion would be especially notable since there were few women in upper business management Wise could count as contemporaries in 1951. Dorothy Shaver was setting new trends at Lord & Taylor. In cosmetics and skin care, Helena Rubenstein and Elizabeth Arden were becoming household names. The late Madam C. J. Walker was already a legend as an African-American who became America's first self-made female millionaire.

Still, from a pragmatic standpoint, the offer was not immediately attractive to Wise. Tupper wanted to establish the new home-party operation just down Main Street from

Farnumsville, in Fisherville, Massachussets. For Wise it would mean having to give up not only her home in warm, sunny Florida after only eleven months but also her lucrative distribution end—all in order to draw a regular management paycheck of $400 a week.

As a compromise, Tupper allowed her to split time between Massachusetts and southern Florida, and she agreed to run the home-party operation at least until it was well established enough that someone else could take over.

On May 3, with Wise now on board, Tupper sat down and drew up a plain-talk letter intended to woo dealers back into the fold and reassure those who'd been holding fast through the Hostess debacle:

> *Dear Tupperware Dealer:*
>
> *We have plenty of Tupperware right in stock ready to ship—And that includes the entire line. You can also look forward to new items soon unless materials become more difficult to get. Rest assured that Tupper will have materials as long as they can be had legitimately. If anyone tells you that you cannot get Tupperware, please let us know.*
>
> *You are in a lusty business; and like in all the old gold rush days, you will make a lot of money if you stake your claim wisely. As in the gold rush days, there seems to be every sort of scheming afoot and everyone seems to be trying to grab off of someone else's claim.*
>
> *Those of you who are selling Tupperware, know that it is pay dirt because it was the first of its kind to be made*

and still is first by far in volume sold and in quality. People remember and ask for it. It is the backbone of plastics parties. No imitation will ever be as good. There is just exactly as much difference between the Tupperware original and imitation, as between an original painting and a copy— or an original in anything and the copy that comes later.

We want Tupperware dealers who recognize that fact; and who will not offer other products of similar appearance at Tupperware Home Parties and lead people to think they are getting all Tupperware. If any person suggests you do that, please let me have the details. You and the buying public are going to be hearing a lot about Tupperware and other Tupper Products.

Later that week, Tupperware announced the appointment of Brownie Wise as general sales manager for the Tupperware Home Parties Division. To round out THP's two-person executive staff, Wise turned to an old friend from her days in Michigan.

While Gary McDonald was still a new marine recruit in California, he and other soldiers had been enlisted to help fight range fires in the southern part of the state. After three days and nights of breathing in noxious smoke, McDonald was "hit with asthma" and could not breathe. In a field hospital, as McDonald was receiving pure oxygen, an absentminded doctor strolled in with a lit cigarette. The attending corpsmen dove out of the room at the sight of it, but fortunately the blunder didn't ignite anything. After McDonald was moved to Pendleton's base hospital, another doctor prescribed an ether enema. "I called that doctor every word I ever learned in the Marine Corps," McDonald laughed. As many of his contemporaries marched off to the Korean War, twenty-year-old

Gary McDonald's asthma and tribulations led to a medical discharge.

The military's loss was Tupperware's gain. Upon his return to Michigan, a wire was waiting for him: "Unpack your sea bag and pack your suitcase, we need ya, Brownie Wise and Earl Tupper." After just a few days back home, McDonald was given the title of sales promotion manager and joined Wise at a Fisherville mill Tupper had purchased to house THP. It started humbly with a couple of offices, four clerk secretaries, and one bookkeeper.

Tupper also approached two stalwarts from the early days, Pete and Elsie Block, to see if they would put the power of their Poly-T business back behind Tupperware where it belonged. "Earl Tupper assured us that we would have a continual flow of Tupperware again," Elsie Block said. "We trusted his word as final. We agreed to cover all the counties north of San Diego County to Madera and Modesto counties. That was roughly half of the Golden State and we were ready to start mining."

Before long, the Blocks promoted three dealers to unit managers, and then divided all of the remaining dealers between them. With that accomplished, they could start their weekly sales bulletin, promotions, and contests, letting the three units battle it out for sales supremacy. That same kind of business-building started to sprout all over the United States.

Once Wise was installed as general manager, Tom and Ann Damigella lost the one-on-one contact they had enjoyed with Tupper. "I give the man credit," Tom Damigella said of Tupper. "He aligned himself with Brownie Wise immediately. She was brilliant. She had the real gift of gab." It would be up to Wise to be a conduit between manufacturing and the distributors, and McDonald would handle scouting and recruiting new distributors in new territories. In the spring of 1951,

Tupper pulled Tupperware from store shelves, gambling that his network of motivated distributors would deliver.

During the first weeks of Wise's tenure, in a show of trust Tupper didn't like to bestow on outsiders, he took her on a tour of the Farnumsville plant, including his development laboratory, pointing out all the equipment he used to design and develop Tupperware. "Walking down the line of work tables," Wise wrote, "I saw this block sitting on a shelf and I guess I asked about it just because of feminine curiosity being as violent as it is."

"Oh that?" Tupper said. "That's the first piece of material they gave me one day at DuPont and asked me if I could do anything with it." It was the ugly piece of slag the DuPont people had seen as worthless.

"It just stopped me in my tracks," Wise remembered. "I think it is the most potent lesson any one of us can have about the power of man's imagination."

Earl Tupper and Brownie Wise at the Tupperware factory in Farnumsville, Massachusetts.

At that instant, in Tupper's laboratory, the determination and vision of her boss dawned on Brownie. "From this," Wise wrote, "came the magic of Tupperware in all its beauty of design, all of its lovely coloring, all the artistry, and think of the imagination it took, the tremendous imagination it took. But always remember that the imagination had to be followed by a great deal of persistence through the years, to turn *this* in to *that* . . . the best sales story I have ever heard in all my life."

Tupper gave "Poly" to Wise, who made it her most prized possession. She gave speeches about it as if it were a person, had dealers and distributors touch it for good luck and be photographed with it, and had Lloyds of London insure it as a valuable artifact. One person was assigned to make sure Poly was where Poly was supposed to be, and God help them if it wasn't. "Just get your fingers on it, wish for what you want," Wise would implore her dealers, "know it's going to come true, and then get out and work like everything . . . and it will!"

Wise toured the length and breadth of the Tupperware empire, including the L'Epiphanie operation in Canada, the Fifth Avenue showroom in New York, and Tupper Texas, which could have been the long-term home of Tupperware Home Parties had the local citizens gotten over their suspicion that Tupper was nothing more than an East Coast carpetbagger. Wise compared her journey to a magic-carpet ride that offered her the awe-inspiring big picture; now it was time to get the sales side off the ground and keep all those factories humming with orders. "Sometime I hope to set up a museum of the first hand-made pieces of Tupperware produced," Wise wrote, "when it was a dream to Mr. Tupper and an impossibility to the rest of the plastics industry."

After her orientation road trip across North America, in Detroit Wise gave what is believed to be her first speech as general manager of Tupperware Home Parties. With an abiding sense of pride and overflowing optimism, Wise addressed a crowd of friendly faces. "It's a new day for Tupperware Home Parties . . . for Tupperware," she told them, "for our distributors, for you and you and you and YOU. It's a new day for our customers in the field, who will be introduced to more and more new, useful, unique pieces, original pieces of Tupperware, designed for modern living."

The speech was vintage Brownie Wise, coaching dealers to be the best "service representatives" they could be, not mere salespersons: "Are you yourself as fresh as you should be—is your hair well arranged and shining and your hands well-groomed? (remember they frame every piece of Tupperware they handle!) Are your white shoes WHITE and your dark shoes gleaming?" she asked the audience. "When you make your delivery, is your appearance as inviting as it was when you put on the party? Have you time to be pleasantly cordial with your hostess, and relaxed, and friendly—or are you in a mad rush, because you got off to a late start?" She urged the audience to keep their minds refreshed and learn all they could from customers, fellow dealers, and managers. "We are not building for tomorrow only," Wise told them, "or next week or next month; all of us are building for the future. To build is to USE all you have."

The new THP Division was also about to embark on an "old, old dream" of their new general manager's: to make a movie featuring a demonstrator and audience. Wise hoped it would be a filmed version of the perfect party demonstration. "Well, 99% perfect anyway . . . we have to save the 1% to grow on," she mused. Wise thought it could be the best possible training tool for old and new dealers, "the most potent ammunition," she wrote, "anyone could have with which to fire the guns of ambition." On August 18, filming began in Norwalk, Connecticut, of a forty-five-minute, full-color feature complete with sound track, at a cost of almost $1,000 a minute. The star demonstrator was Marge Rogers, one of the alumni from Wise's former Michigan branch.

Business was booming with the flow of Tupperware restored, and Elsie Block reported hefty sales among her Golden State dealers. In one week, the Blocks' Poly-T company ordered 1,140 sets of Wonder Bowls and 6,360 cereal-bowl sets. By the end of 1951, Block said her operation had reached $365,000 in sales for the six months they'd been back in the Tupperware business. At their year-end celebration at the Pasadena Elks Lodge, their dealer numbers had grown from 30 to 130. Because of all the money the Tupper Corporation laid out to get the new division rolling, as of September 30, 1951, Tupperware Home Parties was operating on a $32,171.46 deficit. Yet Tupper's expansion plans were undeterred; clearly the early sales reports from operations like the Blocks' indicated good times ahead.

In September, Wise presided over the first sales conference of Eastern, Southern, and Canadian Tupperware distributors. To complete her ascent within the new company, the Tupper Corporation's board elected Wise vice president, also bestowing on her the title of general sales manager. At that conference, Wise announced a contest to award a Cadillac to each of the seven distributors operating in the United States who had the highest sales for the coming year.

In November 1951, an ad in *Salesman's Opportunity* magazine featured a smiling woman holding fistfuls of cash and the promise that Tupperware "must make $10 to $50 for you in one evening—or pay nothing." All people had to do to earn the "quick money" was attend parties, have good times, and expect a shower of "crisp bills and jingling silver."

The same month, acting as "editor, writer, artist and copy girl," Brownie Wise churned out the first edition of *Tupperware Sparks*—the companywide newsletter intended to boost employee morale and motivation:

> First came Earl Tupper's vision . . . beauty of design for kitchenware, plus the unique utility of "material of the future."
>
> Then came his invention in distinction . . . Tupperware!
>
> Now, the third great development is well on its way—Tupperware Home Parties Inc. the modern American plan to distribution.
>
> YOU are the most important single factor in the far-flung Tupperware PLAN.

The inaugural issue, complete with photographs, took "Tupperware Folks" on an eye-opening tour similar to the one Wise herself had taken just months before. Across America, distributors and dealers had to be every bit as impressed at the size and scope of Tupperware North America. Immediately, *Tupperware Sparks* was a public relations bonanza for Tupper. More importantly, *Sparks* became a crucial motivational tool, with dealers vying to get their name in print, their accomplishments recognized, and their picture next to Tupperware big shots like Wise.

For his part, Tupper was still trying to find a permanent home for his upstart Home Party Division. Remaining dead-set on areas where unions were not prevalent and land could still be purchased cheaply, Tupper scoured the Carolinas, Tennessee, and Alabama. "We were urging him to pick Florida,"

Earl Tupper gives members of the THP team a tour of his Farnumsville operation.

McDonald remembered, "because we could have all of our salespeople come down there on family vacations and we could have them there for seminars and big meetings and not have to worry about paying expenses." Wise remembered the morale boosting, team building, and educational aspects of the Stanley pilgrimage and thought Florida could add a hint of tropical sunshine and glamour to the draw. Tupper cared most about finding the most land at the cheapest price, which would explain why one of the first Florida locales he seriously considered was in Starke, Florida—home of the state penitentiary and death row, where condemned inmates met their fate in a native oak electric chair, "Old Sparky."

On slower weeks, Brownie would do her part in the search and load her now thirteen-year-old son and mother in the car and go land shopping around southern Florida. In Jupiter, Wise found the stretch she fancied most: "It's in what is known as the 'Indian Hills' section—rolling land, and closer to the ocean than most," she reported to Tupper. In a hurriedly typed letter, she took time to write in her own hand about this property, "Very nice!" A three-hundred-acre parcel near Boca Raton was also under consideration, right along U.S. 1.

The pragmatic and cost-conscious Tupper told Wise she should shop around Florida for an abandoned airport—not exactly the kind of tropical glamour she had in mind. He once made the fifteen-hundred-mile trip to Miami just to take her to one such airstrip in the town of Stuart. Wise yawned the whole way and made it clear she had better ideas in mind: "If you want an old airport, buy one," she told him, "but my head-quarters won't be at any airport." An old hangar could provide plenty of cheap space to operate, but it would also be hot in the summer, cold in the winter, and noisy almost all the time.

Despite Wise's concerns, at the end of 1951, Tupper took an interest in the Orlando municipal airport, a location steeped in history. In 1935, Amelia Earhart was among barnstormers who took part in the annual Florida Air Party there, and three years later, Eddie Rickenbacker celebrated the grand opening of Eastern Airlines' passenger service to exotic places like Key West and Havana. During the war, German POWs housed there worked the citrus groves and nearby packing plants. Some received such humane treatment that they made central Florida their home after their incarceration. Along with the rich history, the site also appealed to Tupper because un-like his recent experience in Texas, central Florida business leaders were welcoming and willing to help him relocate his company.

During her own barnstorming days with the Patio Par-ties business, Brownie Wise had made a number of trips to Orlando. The small city was far more landlocked and less at-tractive than the places she'd been eyeing as the future home of THP. She tried to discourage Tupper from putting the com-pany there: "PLEASE don't make a deal on the Orlando land right away," Wise implored him. "If you want to go up there, just go in on a temporary basis in the airport building, and wait a few months before you commit yourself to a building site. PLEASE . . . because I honestly think you could be terribly disappointed." Of course, Wise was trying to convince an autocrat who nearly put the home-party operation near Florida's state penitentiary. Shortly thereafter, Tupper also became aware of a cattle baron offering some land near the town of Kissimmee at a very good price.

Tupper mulled his decision: Should Tupperware Home Parties relocate from Fisherville, Massachusetts, to a temporary home at the Orlando municipal airport, with the idea of building a new headquarters somewhere in central Florida? Orlando wasn't the oceanside spot Wise was looking for, but perhaps she could make it work. The warm climate, lakes, and palm trees, as well as area tourist attractions like the Bok Tower, Cypress Gardens, and Gatorland, provided a suitable enough image for Wise to draw dealers. And the beaches were still close enough to suit Jerry. Perhaps, too, Tupperware could play a role in shaping Orlando as much as the city would shape the young company.

At the end of 1951, this still-sleepy, agrarian part of the Sunshine State was just beginning to awaken to the tourism and technological boom the rest of the decade had in store. Despite the promise of the economic and civic transformation that forward-thinking companies like Tupperware Home Parties could bring, Orlando was still entrenched in the ways of the Deep South, including segregated schools, pools, and restaurants—and worse.

On Christmas night of 1951, forty-two miles to the east in a little, forgotten outpost town by the name of Mims, Harry T. Moore and his wife, Harriette, were also celebrating their twenty-fifth wedding anniversary. Harry Moore was an educator, head of the Progressive Voters' League, and Florida representative for the NAACP. To Ku Klux Klansmen, he may have been the most hated man in the state at the time. That night, after Moore turned out the lights in his wood-frame home and fog had settled in around the area, someone detonated a bomb planted directly beneath the Moores' bedroom.

After a frantic drive to Sanford, to the nearest hospital that would accept black patients, Moore died of his injuries. Despite her own devastating wounds, Harriette insisted on attending her husband's funeral, and then died a short time later.

"The state is swarming right now with FBI agents," a newspaperman commented, "and we want the perpetrators caught and punished. Ninety-five percent of our folks are fine, decent-minded people. The other five percent are trash. And it is that trash that causes that kind of trouble. I suppose they do what they do because they feel they have to have somebody to look down on." The Moore bombing remains the most notorious Florida murder case for which no one was ever prosecuted.

These events would undoubtedly have been troubling to Brownie Wise, who had black friends throughout her life and counted on some as mentors during her formative years. In Michigan, some of her early dealers were black and made good sales in their neighborhoods; working-class people more than anyone needed ways to stretch their limited budgets.

Jerry Wise said his mother always opposed segregation despite it being the tradition where she had been brought up. Others followed Wise's example. When she came to Florida for training, dealer Claire Brooks credited her distributor Anna Tate for refusing to book hotels that would not allow black children to swim with white ones. "Mrs. Tate was, to me, way ahead of her time," said Brooks, a divorcée, who made enough money through Tupperware to pay for her home and put two daughters through college.

Despite the Moore bombing, a new day was dawning across central Florida as Earl Tupper contemplated a new home for Tupperware. Pulitzer Prize–winning Associated Press war correspondent Hal Boyle noted that many of the "new pioneers" were young veterans who had fallen in love with the climate while stationed in the Orlando region and returned to launch their civilian careers.

"Florida is a land of reward for almost any fresh talent," Boyle wrote. "Anyone who likes to turn his hand to new jobs might find a real opportunity in a recent newspaper ad offering $75 a week for an alligator wrestler. When I remarked the pay didn't seem too attractive, an old timer remarked: 'Well, the hours are short and it's more than the alligators get.'"

In 1951, Earl Tupper finally found the sales formula he needed to make his dreams of being a millionaire possible, and now he was close to finding the right home for his operation in 1952. The new year would also be a watershed one for Wise, who had two more moves on the horizon—the latter of which would bring her to a waterfront mansion fit for a movie star. However, as 1951 drew to a close, she had her hands full with an upcoming distributor conference, her first as general sales manager. Some long-simmering tensions within the ranks were threatening to boil over, and success at this crucial summit would be the key to consolidating her new, hard-earned power.

A Sunshine State

*O*n New Year's Day 1952, Brownie Wise wrote Earl Tupper from Miami Beach, where the fifteen distributors assembled, including the Blocks and the Damigellas, held the fate of Tupperware in their hands. It would be their responsibility to grow their regions following the plan he had put into place. "These distributors have gone nuts over Florida," Wise gushed. "They're like kids at their first circus . . . never saw anything like it."

If this first conference was generally a success, Brownie also knew that some barely hidden frustrations festered just below the surface. The distributors had built their own businesses and recruited their own dealers without her, but now Tupper was asking them to put their faith in her as he had. Some felt she lacked experience. Her old nemesis in St. Petersburg, J. B. Evans, expressed his own ideas at the summit about how things should be run. Wise insisted that no other sales meetings be held until she called one in June or July. "We're in for a bad session of it, I'm afraid," Wise reported to Tupper. "One sour apple y'know. . . . Not that I think any serious upheaval will result—it's just too bad to waste distributors' time, when they need so much help as they do, with bull sessions on J.B.'s brainstorm." Wise gave all of her distributors the first edition of *Tupperware Know-How,* her primer on how to give better demonstrations and ring up more sales. She called it "the most complete and effective manual of its kind in the direct selling industry."

Despite that milestone, Elsie Block was not impressed. When she and Peter reported to the other distributors that the line they were selling was already 90 percent Tupperware, their peers wanted to know more. Some were just coming into the new party-plan system and carried a wide variety of other "saleable merchandise." Elsie remembered that "We were riddled with questions about warehousing, licensing, recruiting, training, premiums, and so much more." Apparently Wise also noticed the distributors' interest in the Blocks and wasn't pleased. In their hotel room later that evening, Peter and Elsie got a visit from a Canadian distributor.

"I think I should warn you of something that I don't think you're aware of," he said. "I have been watching Brownie's reaction while you are answering questions coming from the folks at the meeting."

Peter asked what he meant.

"It's not sitting very well with her. You folks are getting too much attention." "We were so cautious from then on," Elsie Block wrote. "I could understand her feelings, if it were true about her. After all, she was the newly appointed leader of the pack and coveted their recognition."

If Wise felt a rivalry with the Blocks, she didn't mention it in her New Year's Day letter to Tupper. He needed to know how much demand he might expect on his manufacturing end and wanted Wise to ask her distributors. It was an important question; if they wanted the new plan to work, an uninterrupted flow of Tupperware to their customers was vital. The Blocks projected $1 million in sales for 1952. With that kind of performance promised, even if Wise was competitive with Elsie Block, this early, team-building stage in the company's existence was no time to press the issue.

The tone of Brownie's letter to Tupper was upbeat; she knew he was on his way to Orlando to prospect for THP's new home. "Have a pleasant trip," she wrote. "Be careful . . . these tourists are crazy drivers."

Tupper was further along in his negotiations than he may have let on. Just one day after she wrote that letter, the Orlando City Council unanimously approved a seven-month permit for Tupper Corporation's use of a massive hangar, T-129, at the city's municipal airport. Tupper promised to bring new jobs to the area, and Tupperware Home Parties was just the kind of year-round diversity the area's evolving, citrus-based economy needed. Even at the temporary location, he expected the airport operation to employ close to one hundred locally recruited tool-and-die makers, machine operators, and clerical staff. He also left the impression that Orlando would be the permanent home for his manufacturing and distribution center.

On Thursday, January 17, 1952, the manager of the Orlando Industrial Board appeared with Tupper in Orlando to make the historic announcement to an assemblage of photographers and newspapermen. The next day, the *Orlando Sentinel-Star* newspaper ran the front-page story under the headline MILLION DOLLAR PLASTIC FIRM TO COME HERE. The paper also lauded Tupperware's arrival in an editorial titled "Another Central Florida Triumph." In a statement that had to thrill Tupper, the paper's editors promised, "The organization and its officials will receive every possible assistance from the city and its citizens." There would come a time when Tupper's people would need to call in a few favors, from the newspaper especially.

For Wise, the announcement was bittersweet. She had been in her south Florida home for only a year and a half, and she had had to fight like hell to get her business established. But there was little time for looking back, and Wise always concentrated on what was around the bend, not what was behind it. She had two moves to make: her home from Miami to Orlando, and Tupperware Home Parties' home office from Fisherville to Orlando.

Tupper announced to the newspapers that his people would arrive to begin setting up offices at Orlando's municipal airport on Saturday, January 20. To make that timetable, a lot of grunt work was required. Clerical staff packed up the office, and Farnumsville workers packed the Tupperware into a red truck for the Florida trip, with heavy items shipped by railcar.

Gary McDonald supervised the operation and got a first-hand look at Tupper's stern attention to detail one night when workers were well into the job of filling up the freight car for the Florida move. "I was supervising the thing and went back to the office where Brownie and Tupper were," McDonald remembered. "When I walked in, I told them they were about half-full, and the first thing he said to me was, 'Did you line the thing with plastic film?' I said no. He said, 'Good grief, man, those cartons *breathe;* they *breathe* in and out as it bounces along and will pull all the dirt in from that boxcar, into the containers, and it could ruin everything that's in there. Now get your ass over there and fix it!' "

McDonald sprinted back to the loading platform and had the men pull everything out of the freight car and start all over. "I told the factory guy what Tupper said, and he said, 'He didn't fire ya?' And I said, 'No, not yet anyway.' That's the kind of guy he was—harsh. McDonald was one of Brownie's guys, and Tupper wasn't about to fire someone so crucial to her confidence.

When the Tupperware was all loaded, the Tupperware Home Parties staff piled into two vehicles: the now-famous red truck driven by McDonald, and a four-door sedan with the women and the bookkeeper. With the railcar already bouncing its way down to Florida with its precious stock fully protected with plastic film, this tiny, two-car procession comprised the entirety of Tupper Corporation's executive sales branch. The shocks and front steering on the truck were so bad that McDonald kept crossing the center line. In the Carolinas, a police officer took notice and pulled him over on suspicion of driving while intoxicated. The procession of Tupperware pioneers ground to a halt as McDonald pleaded his case before the justice of the peace. The judge heard the story and released him, saying, "Get out of here, drive the best you can."

On Saturday, January 20, the group finished the 1,260-mile trek down the East Coast. When Gary McDonald made the turn off Colonial Drive and pulled directly into Orlando municipal's hangar T-129, a sense of happy exhaustion overtook any notion of what a historic moment it was. "We were so relieved to be here," McDonald remarked. "It had the magic that all Northerners used to have in their minds about Florida."

The hangar was a sprawling, cavernous space in which the team set up shop. Downstairs, they unloaded all the Tupperware they had into a small area blocked off with chicken wire. Upstairs, they placed the desks, phones, and supplies necessary to start spreading the new gospel of Tupperware across the country. Wise threw herself into the work, getting and making calls from the new office, as well as her new home in the Orlando suburbs.

Wise had sold her south Florida property for a tidy $5,500 profit and picked out a home on Orlando's northwest side. With its pleasing aesthetic lines and art deco influence, the single-story house rented for $100 per month and was situated just off the second hole's green at Dubsdread Country Club's golf course. The buzz at the local social hub the week Wise moved in was that West Virginian "Slamming" Sammy Snead had agreed to play in the upcoming International Mixed Two-Ball Tournament with another woman ahead of her time, Babe Zaharias.

Socializing at places like Dubsdread would have to go on without Brownie Wise for the time being, though—she didn't have the time. Within a few days of her arrival in Orlando, she adroitly began courting the press. She continued to use her married name, but no mention was made of something as personal as her true married status. She took out ads in *Opportunity* and *Specialty Salesman* magazines looking to drum up business, and an article in the January 24 issue of the *Orlando Evening Star* featured a photograph of a regal-looking Wise to the left of a headline that read: PLASTIC FIRM OFFICIAL SPREADS CITY'S FAME. The article noted that Wise had sent notices throughout North America informing the Tupperware faithful of the move: "Like Tupperware Home Parties," Wise wrote, "Florida is progressive and ambitious, it is the third fastest growing state! We sought a location that would lend itself best to national publicity and we felt that many of our people would like to visit us, especially with the wonderland of Florida to add warmth to the invitation."

In late January, aside from the cheerleading PR of Brownie Wise, there wasn't a lot of wonderland or warmth in hangar T-129, the less-than-auspicious home of Tupperware's new queen. Each morning Gary McDonald had to coax an old boiler into warming the place. The old machine began each day's work with such an explosion that McDonald remembered, "I never knew if it was going to be the beginning of the day—or the end of my life." Wearing coats and sweaters, people in the upstairs office waited for the big space to heat up.

The remains of the old air base provided a never-ending source of wonder and amusement for thirteen-year-old Jerry Wise, however. "I had the run of the west side," he recalled. "I used to drive my mother's '51 Hudson or Rose's Ford around the abandoned runways." He also discovered old World War II trainer planes and a "mountain of supplies just sitting there." It was as if the soldiers and airmen had just packed up their personal belongings and left all the government's toys behind. "There was no guard," Wise said. "You just drove in and drove out."

While Jerry explored, his mother busied herself with churning out her first Florida-based edition of the *Tupperware Sparks* newsletter. In a one-inch-high headline, Wise announced the company's relocation and establishment: TUPPERWARE—ORLANDO!

"So, we started in the sunny state of Florida," Wise wrote. "The welcome we received in Orlando made us want to take the time to stop and look around. And what we saw we liked! Orlando, as you know, is in the heart of Florida and is known by many pleasing names such as 'City Beautiful' and 'The City of Camellias.' Within the city limits are 43 lovely lakes. We are not the Junior Chamber of Commerce of Orlando, but we do love it here." The personification of all the Orlando Industrial Board hoped for when they rolled out the welcome mat to her boss, Brownie was already promoting Orlando as if she were on the chamber's payroll.

But Wise was about far more than promotion and public relations. She had a shrewd, almost uncanny sense of what to look for in a prospective "Tupperware Lady," and then how to keep her motivated once she was onboard. Despite her limited formal education, Wise also had a genius for effectively putting her philosophy on paper, instructing managers to use "eight basic qualifications" when scouting new dealers:

Health Her health must be excellent, so that she can work steadily and so that she can work on her feet, as must be done in conducting a party.

Need of Money She must have a real need to earn at least $50.00 a week, and it is still better if she must earn a good deal more than that.

Full Time She must be willing to devote her full working time to this business. Of course, this does not mean that she will have to work forty or forty-five hours a week— as she would have to do in ordinary employment. What it means is that she should have no other employment, to distract her attention from this business.

Evening Work She must be able and willing to devote several evenings a week to this work.

Family's Agreement Her family must approve of her work. For example, if she is married, her husband must be willing to see her give several evenings a week to our work. We must *know* that this requirement has been met. We cannot safely accept her statement that "my husband won't object." We must see him ourselves, explain our work to him and sell him on it, so that we can be sure of his full cooperation. This same principal [*sic*] applies to any other members of her family who are likely to influence her.

*Field Dating** She must be able and willing to do field dating, if and when it is necessary. This is especially important during her earliest weeks, when she may not have developed enough skill in dating Parties at Parties.

Residence She must live within easy reach of you, so that you can visit her personally and so that you can phone her readily—and so that she can attend your training classes and your meetings.

Training She must be willing to spend at least four or five afternoons (or an equivalent amount of time) and at least two or three evenings, in our regular course of training. AND, it must be more than mere "willingness." She must *want* to be well trained. If she isn't eager to devote enough time to her first training, you should not appoint her. Beware of the applicant who thinks she doesn't need thorough training. The odds against her are huge.

Wise also advised her managers to pick a woman who was at least twenty-five or who had "outstanding ability that makes you feel sure she will succeed despite her youth." If the woman had children, she would need someone who

---

* "Field dating" meant making cold calls to friends, relatives, and even strangers with the hope of getting someone to put on a party until the dealer network led from one party to another.

lives in the house to care for them, not just a sitter: "The expense of paying the 'sitter' generally leads the Dealer, in time, to drop out of the work." The prospect also needed to know how to drive and have regular access to a car and a telephone. In many ways, Wise was looking for someone who reflected the need and ambition she had as a young divorcée herself.

At the end of her dealer-recruiting drill, Wise cautioned: "You aren't looking for perfection. *You'll never find it!* All you are trying to do, in selecting new Dealers is to put the odds in your favor—by picking the women who rank highest on those characteristics."

Tupperware Sparks would inform the growing family of dealers and provide Brownie with an opportunity to regularly recognize their accomplishments and stoke their competitive fires. At the same time, Earl Tupper's gamble was starting to pay dividends: Tupperware Home Parties was gelling, distributors were starting to get product on a timely basis, and dealers were selling it to a new generation of customers.

On February 27, 1952, Wise sent out a newsletter to the new distributor network. "Pull out that bottom desk drawer," Wise wrote in a folksy tone, "put your feet in, lean back, and let's visit for awhile." She paid homage to Ann and Tom Damigella just for calling long-distance from Boston to say "hello." Wise lauded Pete Block—no mention of Elsie—for "his" January Tupperware orders totaling $25,353.18 "Number one for the States!" Then came the motivational push: "I'm sure you'll agree with me that sales like these do not just happen! It takes a lot of dealers putting on a lot of parties, demonstrating to a lot of consumers."

Earl Tupper was taking notice of those sales figures and sent a handwritten motivational note of his own to Brownie Wise:

Brownie,

> *Just a little line to be sure you know I appreciate what a whale of a job you are doing in spite of all the many problems. It's the first time I've ever had anyone so good on my team. Believe me it's a* good *feeling. We are going to do a real job.*

Earl Tupper

Wise could use the reassurance. In addition to all of her responsibilities with distributors and dealers, she was in charge of the Orlando office, and she sometimes butted heads with male employees not used to taking orders from a woman. When the machine-shop man came in and asked to use the keys to the company car, Wise asked why. "I want to use it, that's why," the man replied, looking surprised. Wise rebuked him but later fretted to Tupper: "I'm on the spot with him about it. Do you want him to have it? I don't want trouble with him." The company car problem continued for months; it was as if the machine-shop man—who was derisively nicknamed "the big wheel downstairs"—was making his own rules just to get under the boss's skin. Wise fumed to Tupper: "Believe me, I hate these fourth-grade arguments for authority. I'm fed right up to my teeth with this deal. But until I receive further instructions from you, the station wagon is to be used as you originally outlined."

Orlando's stormy spring weather brought with it a more serious problem: a blowing rainstorm flooded the hangar and damaged some of the inventory. The machine shop downstairs had standing water, forcing Tupper to focus, in earnest, on his long-term plans for finding land to build on. Despite these struggles, some photos from that time period reveal that these heady early days had a fun-loving levity that would characterize Tupperware events. One photo shows Tupper and Wise decked out for a costume party, he in a top hat and handlebar mustache, she smiling beneath a flowery hat. Both have on formal retro attire, but with a modern twist. Like loving parents, both hold Tupperware bowls, pitchers, and canisters close to their hearts.

A glimpse of the good times. Wise and Tupper suited up for a masquerade party in Orlando, 1952.

Over the next few months, orders began streaming into headquarters, and by the company's first birthday, on April 5, 1952, Tupperware had been chosen for the Housewares Award in the Modern Plastics competition, given recognition at the Industry and Handiwork show in Germany, and featured at the Modern Living exhibit at the Detroit Institute of Arts.

Most important, the number of U.S. dealers had swollen five-fold to fourteen hundred, which meant that Tupperware was gaining critical word-of-mouth, neighbor-to-neighbor, party-to-party popularity.

Brownie Wise and the Orlando staff celebrated the first birthday of Tupperware Home Parties with a formal dinner. Wearing a bright flower corsage, Wise cut a three-layer company birthday cake complete with a single candle on top. "Now the swaddling clothes have been shed," Wise said. "Our infant has bypassed years and has grown to effervescent adolescence. Adulthood is just ahead." Missing from the party was the evening's honored invitee, Earl Tupper. As a first birthday present, Wise sent him candy, nuts, and a mustache cup with a matching saucer. She also included a couple of photographs from the birthday party.

In a handwritten letter dated April 7, 1952, Tupper sent back a letter of uncharacteristic warmth, even giddiness:

Brownie,

I've just opened your package tonite. The one with the two party pictures! You sure look Super! Anyone that cute has no right to be so smart. I'm eating the nuts and candy right now—the picture of the cake didn't bother me until I started eating . . . but now yum! yum! I'm sorry I missed the party—pounds or no pounds. Where did you pick up the mustache cup? The saucer has a beautiful ring. Many thanks to you, Brownie, on our first birthday . . . for the happiest hours this business has known . . . and for doing the greatest job ever done for me.

Sincerely,
Earl S. Tupper

In May, the Tupperware Home Parties juggernaut surged forward with completion of *A Tupperware Home Party.* The fifty-two-minute feature, filmed in vivid Technicolor, starred Tupperware dealer Marge Rogers as demonstrator and costarred fourteen Tupperware distributors. This was the ultimate training tool Wise had always envisioned, to be shown by distributors at their sales assemblies across North America. Dealers would learn the best way to arrange a table to keep items easily accessible during their own demonstrations. "You will be shown how to say the right words at the right time, how to handle your product with grace and poise, how to deal with your audience and how to get their participation." Wise wrote. "You will be shown how to do a concise but complete demonstration of every item in the Tupperware line in a 45-minute session."

In early Tupperware films such as *A Tupperware Home Party,* dealers are shown how to expel air or burp the product to give it the airtight seal, and how to display it for maximum aesthetic appeal: smaller items in front, larger stackable items in back. From where she sits, the customer, dealers are told, should be able to view much of the display easily, and each piece should be within a short reach. The other striking element of the early promotion films is how formally dressed the women are for what are supposed to be casual neighborhood gatherings—a reflection of the time, and of Tupperware's strategy to emphasize the products' feminine appeal.

Given all the effort Wise had expended on developing a thorough and uniform training and motivational program, she found it hard to sympathize with distributors who weren't keeping pace with the leaders. That unfortunate distinction fell upon Russell Bassett of Hamden, Connecticut. Brownie Wise's letter to Bassett, dated May 3, 1952, showed that, along with being an expert cheerleader and motivator, she could be the taskmaster ready to use her ruler on a student not getting the job done.

"First, I hope you can appreciate fully, Russ, that the only sense of failure we can ever get here at the home office must necessarily come from some failure on the part of one of our distributors. We have in all cases given an equal share of sales aid and encouragement to all distributors," Wise wrote. "I have re-read every piece of correspondence in your folders, and I cannot help coming to the conclusion that you simply have not followed through, Russ. If you had used all the suggestions that have been given you, I truly believe you would have succeeded even without the past experience you have had on the party plan."

Wise warned Bassett that his distributorship could be at stake: "We have not received appreciable cooperation from you in reporting on the leads we have forwarded to you for your territory," she complained. "My serious advice to you (and it is also friendly advice) is to put everything you have into this operation for the next 60 days and prove what you are really capable of doing. I wonder if you fully realize how much money a number of other distributors are making Russ. Let me hear from you."

Wise also went to battle when a letter later that month showed that contrary to popular belief, in 1951, Tupper had not pulled Tupperware entirely from store shelves. He was considering putting a new line of Frosted Crystal Tupperware in department stores. Wise had to draw the line; she felt retail outlets were hurting her distributors' progress and undermining the training program she had worked so hard to install. Wise was not afraid to take issue with her boss and state her case in a forceful and analytical way. "The average home demonstrator does not realize how little is sold in stores where the product is displayed," Wise wrote Tupper. "He simply is conscious that our products are for sale in a store, and that this fact knocks out his punch line in the presentation of Tupperware to the effect that it is sold exclusively on the Home Party Plan. It further knocks out the reason we give for this type of merchandising. . . . Tupperware must be demonstrated."

Wise went on to disagree with Tupper that it was prestigious to have Tupperware in stores, or at least certain pieces of it, even if it did not produce much sales volume. "I cannot agree with you on that," Wise told him. "If you had visited as many stores as I have had to do to buy out what was left of a stock of Tupperware which had gotten dusty, and been reduced to cost, and stacked up any old way, you would realize that unless Tupperware is displayed properly, it is better not to have seen it at all. I believe you do realize this, because I think I have heard you mention some incidents along that line."

Tupper worried that Tupperware's potential for future publicity in magazines dependent on retail advertising could be compromised if the products were not available in stores. Wise was concerned about unrest among the foot soldiers charged with doing the real work of selling the product.

In California, Pete Block was the first to make an issue of the chain Van-Keppel Green still selling Tupperware retail. In Detroit, J. L. Hudson had a supply. Many top distributors blamed the retail stores for undercutting their hard work, confirming Wise's fears. "I feel we're just on the threshold of receiving the kind of recognition that all our efforts have been slanted toward," Wise complained to Tupper. "I hope you realize that I am giving this careful consideration; I am not pulling a mother-hen act with our distributors, most of whom

I could cheerfully kick in the teeth at least every other day. I have truly given this very serious thought for three days before answering you, and these are my firm convictions."

Wise had a good point. Across America new dealers were buying into the home-party plan, and in letters to Wise, Tupper was pleased with the way his new division was performing. And Wise could finally make sure all the new dealers were trained well. Why compromise distributor morale by sticking to the old, failed retail outlets? In this sense, Wise was firmly telling Tupper to let her handle sales, and he was demonstrating why he needed someone like her at the helm.

Tupper's correspondence with Wise showed that his mind and his attention were more naturally focused on inventions anyway. Among the sketches he floated by her was one for a funnel to be used for "feeding or watering an invalid in bed." Like a master guiding his apprentice, he sent her inspirational messages: "The Madness of Genius . . . is only the difference which makes the Genius tackle new things . . . believe they can be done . . . and do them! Quite naturally the plodders consider such a person unusual . . . even mad. E.S.T."

Tupper welcomed Wise's input on sales matters, but followed his own instincts on other matters, like a permanent home for his sales division. While Wise pushed originally for headquarters near the ocean, ever the frugal pragmatist, Tupper settled on more acreage for the money. At the end of May Tupper flew back to Orlando for another historic announcement: He had reached a deal with State Senator Irlo Bronson on a thousand-acre tract of land just north of the city limits of Kissimmee. Bronson, the speaker of the Florida House of Representatives, was also the largest landholder in all of Osceola County, assessing "his holdings in number of townships not thousands of acres." In just two real estate sales, one to Earl Tupper, the other to Walt Disney, Bronson forever changed the central Florida landscape.

Gary McDonald remembered how Tupper wanted to check out the swampy property for himself before making the deal final: "Tupper, true to his own style, walked the property carrying an iron stake with rubber gloves and rubber boots and a hammer, and he would push the rod down in the ground and hit it with a hammer to chase the snakes away."

On May 30, 1952, Bronson and William Bennett from Orlando's Industrial Board joined Earl Tupper and Brownie Wise in making a formal announcement of the land deal. Situated along the main artery bringing tourists into central Florida, the Orange Blossom Trail, the property encompassed a mile of highway frontage. For Tupper, the land's easy access to transportation routes was a big plus. For Wise, the proximity to tourist attractions up and down the Trail could be exploited in promoting the new headquarters to her stable of dealers. On Monday, June 16, 1952, workers started grading the land that would become THP's new home.

Despite their differing opinions about the move, Tupper

Earl Tupper handing Wise the keys to a new Cadillac in front of her Orlando home, 1952.

and Wise enjoyed one of the warmest periods of their professional relationship. Images from the time belie the notion that Tupper was humorless and didn't know how to have fun. One classic photograph taken in front of the Orlando Dubsdread golf course home shows a smiling Earl Tupper handing Wise the keys to a brand-new Cadillac. Tupper rarely posed for any public relations photographs of this kind.

The work on headquarters had to be jammed into the breakneck schedule of cross-country tra ' Wise was keeping. In June, she flew to San Diego, Pasader and Miami to award leather cases to the highest performing dealers. Each carried an inscription, "To a Star Distributor—Compliments of Earl S. Tupper, President of Tupperware Home Parties Inc." In Miami, Wise awarded the case to none other than Rose Humphrey. Nowhere in the June-July issue of *Tupperware Sparks* did Wise mention that Humphrey was her own mother, but Tupper didn't seem to see it as a possible conflict of interest. In San Diego, the biggest of the three winners was the Blocks' Pasadena-based Poly Sales Company, which had done $165,899.02 in sales over the seven-month contest period.

According to Elsie Block, at that award presentation she asked her dealers: "We've got millions of people in our area. Are we going to get out there and get the sales personally or do we all have to recruit new people to do the job?" All over the banquet hall at the famous Biltmore Hotel dealers chanted back, "We'll get all the sales!" "When I sat down," Block wrote, "Brownie turned to me and said, 'So that's how you do it!' I thought, 'She doesn't know?' It was on that night that Brownie got a glimpse into some of the reasons for our rapid growth."

While Elsie clearly intended to minimize Brownie Wise's knowledge and stature here, by this point in time one could understand why. Wise had literally written the book on sales know-how and dealer motivation, but she did some minimizing of her own in the June-July issue of *Tupperware Sparks*. A photograph shows Wise addressing contest winner Peter Block, with, once again, no mention or recognition in the caption of Elsie, despite the fact that she is smiling and very evident in the picture. Given Wise's penchant for diplomacy and attention to detail, this was more than an oversight on her part. She did, however, give both some written recognition: "The Poly Sales family turned out in full force for a giant rally and sales assembly. In honor of the occasion they had run a 'Brownie Wise Week' and their total sales for that week set a new record. Both Pete and Elsie Block paid glowing compliments to the cooperation of their dealers, managers and sub-distributors." The Blocks' distributorship would go on to produce some of the most important and successful alumni in Tupperware history.

Keeping with the new company's habit of holding conferences on holidays, Tupperware Home Parties held its semiannual distributor conference over the Fourth of July weekend at the Alpine Inn in Ste. Marguerite Station, Quebec. Highlights included the introduction of seven new Tupperware products, bringing the product line to thirty-two. Wise had a chance to preview the company's demonstration film featuring the ideal Tupperware party to the audience of almost seventy distributors. Cooperation, not competition, she told them, was the key to their young company's continuing success. "It is a source of sincere pleasure to me to know that I don't have to stand here and sell any of you people on the truth of this," Wise said. "All of you have accepted in this program a wonderful community spirit." Even her relations with J. B. Evans—the St. Petersburg distributor with whom she'd practically gone to war two years before—had come so far that Wise presented him an award "for general cooperation with the Orlando office." In the face of skyrocketing sales figures, it seemed almost anything could be forgiven.

"Brownie has kept me well-informed on your progress," Tupper wrote Evans soon after, "and we are happy to renew your franchise as you request." The August 4, 1952, letter was also Tupper's chance to let Wise's old rival know just who was in charge of the Home Party operation. "I'm happy because this just tells me again, as I've been told in so many other ways, that at last we have someone (in the person of Brownie Wise) who has the knowledge, ability and character to handle the difficult job of liaison between the factory, upon which you depend, and you folks, upon whom the factory depends, for a sound, successful operation." Tupper also gave a glimpse into his paranoia about his proprietary products: "Believe me, we are here, with malicious glee, very busy stewing some vile broths for those who step foot into our domain with products designed to annoy us."

In return for his confidence and praise, Wise had promised Tupper that her THP distributors would double their business in the second half of the year. With that deadline bearing down, Wise penned a memo on August 15 to "All-of-You," where her motivational techniques border on obsession:

> The vacant stare in my eyes is due to the serious contemplation that there are still five months to go before the deadline for my nibbling away at this tasty testimony. Now gather round, chillin, my voice is growing weaker. Self-preservation, they say, is the first law of nature, and I find myself strangely concerned about my own digestive welfare.
>
> I can appreciate that this *personal* matter is of more

concern to me than to any of you, but when a person is backed up to the wall with only a narrow avenue of escape, you can expect him to make the most of that avenue. I can assure you I will do just that. My only avenue of escape is obviously a 100% increase in sales volume from you and You and YOU . . . and from here on, you can expect me to resort to almost any means to achieve it. I may call you at three o'clock some morning to find out how many parties your dealers have coming up the next week.

Perhaps the stifling work environment had something to do with the memo's bizarre tone. "It is, shall we say, quite warm in our office quarters there," Wise said of the home office hangar, "which is another reason for all of us looking forward to September and the move to our own building." As Wise hopscotched around North America speaking of Orlando's glamorous locale, working back home in the central Florida summer with no air-conditioning was pure hell. The upstairs office in the metal hangar was cooled by huge, noisy box fans. To keep papers and files from blowing away, the staff weighed them down with two-by-fours.

In September, Wise was encouraged on two fronts: The shell of the modern, spacious, and air-conditioned new headquarters was nearing completion, and sales during the month of September hit an all-time high. In San Diego, Esther La Venture recorded a "sensational" $1,303.67 sales week.

La Venture had had a hunch that it was not too early in the year to include a small Christmas tree in her presentation: "I had the smallest pieces of Tupperware tied with ribbons and placed beneath the tree. This must have been a good idea as the guests did buy, plan and talk Christmas shopping with their friends. My party sales climbed, I mean leaped." *Tupperware*

Sparks featured a picture of a California dealer smiling proudly, a tiara on her head after being named "queen of the week." Wise seized upon the accomplishments of star dealers to urge on others. "Hitch your wagon to a Tupperware star," Wise wrote, "and begin breaking some sales records yourself."

On October 15, Tupperware made headlines by awarding a new Cadillac to each of the seven highest-performing distributors over the last twelve months: Peter Block of Pasadena; Tom Damigella of Everett, Massachusetts; J. B. Evans of St. Petersburg; Rose Humphrey of Miami; Eli Schofield of San Diego; Mildred Thompson of Lindenhurst, New York; and Ronald Tremblay of Montreal. The scope of the prizes awarded reflected how far the company had come since the previous year, when they'd had an operating deficit of $32,000.

Reactions were quite different among some of the winners: "When we saw the Cadillac we could not help but gawk at what we saw. There had been mounted on each of the front fenders long bugle horns," Elsie Block wrote. "We even kidded about entering it in the Rose Parade. That would have been a great way to advertise Tupperware." Rose Humphrey never even drove hers, preferring to trade in the Cadillac for a more modest Ford; her vehicle of choice dated back to the family's Detroit days. Tom and Ann Damigella wrote Earl Tupper a letter of thanks: "In spite of your absence, we could not help but feel your presence there in Orlando, especially since most of us present there had had the pleasure of your personal acquaintance and also the happy experience of growing with Tupperware."

These were some of the best times Wise would ever experience at Tupperware. In 1952, Tupper paid her a salary of $20,933.33, far more than she had ever made since being on her own. He also agreed to provide her a home near the new company headquarters. That concession might have helped Wise get over her initial impression of Kissimmee, with a population hovering around four thousand, as something of a "hick town." Lake Tohopekaliga, a 19,000-acre lake just south of the city's small downtown, caught her eye especially.

Jerry Wise remembered his mother driving him around the northeastern edge of Lake Toho—as the locals called it—to their new home. Off in the distance on a peninsula, "it was all you could see; it looked like a castle." It was a home Hibiscus would have been proud of, only this time there was nothing fictional about it. It would provide a kind of regal Southern lifestyle Brownie Wise could have only dreamed about that cold spring day in 1950 when she left Michigan for an uncertain future in Florida. It was Tupper's payoff for all Wise had done to bring Tupperware Home Parties to fruition and another setting Brownie Wise would use to attract homebound housewives to Tupperware. She called her mansion Water's Edge.

Water's Edge, on the shores of Lake Toho in Kissimmee.

"There's Gold for Me in '53"

In 1952, the first full year of Tupperware Home Parties' existence, the pride of Abilene, Kansas, Dwight David Eisenhower, was elected president, and less than a month later he made good on his promise to visit the war zone in Korea. Dave Garroway hosted the first-ever edition of the *Today* show on NBC, the first open-heart surgery was performed, and Siamese twins were successfully separated for the first time. But what perhaps mattered most to Brownie Wise was the news that distributors had sent in wholesale orders totaling $2,170,617.62. And there was every indication that those numbers would continue to grow in the new year.

On the Orange Blossom Trail north of Kissimmee, workers had dug a reflecting pond to provide fill material on which to build THP's new 40,000-square-foot headquarters. In late November, as soon as the shell of the building had a roof, Brownie Wise and her team moved in. In many ways, the huge space was reminiscent of the airplane hangar they had left behind in Orlando—there were neither walls nor dividers nor proper office space. There was still much work to be done to complete their new home, but mercifully, from the beginning it did have air-conditioning. Workers installing the metal roofing overhead made such a clamor that each strike of the hammer sounded "like a rifle going off." For Wise, with the move it finally felt like the company had arrived:

We now have our roots firmly down in Florida's tropical soil, our new building has attracted wide attention and is a modern, efficient and comfortable home for our operation. In that home, large enough for us to spread our wings, we will be able to do a great deal more in the way of promotional work for our national program. Now that it is over, we can look back with even a smile at the handicap under which we operated during the first year of Tupperware Home Parties Inc.

Her choice of residence ensured that Brownie Wise would live a regal existence compared to most of the Florida natives around Kissimmee and Osceola County. On November 14, 1952, the *Kissimmee Gazette* ran a front-page story reporting that the Tupper Corporation had bought, for a hefty $35,000, the sprawling home Brownie Wise had spied along east Lake Toho. The house featured "eight spacious rooms" and nineteen hundred feet of lake frontage, "the most of any other property in this area." The architecture showed Spanish influence with red tile shingles surrounded by tropical palm trees. The home featured one of the few indoor swimming pools in the area. There were sweeping staircases, broken-tile floors, and plenty of entertaining spaces. According to local legend, the home had been built in the 1930s for a film star whose name no one could recall. As it turned out, the star had a change of heart and never moved in anyway.

For fourteen-year-old Jerry Wise, the home was awe-inspiring. His mother almost changed her mind about moving in when she spied some squatters who'd already taken up residence outside the estate. "Gators," Jerry said, "big ones." Brownie and Jerry soon learned, however, that alligators, no matter how big, have a natural fear of humans. As a last resort he and his mom could always, "shoot 'em if they got too close."

Wise swept into action, hiring a maid, surveying what renovations and repairs were needed, and installing a dining room table fit for a queen. "Good Lord," Jerry remembered, "that thing must have been fifteen feet long, with matching chairs." Brownie painted her bedroom pink and quickly assumed an aristocratic mantle in a very small, out-of-the-way cow town.

Inside the luxurious Water's Edge, Brownie Wise has her portrait painted.

During this period, another key player in the early days of Tupperware Home Parties came on board: Jack Marshall. Dark-haired and broad-shouldered, Marshall had a salesman's smile almost as big as his personality. He'd worked in the trenches with dealers, managers, and distributors dating back to his days as a brash Stanley man. Notice the unusual tack Wise takes in describing Marshall's hire:

He studied Brownie's vision, her product and her plan. What other company had ever built a dealer strength of 3,000 in so short a time? How had they done it? As Brownie talked, he realized that she had made sound plans in the beginning . . . and followed them. It indicated solid foundations. So Jack Marshall decided to become a part of Tupperware's growth. He was appointed general sales manager.

Another key personality in the worldwide spread of Tupperware came on board during this early growth period: a humble, diminutive, and soft-spoken Deland, Florida, housewife named Elsie Mortland, who personified Tupperware's potential for changing the lives of common working women.

Some friends from a nearby self-service laundry had recommended Mortland the day a woman came around asking if anyone might be interested in becoming a dealer, "mostly to get rid of her," Mortland laughed. In those days, Mortland, like many housewives, thought plastic products coarse and inferior. When you poured hot water in them, "they would almost melt." Tupperware was different; "that's when women started using it and telling each other how wonderful it was." Before long, Mortland became a star dealer in Rose Humphrey's distributorship. Through hard work and practice, Mortland perfected demonstrating the Tupperware burp. "I remember one of the early parties in Deland; a woman came in and the first thing she said was, 'I want a set of those salt and pepper shakers with the toilet seat tops."

As Tupperware found its way into the hands of more and more ordinary women like Elsie, something happened. "No women got praised for scrubbing floors, mopping floors," Mortland reflected. "But when they got praised for selling Tupperware, they had something to be proud of." That simple yet profound concept was resonating nationwide, as demonstrated in an important piece of publicity Tupperware received from *Salesman's Opportunity* magazine. An article entitled "How a Typical Homemaker Learned the Secret That Can DOUBLE Your Family's Income" delves with a sense of wonder into the very notion that a salesman's opportunity could come to an average, yet enterprising housewife—Tupperware dealer Eleanor Sterhan.

Lest the reader jump to too many conclusions, the article begins by reinforcing where a woman's place remained: "The orderly five-room Sterhan bungalow in a quiet residential section of Detroit, her well-mannered youngsters, and her proud husband are ample proof of her success in every woman's most important job . . . that of wife and mother."

However, the piece also goes on to conclude that what makes Eleanor exceptional is "her top-flight success in the dual role of homemaker and career woman. . . . For although she is not a career-woman type, Mrs. Sterhan has been operating her own business for more than three years." Whatever the "career-woman type" was up to that point, articles like this one reveal how revolutionary the female-based Tupperware home-party sales system was.

The article describes how Sterhan overcame her first party jitters, despite the absence of the experienced demonstrator assigned to her, who was too busy with her own parties to show up. To enhance the upbeat, soft-sell Tupperware philosophy, "[Sterhan] began by dividing the group into two teams. Then she placed an orange under the chin of each captain, instructing them to pass it chin to chin, to the members of their teams without touching it with their hands. The team that returned the orange to the captain first was the winner." Only after several games were played and prizes awarded did Sterhan start her demonstration of the Tupperware samples she'd set up on a card table.

Mrs. Sterhan was not a natural salesperson and didn't know how to give a so-called "sales talk." Yet she described the plastic products, their uses appropriate for every room in the house, and their pastel colors: lemon, lime, peach, raspberry, plum, and frosted crystal. She demonstrated the patented Tupper seal, passed the samples around, and then "chatted with her prospects while they drank their coffee and placed their orders." That first party netted her a respectable $80 in sales, of which she kept $25. From that point on, the Sterhans went into the Tupperware business as a family team. The two teenage daughters pitched in with the housework, and Mr. Sterhan "packed and unpacked merchandise, made deliveries," and even "prepared many a dinner for the family."

Before long, Eleanor was putting on five parties a week, earning around $100 in weekly profits, and "practically" doubling her husband's postal service income. Even more appealing to post–World War II baby boom families, "the Sterhans quickly replaced their 1937 Packard car with a new automobile, practically refurbished their home, bought a TV set, took a motor trip to California, and made financial problems a thing of the past." Beyond the comfort of money, Sterhan says her main sense of satisfaction was the feeling of "security and independence" she had achieved. "There's as much money to be made as anyone needs," Sterhan reflected. "All you have to do is put a little effort back of your desires. There is no profit in hoping . . . but there is profit in selling." It is a quote that could well have been written by Brownie Wise herself.

With these kinds of typical, yet extraordinary, women coming into the Tupperware family daily, and with the kind of publicity this phenomenon was generating, the 1953 catchphrase of Tupperware Home Parties was "There's gold for me in '53." For Tupper and his manufacturing division, it was a call to arms, but orders flooding in did not always translate into product rolling out. In a memo early that year, Tupper addressed his "Fellow Workers" about the need to keep up with ever-increasing demand. "From what you have seen lately, you know we have a real live-wire sales division. We have a hard job ahead of us to keep up with them," Tupper wrote. "That means you and I all have that job—but it offers a dandy reward in the way of greater success and promotion and better pay—if we come through. I need your help!"

On the sales end, Brownie Wise closed out 1952 with another cross-country trip to California to award THP's first-ever National Merit Award, which Wise had designed to recognize Tupperware's top dealer in the nation. "The qualifications of so many were so high," Wise wrote, "we pitied the three outside individual judges who had the problem of choosing the winner." The judges decided on Corliss Levitt of San Francisco, the mother of three young children who had to borrow the down payment for her Tupperware sample case. Wise called her on New Year's Day to pass along the good news. "I was in heaven!" Levitt wrote. "What I did, others can do and will do . . . just as soon as they have the want to!" The December-January 1952–53 issue of *Tupperware Sparks* shows a photograph of the smiling winner, with flowers on her arm, accepting the engraved silver-vase trophy. As was the case with many super dealers, Levitt would go on to be awarded her own distributorship.

At the Pasadena distributor conference held at the posh Huntington Hotel, Wise made the "thundering announcement" that sales for the last half of 1952 were triple those of the first. Part of the credit has to be given to Wise for standing up to Tupper when it came to keeping his product out of department stores, a strategy that still went contrary to his instinct, regardless of what he might have been saying publicly. Appropriately festooned with flowers, Wise awarded Hawaii trips to the two distributors who most exceeded her goal of "double-in-the-last-half of '52."

In typical Brownie Wise fashion, she found a way to congratulate her distributors' success yet ensure that no contented stagnation would set in:

> There are outstanding examples, of course, of distributor growth during the last six months. Amazing examples of dealer sales records broken, of high weeks, of high parties. In spite of all this, and it is all good, we still have a long, long way to go. We still have territories unfranchised . . . and a lot of growing to do; for all of our growth and development and achievement—and for all of it we must be happy—we still have not scratched the surface.

Wise compared Tupperware dealers and distributors to miners from the nineteenth-century gold rush days and concluded with a quote from Earl Tupper on how to prepare for success: "The first step is learning to realize how little time you have in the world . . . the second step is pushing yourself to hurry and make the most of that time." Judging from her own schedule and workaholic tendencies, Brownie Wise had taken that message as gospel.

Back at the company's new home near Kissimmee, work was going "full blast" to complete the building in time for a big July conference. The "ear splitting blasts" that Gary McDonald compared to rifle rounds were actually .45-caliber shells used in what Wise described as "specially-designed guns to attach metal to cement block." On the grounds, steam shovels and cranes positioned tons of sand, gravel, cement, and landscaping. Outside, the placing of "giant *cocos plumosus* palms" added a windblown, tropical look.

Wise in front of Tupperware's first permanent building along U.S. 441 near Kissimmee, 1953.

Photographs show accountant Herb Young trying to concentrate on processing orders despite all the construction commotion. The largest image on the front page of *Tupperware Sparks* features Brownie Wise smiling peacefully, and she is quoted as calling the noise "music to our ears." The headline of the March issue, written by Wise as always, reads: BROWNIE WISE CREATES STARTLING NEW LOOK FOR WORLD-FAMOUS ORANGE BLOSSOM TRAIL. As Earl Tupper took to including just his initials, E.S.T., at the bottom of some correspondence, Wise was starting to use her own, B.W., to reflect her growing status.

Some distributors felt Brownie was taking on too much, however, and that their orders were getting muddled in the process. In California, the Blocks received the following message: "Upon receipt of this notice, all further orders are to be sent to Tupperware Home Parties, Inc. in Florida." For long-timers already smarting over the loss of one-to-one contact with Earl Tupper and the manufacturing operation in Far-numsville, sending orders to Massachusetts by way of Florida increased the chances of delays or mistakes. "Our concern was soon justified," Elsie Block wrote. A first order to Kissimmee went in with neither acknowledgment nor ensuing shipment of product, then another. Time was money, and Peter and Elsie Block were running out of patience.

Peter called the factory in Farnumsville. "I'm sorry," the voice on the other end of the line said, "you'll have to call Florida." When he did that, there was still no satisfaction from the operator. "Nobody can help you with that information except Mrs. Wise." Problem was, Mrs. Wise was out attending to something on the grounds and wasn't reachable. Exasperated, Elsie finally gave the Florida operation an ultimatum, "Tell her that if I don't get a call from her in twenty-four hours we are going to send a message to all our dealers to stop putting on parties." In less than an hour, Block says Wise called her back: "Don't do that please," Wise begged, offering that the ordering delays were due to a mold that had broken down at the factory. "One mold?" Elsie asked. "Is it true our whole order was held up because of one item? Dear Brownie, why wasn't everything else sent? Why weren't we notified?" Later, Elsie Block said, "I learned from employees at the Florida office that Brownie Wise hadn't delegated authority to anyone other than herself." It was only after Peter Block's persistent phone calls to Farnumsville that their company had a constant flow of product restored.

There were more problems with the new headquarters. Tupper felt the phone service and drainage were too poor to proceed with plans for the second phase of construction on the Orange Blossom Trail site. He had already sent down a freight car full of equipment to set up a tool shop in hopes of the problems being cleared up and construction proceeding on the new addition.

Despite those issues, Wise charged ahead with getting the headquarters ready for the July conference. In May, she hosted a tour of the new building for Stan Tasker and Caryl Bailey, husband and wife art professors at Rollins College. It was Bailey whom Wise commissioned to paint a forty-two-foot, ten-panel mural inside the headquarters building. "The mural will portray in a modern rendition the evolution of dishes," the *Kissimmee Gazette* reported, "from their earliest beginnings and continue through the centuries to a typical Tupperware mold. The hands of Earl S. Tupper, president of the firm, will be used as a model for the final panel."

Wise in front of Tupperware's Evolution of Dishes mural, ca. 1956.

Wise believed that business should support art in public places, a conviction that in 1953 was ahead of its time. She would go on to establish Tupperware art fellowships and hire a director for the Tupperware Art Fund. Recipients were chosen on the basis of their work, regardless of race, creed, or color. They could use the money for study, travel, or supplies. When asked why Tupperware was interested in promoting art and painting, Wise replied: "It's just one of the ways we've chosen to help pay for our room on earth. We believe that a company should exist for more than just to supply useful products." The notion of "paying for our room on earth" came from a phrase Wise remembered and often quoted from her own grandmother.

April brought THP's second birthday, which Brownie and her staff celebrated at headquarters and Water's Edge. *Tupperware Sparks* included the musical serenade "Happy Birthday Dear Brownie, Happy Birthday to You," as well as scenes of the revelry: Brownie sits at her desk, smiling at the congratulatory telegrams and flowers as staff stand around her; Brownie, in her party dress, beams as she prepares to cut into the five-layer birthday cake with the "2" on top; Brownie "cuts a rug" with Gary McDonald at the after-hours party at Water's Edge; Brownie poses with the cake again at Water's Edge, this time surrounded by the Tupperware men; Brownie mocks surprise at receiving a congratulatory phone call. It's unclear if Tupperware's photographer, Jack McCollum, insisted on Brownie being the focal point, or if Wise herself felt she deserved such recognition for all THP had accomplished.

Further establishing a sense of the company's growing national momentum, in the spring of 1953, Wise and her THP team barnstormed into Boston's Somerset Hotel for a sales rally. Leading the cheers was sales-promotion manager Gary McDonald with his trademark bow tie. Brownie Wise took the opportunity to pay homage to the East Coast's longest-running distributors, Ann and Tom Damigella. Her new right-hand man, Jack Marshall, gave an award to Artie Watts—an African-American unit manager. In 1953, it would have been hard to imagine a black woman holding even a low-level managerial job in many other companies, especially if it were located in Birmingham rather than Boston.

Despite supply problems, the slogan "Gold for me in '53" was coming true. Each dealer who had registered at least one so-called "Victory" week—where sales totaled at least $300— had his or her name listed on an honor roll. The list of names, flanked by gold columns, numbered three hundred. Some had enjoyed more than six Victory weeks; others had rung up weekly sales of more than $1,000. Sixteen of those on the honor roll ended up getting their own distributorships.

When Wise returned home from many miles on the road, she and Jerry each shared a milestone birthday. On May 25, 1953, she turned forty and her son, fifteen. To mark the occasion, and in a show of the esteem in which he held Wise, Earl Tupper sent her a Palomino horse on which to ride the grounds of Water's Edge. On her birthday card, he included a poem:

A Verse for Brownie Wise
I have a Palomino
Named Golden just for me
Because the way the tale goes
There's Golden '53.

Introducing Golden, the 5-year-old Palomino
Gelding

from Earl Tupper
to Brownie Wise on
her May 25th Birthday

Earl Tupper shopped around Kissimmee before settling on the "golden" Palomino, but it wasn't until later that Jerry Wise discovered Mr. Tupper hadn't gotten all he'd paid for. During a rainstorm, the horse's color started to run. Unbeknownst to Tupper, the previous owner had taken the liberty of filling in discolored spots. "Golden" was part gelding and part painted pony.

Good-natured and precocious, Jerry found this all very amusing. While his mother kept up her breakneck schedule, he had the run of a curious teenager's paradise. His main hobbies during the carefree days at Water's Edge included "riding horses and chasing girls," as well as aggravating his mother. He'd often play a practical joke on Brownie or spout off a dirty word just to get her reaction—always the same disgusted look, a pointed finger, and sharp rebuke, "I don't like that word!"

These playful interactions were particularly memorable for Jerry because they had become increasingly rare as his mother's career took off. Despite the move to Kissimmee, he still attended Seese private school on the shores of Orlando's Lake Eola, and for forty-six cents—to Orlando and back, twenty miles each way—the Greyhound bus picked him up and dropped him off at Tupperware headquarters. "That was the only place Brownie would be," her son remembered.

During these years, Jerry Wise also had a ringside seat to the spirited brainstorming sessions his mother and her staff held to try to come up with the next great marketing idea, dealer incentive, or training technique. In those days, Brownie's process was democratic, with a hint of a family dynamic and little attention paid to the long hours. After the workday was over, Wise and her small team of managers would head back to Water's Edge for more hours of strategizing, some of them quite intense. "It was interesting," Jerry remembered, "because they were arguing with each other and really fighting, and I was afraid they were gonna kick each other's ass." But Wise channeled the energy by requiring those around her to write down what they said. "She wanted everyone to sit down with a piece of paper," Jerry said, "and at the end of that meeting she wanted that paper full. And don't throw it away—it's going in the file with your ID number on it."

That summer, some of the suggestions that emerged from those brainstorming sessions bore fruit: THP produced a new game booklet to give dealers ideas for anniversaries and parties; a new product brochure kept them up-to-date on the Tupper Corporation's ever-expanding line; and new color recipe cards brought "ideas for dishes from across the land, and additional uses for Tupperware." The team also decided on what would become Tupperware's new symbol: the Tupperware Beauty Rose. To make it official, the July-August cover of *Tupperware Sparks* featured the rose surrounded by an antique frame and this caption: "Both symbolic of enduring perfection—the exquisite artistry of Tupperware . . . and the matchless and delicate beauty of the regal rose." Standing larger-than-life to the left was Brownie, dolled up in a shimmering gown and pearls.

On Tuesday, June 30, 1953, to kick off the distributors' conference, Brownie Wise hosted a buffet supper and cocktail party at Water's Edge. It was a chance to give dealers and distributors a first look at her "palatial home." Subliminally, it was yet another motivating tool: work hard, sell Tupperware, and a life like this is within your reach, too. At the same time, just to buy into a piece of this fantasy, the Tupperware faithful were expected to make these trips on their own dime.

Hence, the importance of a location that people regarded as a travel destination, where their children could enjoy the sunshine while they attended long days of speeches, training, and workshops. Often it was left to Jerry Wise to be tour guide for younger members of the Tupperware family.

In the headquarters' Pacific Hall, during that conference, Wise delivered a speech entitled "Our Place in the National Selling Picture." While she would gladly play the part of aging debutante for the cover of the company's in-house publication, Brownie Wise was also an astute businesswoman. She kept in close touch with regional employment trends, gave long-range sales projections, and analyzed the effects of explosive growth on the company's relations with dealers and distributors, as well as a host of other less glamorous minutiae that came with the job. When the legions weren't coming to her, Brownie Wise was going to them, logging an exhausting amount of travel in 1953.

Soon after the conference wrapped up on Sunday, July 5, Wise and Jack Marshall embarked on the most grueling travel schedule of their days at Tupperware Home Parties. Starting in Hawaii, the vice president and her general sales manager intended to put in 100,000 miles to personally tour Tupperware distributorships across North America and meet thousands of new Tupperware dealers. Wise wrote in 1953: "Our ties are particularly strong with our people because we have planned it so. The close personal contact of rallies, assemblies, seminars etc. have kept us very close to the dealers." It also sent the message to dealers that while distributors ruled the region, Brownie Wise and her Kissimmee office ruled the entire sales end of the Tupperware roost.

During the first three days in Hawaii, Brownie Wise hosted what has become, in company circles, a famous Tupperware party—right on the Pacific Ocean. In a photograph later run on the cover of *Tide* magazine, Wise stands next to a well-appointed table of Tupperware products, and the tablecloth has "Tupperware Home Parties" in plain view. While the nine others in attendance are dressed in casual clothes and bathing suits, Wise is the quintessential Tupperware Lady with coiffed hair, pearls, earrings, and a not-too-casual summer dress. This was just the beginning of an all-out publicity blitz for the woman soon to be America's executive "it" girl.

Wise giving a Tupperware party in Hawaii, 1953.

"I have the feeling," Brownie Wise wrote in a memo to Earl Tupper, "that you don't realize how close you are to rocking this whole direct-selling picture right back on its heels." Sales for 1953 were on a course to far surpass the previous year's, and in 1954, Wise forecast to Tupper that the number of Tupperware dealers would top ten thousand. Tupper himself had already made a shrewd move of his own that would help Poly-T reach the coveted "next level" in 1953. He hired a Madison Avenue public relations firm in New York by the name of Ruder and Finn to help guide his company's corporate strategy. They, in turn, locked arms with the formidable and enthusiastic public relations machine from THP, Brownie Wise and Gary McDonald.

Wise and her young protégée were about to embark on a difficult test: impressing editors from some of the most important and influential national magazines. With the backing of Ruder and Finn, Tupperware Home Parties was planning to host its first-ever New York press party. Bigwigs had been invited from many major magazines, newspapers, and wire services, including *Business Week, American Journal of Commerce, Newsweek, Tide, American, Ladies' Home Journal, House Beautiful, House & Garden, Mademoiselle, Cosmopolitan, Coronet, Retailing Daily, Opportunity, Glamour,* King Syndicate, the United Press International, the *Philadelphia Inquirer,* and many others.

To present Tupperware in the best light, they chose one of the most glamorous and ornate hotels in the entire city, the St. Regis on Fifth Avenue, which was within walking distance of Tiffany's, Rockefeller Center, and Saint Patrick's Cathedral. Just five years earlier, Wise and McDonald had been selling mops and floor wax in working-class Detroit neighborhoods. Now the former secretary and her young twenty-something sidekick were about to take on the Big Apple and a bunch of big-city editors. "My knees," Brownie remembered, "were shakiest of all."

Besides the date and time—Wednesday, October 21, 1953, at 12:30 p.m.—invitations to Brownie Wise's long-awaited press party featured a whimsical cartoon of a dozen women smiling and chatting while holding their stackable Tupperware. "I believe you will notice that the layout man for Ruder and Finn developed very quickly a real feeling for Tupperware," Wise wrote Tupper. "Notice its apparent light weight by the

way in which the feminine figures hold it in the sketch!"
The invitations added:

> We're having a party and we hope you'll come to meet the
> newest members of the famous TUPPERWARE family of
> Polyethylene table and refrigerator ware and hear about the
> plan that is revolutionizing the buying habits of American
> women.

Far from the Pacific Ocean shores and swimsuit-clad guests,
Brownie Wise would host this Tupperware party at the famous
St. Regis Maisonette, a posh dining room one floor off the hotel's main lobby. Built in the French Beaux Arts style, the St.
Regis had been a landmark in New York City since 1904, but
it looked like it could have just as easily been situated along
the Boulevard St. Germain in Paris. If Brownie felt at all out
of place in such rarefied company, she could take solace in
knowing that she wasn't the first Floridian to hold court at the
St. Regis. In the 1940s and 1950s, Dorothy Shay, the pride of
Jacksonville, became a fixture there, wowing the audience with
her smoldering charm and entertaining rendition of "Uncle
Fud." The song so delighted her audience that they often asked
for more like it, and Shay soon came to be known to the sophisticated New York crowd as "the Park Avenue Hillbilly."

As Brownie Wise moved with ease from the boardroom,
to an assembly hall packed with dealers, to an ornate dining
room like the Maisonette, she drew upon her Southern roots.
Her years spent speaking to crowds as a young teen prepared
Wise for the big moment, and she did not disappoint. She
wrote, "The setting for the Party was the most beautiful,
undoubtedly, that I have ever seen." The Maisonette's small

round tables were set on blue-gray linen, and vases filled with Tupperware's new Beauty Rose made striking centerpieces. A "rosarian" who had patents on such flowers as the first thornless rose had been brought in to make the arrangements himself. In all, 130 press people, many of them men, packed the room for cocktails, lunch, and the Tupperware "pitch."

In her fifteen-minute presentation, Wise masterfully blended information relevant to the various audiences present, including details of the company's method of distribution for business editors; arguments for the versatility, stability, and utility of Tupperware itself for women's editors; and "a little personal glamour" for the benefit of the editors of such magazines as *Vogue* and *Glamour* who were primarily engrossed in determining just how any appreciable amount of honest-to-goodness business was conducted by "a mere woman."

Wise also addressed why Tupperware was available only on the home-party plan, and then introduced the new Beauty Rose—just before Gary McDonald demonstrated how to apply Tupperware's patented seal. According to Wise, Ruder and Finn's people said the affair was "undoubtedly the most successful press party they had ever had." Wise agreed in her letter to Tupper: "I am sure that you would have been proud of every separate detail of it."

Ruder and Finn saw considerable potential in Wise as a revolutionary marketing figurehead. In-house, consciously or subconsciously, Wise had presented an image of herself as the ideal Tupperware Lady to her dealers. She did the same in the Orlando and Kissimmee newspapers, having herself photographed while explaining Tupperware to State Senator Bronson and giving speeches to myriad civic groups. When Ruder and Finn looked at Brownie, they saw something new and different to present to America's rapidly developing, suburban-based, consumer culture. What she had started doing herself months earlier, they wanted to amplify on a national level.

At a meeting with THP executives Brownie Wise, Gary McDonald, and Jack Marshall, the Ruder and Finn people talked about the "three *P*s" to consider in a campaign: the Product, the Plan, and the Personality. "They made a case that we had all three things that made a product unique," McDonald remembered. Two of them would be a tough sell, though: People still had a negative opinion of breakable plastics, and they saw parties as potentially high-pressure and an imposition on their friends. "It's the third one," McDonald recalled them saying, that was the easier sell: "the *woman* who's the leader of this company, and we could position her as such and build her up. We'd get great press on the fact that she's the leader of a company and that it's a company of women all across the country."

It didn't take much to convince those at the meeting. "We agreed," McDonald said, "and then Brownie talked to Tupper on her own and sold him on it." Earl Tupper himself signed off on the idea of making Brownie Wise the national pitch-woman for his beloved Poly-T. And why not? With the exception of a few supply hitches Tupper planned to address with the factory expansion, the party plan was working: Dealers were signing up, dollars were rolling in, and more and more people were seeing the need for Tupperware in their home lives. As evidenced by all the traveling and promoting she'd done that year, Wise was making Earl Tupper's invention a household name.

Tupper rewarded Brownie with a $10,000 raise, and by 1953, she was making $30,800 as an executive. By all accounts, his investment was paying off. Wise was exceeding expectations, and, as always, she wasn't afraid to let Tupper know when he wasn't. On November 21, 1953, Wise typed an eight-page, single-spaced interoffice memo to Tupper, challenging him on his decision to avoid an active role on the sales side.

"If this company had a President, who was active at all in the sales picture or would even permit his name to be used," Wise complained, "we could have a President's Club like Avon, Fuller and Real Silk have. . . . This is a club for star salespeople who qualify by meeting a certain required volume, but since we don't have that kind of President we make do with other gimmicks."

She also stressed how important it would be to take care of supply problems if he wanted more expansion in 1954. "If you intend to carry on this selling program," Wise lectured her boss, "I certainly hope that you have already laid a good groundwork for a greatly increased production output for the next year."

She told Tupper that all the positive sales projections could be out the window if he didn't: "This is so serious an affair and the outcome can be so explosive that I would be a fool to try to forecast now what will happen next year without knowing whether it will be necessary tomorrow or the next day or the first of next week to call our distributors off from further sales."

Wise knew better than to complain and criticize, however, and the tone of the memo is generally upbeat. In the coming year, Wise expected the number of Tupperware dealers to increase substantially—which it would—and for sales to more than double. And yet, she admitted, "We have at this time less than half the country franchised." There was a lot more gold to mine.

"I think it is time for you to decide whether you want Tupperware to step into the big time," Wise declared. "You have the possibility of an amazing amount of orders . . . pouring in a steady stream and increasing on a regular basis if you can outline a program without delay that will give you the assurance you can handle it." For the direct, take-charge Tupper, it had to feel strange for anyone to question his abilities.

"And then," Wise concluded, "for the benefit of everyone concerned, I think it is time we received a forecast from you. What can you do next year? That's all. B. W." During another year of explosive growth, Tupper could tolerate his sales maven's hubris. But he was reaching his limits.

To close out 1953, Wise initiated a program called "Operation Doorbell" that encouraged dealers to knock on doors or phone willing friends with the goal of throwing as many parties as possible. Elsie Block reported that some recruits told her: "Not on your life! I thought I was going into a business that would never subject me to such demeaning things to do."

Finding someone to hold a Tupperware party sometimes required dealers to make cold calls or phone up women who had hosted one in the past. "I stopped at the same gasoline station several times, with my station wagon loaded with Tupperware," Wise remembered of her South Florida days. "The station man got curious, asked me about it. It wound up with his wife putting on a party." Despite the reticence of the faint of heart, like everything else Brownie Wise initiated in 1953, the dating drive surpassed even her lofty expectations. "Telegrams from nearly every distributor . . . told the story of all-time dating records being broken," Wise gushed. In 1953, distributors had more than doubled their sales output from 1952. It was a fitting end to a record-breaking year.

To the Stars

If 1953 was Tupperware's coming-out party, then 1954 would herald its arrival on many fronts: The new national headquarters would be dedicated through an inaugural jubilee; Earl Tupper would embark on an enormous expansion of his New England manufacturing operation; Brownie Wise would make history in the business world; and the number of Tupperware dealers would skyrocket.

The onward and upward drive to "Tupperize" America was embodied in THP's slogan, "10,000 more in '54." In her November 1953 memo, Wise had told Tupper she thought it entirely possible to bring the number of Tupperware dealers to twenty thousand by the end of 1954 and to double sales yet again. To kick off her plan for accomplishing that lofty goal, she initiated a "Full Steam Ahead" contest in which five "lucky" dealers and one "outstanding" manager would win a six-day transatlantic cruise to Paris on board the *Queen Mary*, one of the most luxurious liners in the world—"a lifelong dream trip come true," according to *Tupperware Sparks*. "Winners will find that Paris is fascinating . . . fun . . . and French!" the article gushed. "Dealers and managers will sit in the sidewalk cafes along the Rue de la Paix and watch the Kaleidoscope of Parisian life flow past."

In popular culture, the film *An American in Paris* had been released in 1951, reintroducing the city's magic to Americans. Featuring the music of George Gershwin and lavish dance numbers by Gene Kelly and Leslie Caron, the film spoke to women's dreams; Wise was putting those wishes within reach.

With that kind of prize in play, some dealers booked frenetic party schedules. In the Blocks' Poly Sales Company, dealers held "six-party fetes" that started at 9 a.m. with parties held at two-hour intervals until the last one was held at 7 p.m. "During those marathons the dealer engaged a helper," wrote Elsie Block. "There had to be two sets of displays. The helper set up a display for the dealer at the first party destination before she got there and then proceeded to the next party address to set up a display for the dealer while she was putting on the first party." The hopscotch continued with the helper then going back after the first party was over, to take the display to the third house, while the dealer put on a second party. Then, after the all-day home-party blitzkrieg, participating dealers would meet that night for coffee to see who had tallied up the most sales. Elsie Block reflected, "It was an excellent way to learn how to cut down on time spent at a party and not sacrifice good results." So much for Brownie Wise's axioms about a Tupperware Lady showing up early and never being rushed.

In January 1954, Wise welcomed a crowd of two hundred students to the second managers' training seminar. In order to become an "Accredited Tupperware Manager," they were obligated to attain the "know-how and training that could be obtained nowhere else." The newspapers described the feel of the seminar's commencement: "Organ music and a candle lighting ceremony lent an atmosphere of dignity and emotion . . . more like a college graduation . . . than the commercial feeling one might expect in a sales conference. Tupperware officials said this serious tone of the graduation reflected the earnest purpose with which the managers had come here." As a *Business Week* correspondent once observed, "Emotion is the high-octane fuel of direct-sales success."

On January 11, 1954, THP's National Promotion Day, 345 dealers were promoted to manager, and four managers were made distributors. Six days later, Wise wrote a congratulatory, yet characteristically all-business, note to a longtime member of the Tupperware faithful who had relocated her franchise to Orlando: her own mother, Rose Humphrey. Humphrey's distributorship, Hibiscus Sales, had taken the roots of her daughter's Patio Parties business and seen tremendous growth throughout Florida and Puerto Rico.

"Dear Rose," Wise wrote. "We would like to take this opportunity to point out to you the responsibilities and duties of a Tupperware distributor go far beyond the usual meaning of the term, 'distributor.'" It wasn't enough for a distributor to go about the business of cultivating the region by holding his or her own contests, recruiting new people, and ringing up higher sales. "It is the responsibility of distributors," Wise wrote to her mother, "to help in Tupperware Home Parties Inc. as a national concern as well as to build their own local distributorships."

In 1954, everywhere you looked within the Tupperware empire, the main theme was expansion. Charles McBurney joined THP'S new Public Relations Department with a singular mission: "To make Tupperware a household word." Responding to increased manufacturing demand, as well as Wise's November challenge, Earl Tupper unveiled a new 25,000-square-foot expansion to the Farnumsville plant. Wise, McDonald, and other members of the THP staff "dug their overcoats from the mothballs" and flew up for a tour. It was, they knew, a rare invitation from the guarded and occasionally paranoid Tupper.

"That's manufacturing, and I've got all kinds of secrets," he would protest, and he took extreme measures to protect

them. When product started disappearing inside the factories, Tupper ordered the workers strip-searched. For women,
McDonald said, "it was very easy to put bowls in their bras and
walk out with them." Far from some sinister plot to try to steal
Tupper's hard-earned designs and patents however, the employees often just wanted the Tupperware for their own use.

Tupper also worried about New England's vulnerability to
attack from unknown forces overseas. In response to the possibility that his own workers or union rabble-rousers could
start any kind of trouble, Tupper had small living quarters
added to his office where he could hunker down if need be.
Compared to the sunshine, palm trees, and exuberant atmosphere in Florida, the Massachusetts operation was staid, Old
World, and low-key. That's how Earl Tupper wanted it.

To understand why Tupperware took off so quickly in the mid-
fifties, one must also understand the context from which it
emerged. Beyond the general optimism of the postwar years,
in 1954, the can-do attitude and Tupperware team building—
the all-for-one-and-one-for-all spirit—contrasted with other
events happening in the country. On March 9, 1954, legend-
ary newsman Edward R. Murrow dedicated his entire *See It
Now* program to skewering Senator Joseph McCarthy's Com-
munist fearmongering. Regarded as one of the great early
milestones of television news, the program rocked McCarthy's
credibility and hastened his downfall.

In the U.S. Supreme Court, Chief Justice Earl Warren
wrote the historic majority opinion on the case *Brown v. Board
of Education of Topeka,* declaring as unconstitutional the so-
called "separate but equal" racially segregated schools. In

seventeen states, including Florida, where such schools were the norm, the ensuing months and years were tense as the court's decision was enforced, sometimes with black students escorted by soldiers.

With so much fear and uncertainty pervading the American landscape, people were ready for a dose of wholesome distraction. As such, THP executives kept the pressure on themselves to come up with the next great contest, incentive, or publicity initiative. Brainstorming sessions would continue late into the night, often out at Water's Edge, which could be a problem for staff who lived a good distance away from Wise's isolated home. "We'd be out there late into the evening, then have to go home to wherever home was, Orlando or Kissimmee," McDonald recalled, "and we'd have to be in at eight the next morning." The team discussed at length how to make THP's annual birthday party a much bigger event.

"We talked about the 'pilgrimage,' "—a fond memory from their Stanley days—"and Brownie came up with the name 'jubilee,' " remembered McDonald. "Then we started working on how we could add a lot of pizzazz to it." The event they hatched, the first annual Tupperware Homecoming Jubilee, would have a western theme, and like miners at a gold rush, top dealers would have the chance to prospect for $75,000 worth of prizes in an event created just for them. That wasn't all. In concert with the long hours of training, speeches, and graduation ceremonies, attendees could win one of a fleet of automobiles, mink stoles, or "freezer units." THP's Public Relations Department sent invitations to the national press and media, hoping they might be interested in the spectacle, and their hunch paid off.

Before the jubilee could begin, however, plans had to accelerate on several new facilities at headquarters: Workers welded together steel beams on the roof of the new Garden Pavilion, a venue they designed to seat one thousand people. They also poured concrete into a quadrangle and planted shrubs and trees for the Garden of the Palms. In the Magic Kitchen, visitors could take in the glory of Tupperware products and their many uses. With the ten-panel mural complete, the Museum of Art focused on a first-of-its-kind exhibit featuring the evolution of dishes. Tupperware headquarters was set to become the world-class tourist attraction Brownie Wise hoped it would be. As a finishing touch, floodlights bathed the headquarters building in dramatic light for those who drove by on the Orange Blossom Trail.

On April 2, 1954, the *Kissimmee Gazette* ran a front-page story, with an accompanying photograph of Tupperware headquarters, heralding the "Cinderella" company's plans for its first jubilee: "Mrs. Wise has led the company in its rapid growth to second place among all sales corporations merchandising on the home party plan. The multi-million dollar corporation has doubled its business during each of the past two years and is expected to triple this year." Often, articles like this jubilee announcement were little more than company press releases reprinted verbatim, even if the sales accomplishments were a bit overstated.

Curiously, the *Kissimmee Gazette* piece also notes that Tupperware Home Parties Inc. had been founded three years before by "the Tupper Corporation of Massachusetts." Nowhere does it mention founding father Earl Tupper, still the president of Tupperware Home Parties. Nor did Tupper accept a role in any of the inaugural jubilee activities.

On the opening day of Tupperware's first jubilee, Monday, April 5, 1954, the Edgewater High School band played, and Brownie Wise cut the ribbon on a new era of prosperity and recognition for Tupperware dealers and distributors; her boss, Earl Tupper; and herself. False-front, frontier-style buildings were constructed, and Brahman bulls and horses were carted in to give the grounds a western feel. If there was ever a golden age of Tupperware, it began on this date.

Service to others was the apt theme of Wise's welcome speech to the 633 dealers, managers, and distributors assembled in the new Garden Pavillion. Without people near the top bringing along eager, but inexperienced, people near the bottom, Tupperware's success could not have happened. "It is a time for gratification and it is a time for Thanksgiving," Wise told them. "We would not be human if we were not gratified at the success the last three years has brought us. We would not be very worthwhile human beings if we were not thankful for it. Thankful not for luck, in which I have very little confidence, but thankful for the strength which has been given to our hands and the ingenuity that has been given to our minds, and the willingness with which our spirits have been enriched."

The next day brought the fun and excitement that many of the Tupperware faithful had traveled hundreds of miles at their own expense to experience. On an unseasonably warm, ninety-degree, sun-drenched day, hundreds of Tupperware people dressed in cowboy hats, boots, and other western wear—"90% of them women"—were led to an area referred to as the "Forest of Spades." Shovels that McDonald and his team had borrowed from the Kissimmee street department stuck out of the ground, waiting to be chosen and used. Each person in the assemblage would get a chance to dig until they unearthed a hidden treasure, sometimes sealed up in Tupperware containers. The better-performing dealers would dig in roped-off areas with higher-end loot.

A group of revelers, headed for the 1954 jubilee.

For five-and-a-half hours, with Brownie Wise barking encouragement through a loudspeaker, women hopped on shovels as if they were pogo sticks, prodding and pulling hidden treasure from the sandy Florida soil, while their curious, bewildered family members looked on, screamed, shouted, and exalted in one of the most unique and truly joyous experiences of their lives. Four women who fainted in the heat were carried off on stretchers and later revived with smelling salts.

Betty Long of West Rushville, Ohio, preened after unearthing a carefully wrapped mink stole; Collette Maniaci of Dearborn, Michigan, beamed with pride at the $60 gold watch she prospected; Edith Berkenbile of Oklahoma City needed a titanic effort to pull a $70 radio from the ground; and Fay Maccalupo of Buffalo, New York, sat exhausted atop a toy Ford she had finally exhumed. When the Tupperware team showed her the real-life car it represented, Maccalupo pressed her face against the hood and, sobbing uncontrollably, kept repeating, "I love everybody."

Originally, McDonald and his team had buried the prizes eighteen inches deep. Some of the soil was so swampy that items like diamond rings and pen-and-pencil sets that had been buried in small containers weren't recovered until Vanguard Lake was created years later. "They dug the lake, ran the dragline," McDonald chuckled, "and came up with the Tupperware with the gift items still in them."

The treasure dig had been a sensation; the press and media loved it, too. The leading television news network at the time, CBS, carried film footage on its evening news, and the British Broadcasting Company aired the story in England. *Life* magazine documented all the zany events in a multi-page photo spread entitled "Life Goes on a Big Dig." The magazine reported, tongue-in-cheek, that the women, along with digging up thousands of dollars in prizes, "raised a crop of bonus blisters as big as doubloons."

Wise spun news of the coming national publicity about Tupperware's first jubilee into more acclaim within the local community. "Brownie Wise, brilliant chief of Tupperware Home Parties Inc., called us Wednesday morning and she was so jubilant," the *Kissimmee Gazette* gushed in an editorial after Wise contacted them with news of the upcoming publicity. "And it all can be attributed to Mrs. Brownie Wise, who is fighting for Kissimmee heart and soul, day and night."

As exciting as the *Life* spread and resulting local acclaim was, Brownie Wise received an even more significant honor as a result of the first annual Tupperware Homecoming Jubilee. In its April 17, 1954, issue, *Business Week* devoted seven pages to an article so complimentary to Tupperware and its home selling system that it could have been written by Wise herself. In a move that might as well have been a coronation of Wise as the queen of home-party sales, the magazine featured her smiling face on the cover—the first woman *Business Week* ever gave that recognition. In the photograph, Wise holds a polyethylene block like the one Earl Tupper was given all those years ago, and from which he invented Tupperware. Beneath the cover photograph runs a phrase that through the years came to be known as the Brownie Wise sales mantra: "If we build the people, they'll build the business."

Brownie Wise was the cover story of *Business Week*, April 17, 1954.

The magazine described Tupperware's jubilee as being a three-part combination of "sales training session, circus, and a revival meeting." At the center of it all was the woman *Business Week* called a "Prophet in Plastic," the charming forty-year-old "widow" whom the magazine identified as "the heart and soul" of the three-part hoopla. Wise chose not to reveal her divorce for fear it could lead to her unstable ex-husband—and the real possibility of personal and professional embarrassment.

With *Business Week* comparing her to Aimee Semple

McPherson—an eccentric evangelist who garnered a huge following in the 1920s and 1930s—some grumbled behind the scenes, yet again, about Wise becoming the sole focus of so much attention. But the Tupperware believers, including her own staff and dealers spread across the land, would support the magazine's conclusion: "She's the greatest person in the world."

Business Week also showed Wise throwing a container of polyethylene into the small lake dug out in front of headquarters. From that point on, it was called "Poly Pond," and all dealers had to do was dip their hand in the water for good luck. "There's an alligator in the pond," THP staffer Jack McCall joked, "for the dealers who don't work." The article described the long, thirteen-hour training sessions: "Everything from a Dale Carnegie course on public speaking to brass tacks discussions of how to display premiums to lure the hostess."

The article of course mentioned Tupperware's impressive sales performance—an estimated $25 million in retail sales (roughly $175 million today)—as proof enough that their system was working. Jack Marshall, Tupperware's hard-charging general sales manager, reminded writers that, through it all, the one "safety valve against competition" was the Tupperware patented seal. And to keep dealers inspired, the article pointed out, THP's home office worked "indefatigably" on new contests and promotions culminating at the end of the year in "an orgy of prize giving." Finally, the writers noted a conspicuous trend in the female-driven company's management ladder: Once a woman was ready to be promoted to distributor, that's when her husband would usually "horn in" on the business. Some of her critics say Wise helped perpetuate that glass ceiling by having only men around her in THP management even though she had left Stanley five years earlier because of the lack of managerial opportunities for women.

With the choruses of "I've got that Tupper feeling down in my heart" sung, the treasure dug, and the lessons learned, the historic five-day affair culminated with graduation. On a stage adorned with a row of ornate candelabrums, her male executive staff dressed in dark formal attire seated behind her, Brownie Wise cut a striking figure as she stepped to the lectern positioned between two large flower arrangements and delivered what was arguably her most memorable speech as the head of Tupperware Home Parties. It was entitled *"Ad Astra,"* Latin for "to the stars":

> I am glad that a graduation ceremony is termed Commencement. I believe that people sometimes make the mistake of considering a graduation a climax, an ending, a fulfillment. Actually, it is none of those things. This graduation is not an ending of anything. It is truly a beginning, a commencement; the commencement of a new course of study for you; the commencement of a new way of thinking, of new plans ... definite plans; a commencement of goals, of new confidence and new growth.

Wise told the audience that she chose the *"Ad Astra"* because she was primarily concerned with "reaching to the stars." In doing so, she was rapidly becoming a national sales sensation herself. "Since the earliest days of our recorded history," she told the rapt attendees,

> the stars have always been an inspiration to man; partly, perhaps, because they constitute an unknown quality that appeals to the imagination, to the adventure spirit, to the curious mind; partly, also, because in their distant far-off splendor, they are a source of steadfast wonder. Through the

ages they have been in their appointed places, far beyond the reach of men, but not beyond their dreams.

She spoke of challenges, accomplishments, positive thinking, and the tendency to look back:

All of us have to believe to live; and the more we are able to believe in with *firmness* and *conviction;* the more abundantly, the more prosperously, the more happily we live. What is it that prevents some people from realizing this amazing force in their own lives? Only one thing . . . the terrible tendency of the human being to look back. Like the biblical wife, some people keep turning to the past, and give it the power to destroy the present and the future.

"*Live* this day. Make it work for you; for in the magic of *this* day walks *tomorrow*," she implored them. "Being completely satisfied would be a little like death. What *we* want is growth, progress, the consciousness that we are getting somewhere, and helping other people get somewhere." She closed by advising the new graduates that they should embrace the problems they would face, for "the *knowledge,* the *ability,* and the *desire* to *handle* the problems will give us what we need for happiness."

Business Week observed, "When Brownie Wise made a farewell, inspirational address called 'Ad Astra,' there wasn't a dry eye in the house." As a highly successful distributor put it, "I don't know how it is, but Tupperware has become a religion with me." Brownie Wise had devised a way to build a better life for women and their families, and as in any sales program, success was limited only by how willing they were to let it consume them. In Brownie's case, Tupperware had become her raison d'être, and she was shepherding the flock. "When she was on the lectern, on the platform," Gary McDonald reflected, "she would mesmerize them."

Top distributors Peter Block and Harold Feinberg were awarded Cadillacs, and Rose Humphrey was one of four others who happily took home a less showy Ford—her second as a successful distributor. To cap off the gift giving, "the company" awarded Brownie Wise herself a much-deserved pink Lincoln convertible. In typical style, she didn't take many rag-top days off to tool around Lake Toho.

Nor did all the press and media accolades, she felt, get the creative juices flowing adequately as the THP staff tried to plan for the rest of 1954. As Wise liked to do when her team wasn't coming up with what she wanted, she ordered all of them, herself included, to get a weeklong change of scenery. On Friday, April 30, 1954, the THP staff boarded a plane for Havana, Cuba. Once ensconced at Havana's five-star, twin-spired, art deco masterpiece, the Hotel Nacional, Wise and her entourage mapped out sales, promotions, and public relations for the rest of the year. For fun, they took in the hotel's Parisian-style cabarets and the ambiance that had charmed famous guests such as Winston Churchill and Frank Sinatra. They also toured the new Tupperware operation in pre-Castro, U.S. commerce–friendly Cuba.

The 1954 Homecoming Jubilee, the *Life* spread, and the *Business Week* cover story were the high points heralding the arrival of Tupperware on the American scene. That recognition would continue to pay dividends throughout the rest of Tupperware's golden year.

Victory Behind Us, Success Before Us

To Earl Tupper, the decision to let Ruder and Finn push Brownie Wise to the forefront of company publicity had been an obvious triumph, but it had also pushed him further into the background. Tellingly, the *Business Week* article had somehow managed to minimize Tupper's role in his own product's revolution.

"Nominally," it read, "he is president of the sales company, but actually Brownie Wise has just about carte blanche to run the organization." In a memo he wrote to Wise, Tupper didn't seem to mind her getting the credit as long as the publicity meant more people "hugging his baby." But while the two mostly hashed out business during this time period on the telephone, he made a point, in writing, to remind her where the true focus should be.

"Thanks for the pictures with the interesting quotes on the back," Tupper wrote. "The one with your elbows on the ledgers, fingers interlaced with chin resting on fingers and smile on your face, looks like a very good executive in a very good frame of mind. Apparently the books balanced. However, good executive as you are, I still like best the pictures as a woman, of course with TUPPERWARE!"

Wise should have read Tupper's memo as a word of warning not to get too caught up in her own publicity, but that's not what happened. The 1954 *Business Week* cover story marked the beginning of Wise's ascension from general sales manager to Tupperware figurehead. Ensuing articles would follow this theme to Tupper's growing chagrin.

After the Jubilee hoopla died down, the executive team opened the doors of their swank headquarters for public tours. An estimated five thousand area residents took in the new gardens outside and exhibits inside. Next in line were Spanish-American War veterans inspecting the Museum of Art, the Magic Kitchen, the auditoriums, and the offices. Wise beamed. "We were very pleased to welcome so many of our neighbors to the Tupperware national home."

The team used tours as yet another advertising and recruiting tool. Long before Walt Disney put down roots nearby, THP headquarters became a regular stop for tour buses heading south for Cypress Gardens in Winter Haven. From 8:30 in the morning to 4:30 in the afternoon on weekdays and 8:30 to noon on Saturdays, one thousand visitors came through every week. Each got the Tupperware pitch, and their names and hometowns were duly noted and sent to area distributors who would follow up for party dating.

Wise and THP had every intention of keeping that juggernaut going. Tupperware dealer numbers across North America were taking off, with their numbers soaring past ten thousand in the summer of '54, and Wise kept adding to her team. To help Charlie McBurney churn out more stories, the public relations department added a young Tampa newspaperman, Glen Bump. As the maintenance manager for the ever-expanding grounds, Wise brought in George Reynolds, who also had a say in executive brainstorming sessions. A former sales executive from Safeway, American Airlines, and

Stanley, Hamer Wilson joined the company as sales counselor, to help manage the growing dealer ranks. Elsie Mortland, the soft-spoken housewife from Deland, had become so
proficient at giving Tupperware demonstrations, Wise hired
her as "hostess demonstrator" to run the new Magic Kitchen
at headquarters.

Mortland also became a rare friend and confidante to Wise.
While waiting for their Kissimmee home to be built, Mortland and her family moved into a guest house on the grounds
of Water's Edge. "She was quite the fairy godmother," Mortland recalled. "She just loved the recognition, and I remember
when her mother told me about the time Brownie was in a
high school play. She wanted the role of princess and if she
couldn't have that part she wouldn't be in it."

Wise was also a very caring and maternal boss to some
of the young women hired right out of high school for entry-
level positions at headquarters. "After my mother died," one
former secretary remembered, "Brownie came to me and
said, 'I'll have food made—take some time off and come back
as soon as you can.'" She never forgot the level of genuine
kindness Wise extended.

On June 7, 1954, came what Wise called "the most outstanding event of the summer." At the National Association of
Direct Selling Companies convention in New York City, Wise
and her staff received a plaque in recognition of the "most
outstanding public relations program in the country." And
who could argue with THP's success in that area? Tupperware
was everywhere, and Brownie Wise was quickly becoming a
media darling. As the company's profile grew, so did hers.

"I thought it was sensational," remembered Gary McDonald. "The more I saw, the better I liked it." And there was
plenty of press to see, with articles in *Specialty Salesman*,

Premium Practice, Printer's Ink, American Business, Fortune, Life, Business Week, and *Woman's Home Companion.* In the August issue of *Woman's Home Companion,* an article entitled "Help Yourself to Happiness" brought a flood of calls and letters to headquarters. "The article attracted more dealers than any previous publicity piece," Wise noted.

To capitalize on the success of the article, the ever-expanding THP team launched its "Top of the World" drive. With more people than ever showing an interest in Tupperware, THP challenged team members to again double dealer ranks by the end of the drive. Recruiting cards were issued to dealers to keep on the visor of their cars, where they could "remind you at all times of the people you are about to see becoming Tupperware dealers in the Top of the World Drive."

Successful dealers could win cufflinks and tie tacks commemorating their achievements, and their names would represent links in a shining chain being added to the new "Garden That Loyalty Built" at headquarters. The THP team kept up the relentless push for success, asking, "Will you have had a part in it?" At the end of the contest, Wise and her executive staff planned to fly out and personally congratulate the highest-performing distributors at rallies throughout the country.

At the beginning of September, as the "Top of the World" drive kicked off, Brownie, Jerry, and the well-traveled THP royalty headed off to Paris with the six highest-producing dealers who had won the 1953 "Full Steam Ahead" contest. The September 10 edition of the *Kissimmee Gazette* showed the party of beaming executives and dealers preparing to board the *Queen Mary* in New York. "Would any of these Paris-Rome travelers have believed when they put on their first Tupperware Party," Wise reflected, "that within a year or so they would be putting on original Paris gowns in the fashion capitol [sic] of the world . . . or seeing their names in one of America's leading magazines?" Ever mindful of free advertising, THP invited along Ludwig Bemelmens of *Coronet* magazine to cover the journey.

Beneath the "everything's great" veneer, Jerry Wise said his mother found the trip excruciating: "That was a mess," he remembered. It was one thing to take dealers to New York or Hawaii, but Europe proved a much greater culture shock. Dealers didn't speak the language or understand the cuisine, which opened the door to some classic "ugly American" moments. At a restaurant in Paris, one unnamed dealer stood up and demanded, "I want the *real* Franco-American," not realizing they were in the very spot the dish originated. "From now on we'll pick the winners," Brownie groused to her sixteen-year-old son. "These people are so stupid it's pitiful."

While Wise might have been annoyed by her dealers' lack of sophistication, she also knew well that they were the people driving Tupperware's enormous home-selling engine. On Saturday, October 16, hundreds of dealers from all over Florida gathered in Tupperware's Pacific Hall to celebrate the culmination of the "Top of the World" drive. Thirty-five phones were brought in so dealers nationwide having their own regional "auction" parties could call in with the number of new people they recruited.

As the phones rang, the flashbulbs popped, and the executive team tallied up the numbers pouring in from everywhere. As Brownie Wise mugged for the camera in mock amazement with a phone in each hand, like everything else in the golden year of 1954, the recruiting drive was a success.

"We're 20,000 strong!" Wise and company announced. After starting the year with a force of about seven thousand

Tupperware dealers, the avalanche of national publicity had helped THP nearly triple that number in nine months. Like it was New Year's Eve in October, dealers from Rose Humphrey's Hibiscus Sales wore hats and sang, "We're sittin' on top of the world." Wise broke into an impromptu victory dance with McDonald, McBurney, and Marshall. A photo from that night shows the early THP all-star executive team clowning around on telephones, another big goal realized.

The drive's success also brought victory celebrations from all over the world of Tupperware dealers. In Chattanooga, Mattie McNutt rejoiced with her team from Green Valley Sales; in Spokane, new distributor Corliss Levitt celebrated by promoting a new group of managers in her company, Live Oak Sales. In New York City, all-star distributors Edith and Jack O'Reilly posed for photographs with a team of five male branch managers.

Wise boasted that the Tupperware dealer force had grown from ten thousand to twenty thousand in just thirty days. Even if that was a bit overstated, it testified to the effectiveness of the company's public relations campaign and to the strong chord it struck with prospective dealers. Not bad for a company that just three years earlier had risen from the ashes of the failed Hostess Division.

To handle that enormous growth, Hamer Wilson brought in a "tabulating systems specialist" to help organize THP's new IBM department. "These magic machines could do in a minute," Wise marveled, "what clerks could not do in months!" New offices were built to accommodate the cutting-edge equipment.

In November, bestselling author Napoleon Hill, whose work featured prominently in dealer training sessions, was brought in for the company's distributor training sessions.

Within a few weeks, 6 of the 135 attendees became distributors and claimed new territories to conquer. Hill would later pay homage to Wise and Tupperware with a spread in his pocket-sized national publication *Success Unlimited.*

"The year 1954 drew to a close with the distinction of being the biggest year in the history of Tupperware Home Parties," Wise wrote. But that didn't mean she'd let the sales force sit back and enjoy it for long. "If you have met your last year's goal, set a higher one for next year," she urged. "Great things are behind us in Tupperware. But because we are young and we have so much to offer, the greatest things are ahead—many of them to come this year."

It would be hard to top such a watershed year. The *Business Week* cover story had established Brownie Wise as an icon for women who by choice or necessity sought a life and income of their own.

However, unlike Tupper and other high-level executives, who were aware of the choice they made to use Brownie Wise as a focus for publicity, other key players in Tupperware's success from its earliest days still bristled at the turn of events. After years of increasing resentment, in 1955 some key distributors who weren't happy with all the focus on Brownie Wise decided to do something dramatic—and Earl Tupper wouldn't be far behind them.

A Revolt from Within

At infrequent intervals, a commanding and well-dressed gentleman whom the great majority of employees didn't know showed up at Tupperware Home Parties' headquarters. These appearances never happened during jubilees, and rarely during seminars or large-scale public events; he hated crowds. Even worse, the idea of having to speak publicly in front of a large gathering made him sick to his stomach. Occasionally he announced himself as "Mr. Esty." Other times, he'd just show a business card with the initials "E.S.T." on it. Such was the low-profile way Earl Silas Tupper made his presence known to the sales division.

Sometimes he came just to take care of a business matter or to see how the Florida operation was shaping up. Other visits, however, would center on a new idea for the product line. On those occasions, he would come face-to-face with the commanding personality of Brownie Wise.

Coming to Florida with his mysterious air, conservative seersucker suits, and take-charge attitude, Tupper was known simply as "The Boss." Holding court and reading letters from adoring dealers in her regal, peacock wicker chair, Wise was "The Queen." If Tupper thought one way about a product, and Wise thought another, a battle ensued. Jerry Wise witnessed one such face-off after the bus had dropped him at headquarters, "in the big front room," he recalled, "at that big kidney-shaped table, the rest of the staff sitting there afraid to say anything."

This fight wasn't just two heavyweights sparring over a product idea; it was two parents battling it out in front of their children. When challenged, Tupper could often blow his stack, but where other employees would have been intimidated by his temper, it only gave Wise more fuel. "She wasn't afraid of him at all," Jerry remembered.

At issue was Tupper's notion of making Tupperware pet food bowls. Given all the energy the company devoted to positioning their product as something closer to fine art than the cheap, brittle plastics of the past, Wise loathed the idea.

"It's time to calm yourself down and sit down and listen to me for a minute," Brownie lectured him. "It's going to be too expensive to manufacture."

"Now listen to me, woman, I do the manufacturing and you do the selling!" Tupper shot back.

"Woman?" Wise dressed down her company president. "Is that the way you address your wife?"

Tupper left the meeting red-faced, but with the money his sales department was raking in, he wouldn't stay mad for long.

Outside the office, Tupper had a softer, more adventurous side that included taking young Jerry under his wing as something of a father figure. During Florida visits, Tupper often invited Jerry to look at foreign sports cars at used-car lots. "He loved Jaguars," Jerry recalled. "I remember taking rides in thirty different Jaguars." When Tupper opened up his billfold, Jerry said, he had "nothing but hundreds."

"With that kind of money," Jerry asked, "why don't you just get a new car?"

"That just tells everybody I have too much money," Tupper replied.

Tupper also used his cars to show employees his fun side. As an employee incentive program at Farnumsville, top performers could take one of his high-performance cars for a weekend.

In his mid-forties, Tupper was completely bald except for a few wisps of hair that often tempted the precocious teen's sense of humor. "I always wanted to call him 'chrome dome,'" said Jerry, "but Brownie said, 'Don't you *ever* call him that.'" As much as the top of Tupper's head made Jerry laugh, what happened inside the inventor's mind impressed him more. "He brought me the plans for a three-wheel car with a V-8 engine in it," Jerry marveled. "It was designed to be a police car . . . [and] would take a corner at ninety miles an hour because the front-end was cantilevered." Instead of turning one way or the other, the vehicle's wheels would lie down. "I'm thinking, this guy's brain never stopped," said Jerry. "His mind was just like Brownie's, working all the time."

Given Tupper's propensity to draw as little attention as possible to his comings and goings at the Florida headquarters, some of his top executives had no idea when Tupper was there. That led to some memorable first encounters.

Tony Ponticelli, who was hired to take over as Tupperware Home Parties' special events director, remembers his first meeting with Tupper as a chance encounter. "He met me in the hallway and said, 'Who are you?'" Ponticelli remembered.

Barely in his thirties at the time, Ponticelli had been a VP of sales promotion and public relations at a Madison Avenue firm and brought with him a flair for showmanship and creativity. He designed a new wing at the Kissimmee headquarters and was point man in planning some of the most spectacular shows in Tupperware's early jubilees.

As a worldly, streetwise New Yorker, his first impressions of the company and its people were indelible: "These are way-out nuts," he recalled thinking. "Where do they get off singing, 'I got that Tupper feeling'?" His most distinct memory of the opening day of his first jubilee was watching "all these flaky people singing." By the second day, though, he noticed that he had begun "listening to it, not criticizing in my mind." And that's when his attitude started to change. "In New York, you think you know it all," Ponticelli offered. "You're only with executives. So you're not down to earth with the people. The third day I was singing the song with them."

Why the change of perspective? Without a note of cynicism, Ponticelli replied: "I was converted. It wasn't a phony, staged kind of thing. This was spontaneous. People would get up and sing and people would join in. And before you know it, you had a new religion of helping other people." For the first time, he was overtaken with the feeling of wanting to climb the ladder and bring other people with him. "That was the idea that permeated the sales force," Ponticelli said.

Ponticelli was also struck by his first impression of Brownie Wise, who sat in her customary wicker chair, surrounded by her team of male executives, at his interview luncheon. "In viewing her, sizing up her body motion," he recalled, "I thought 'she really thinks she's a prima donna.' But I watched how the individuals responded to her, and I had to give this woman some credit.'"

To gain that respect in the male-dominated business world of the mid-1950s, Wise was "all business." She never discussed personal matters or private concerns. "She struck me as an individual who was over men," Ponticelli said, "and she never wanted to let her guard down as some individual male might try to take advantage of her weakness." Beneath the image of a vibrant, on-the-go, rising star executive, however, Brownie Wise had many personal challenges to overcome.

Since her divorce, Wise had continued to use the last name of the alcoholic, mentally unstable ex-husband who'd long been out of her life. What most in the Tupperware family didn't know—and Wise worked hard to hide from the press—was that Robert Wise eventually moved to central Florida and was a frequent cause of concern. "You just never knew when he was going to pop up," Jerry Wise remembered. Jerry once had to wear a disguise when there was word his father might try to kidnap him. On another occasion, Jerry found out from the local sheriff that Bobby Wise was back in town—and in the drunk tank.

"Your dad's in jail here. You want to see him? His car's right out there in the lot," the sheriff said.

Jerry declined. "I went through his car, and it looked and smelled like he'd been living in it for six months."

Bob sometimes pressed the issue, calling headquarters trying to reach his ex-wife. On one occasion, she came out of her office and told her new PR man, Don Hinton, that "Bob Wise" was calling from the Angebilt Hotel in Orlando, and that he wanted to come down and see her. "I don't think he belongs down here at this time," she said coolly. With that, Hinton and a couple other staff members drove up to see him.

"We assumed it would be embarrassing as hell for her," Hinton remembered. So he and his men assured Bob that his now-famous ex-wife was far too busy to see him. They were prepared to restrain him physically if need be, but that wasn't necessary. Wise looked in no shape to go anywhere. By that time, he no longer had a car, and he wasn't even quite sure where the THP headquarters was.

According to Jerry, Bob Wise was an intelligent man who had suffered many thwarted attempts at starting a business. Again and again his ventures would go by the wayside, sacrificed—like his family life—to a river of destructive, sometimes violent binges. "My dad just couldn't get it together, and he couldn't stand it that his ex-wife did," Jerry reflected. "Brownie basically had a kind of standing restraining order on him." Because of the goodwill she and Tupperware had built up with law enforcement, Brownie could count on the authorities to pick up Bob if he crossed the county line drunk, keep him in jail, and then quietly transfer him to another lockup farther away. During big events like the jubilees, Hinton always had to keep a wary eye out to make sure Bob didn't show up to embarrass her.

An ex-husband who refused to disappear wasn't the only personal problem Wise had to mask from her adoring dealers, coworkers, and members of the press, however. During Tupperware's early days in Kissimmee, after giving a speech at headquarters, Wise backed away from the lectern—different from the kind to which she was accustomed—and fell directly onto the concrete several feet below, injuring her back so severely it required traction. After treatment she still needed a back brace, and the injury became a source of chronic pain. Making matters worse, sinusitis and stress sometimes brought back the migraine headaches that had plagued her enough to seek surgery while she was first living in south Florida.

Still, the new year had arrived, and the pressure was on

Brownie to keep the 1954 momentum rolling. With so much at stake for THP, she couldn't afford to share any problems or anxieties that plagued her; she had an image to maintain. Wise lived like a movie star in a glamorous lakeside estate and traveled to exotic places all over the world. Her name was being mentioned in the same breath with the few other emerging executive businesswomen in America, luminaries like Estée Lauder in cosmetics and Olive Ann Beech in aviation. As her stature rose on the national scene, Brownie Wise was also becoming a central Florida icon. Like other celebrities so well known they needed no last names, "Brownie" was big news in the local papers. On January 9, 1955, the *Orlando Sentinel Sunday Magazine* ran an article entitled "What a Woman!"

"A trim, brown-eyed ex-secretary who efficiently and swiftly moved into Orlando's back yard and established a multi-million dollar corporation in less than three years," the article begins, "that's Brownie Wise, vice-president and general manager of Tupperware Home Parties Inc." The piece goes on to describe the career and personal life of a star business executive who was trying to balance a twelve- to twenty-hour workday, while logging 150,000 miles a year traveling to seminars, rallies, and contest ceremonies. Considering her travels from 1954, it likely was not an exaggeration. Yet, the writer marveled, Wise still found time to "do a bit of fishing, boating or horseback riding" with her sixteen-year-old son. The article described their "rambling" home as a virtual paradise, with two dogs, three horses, and a twenty-acre estate. "She's not famous," Jerry observed in the piece. "Famous people are movie stars and people like that. She's just my mom." But to the typical homebound woman of the 1950s, years before Mary Kay, Martha Stewart, and Oprah, Brownie's life must have been the stuff of fairy tales.

Wise loading into the car for one of her many business trips, ca. 1955.

The article also described how Wise managed to take the business "by the heart instead of the purse strings." A generous helping of photographs shows Wise in front of the Eiffel Tower on the recent Europe trip; Wise in front of headquarters; Wise reading to her son, chatting on the phone, and talking to dealers on the '54 trip to Hawaii. While the article does mention the Tupperware line reaching close to one hundred "plastic houseware items including dishes, refrigerator storage containers, salt and pepper shakers, combs, even fly swatters," there are no product photos. There is only one mention of Tupper, and it's dismissive, as in the breakthrough *Business Week* cover story. "Brownie's title indicates she isn't the top rung on the company ladder, in reality Earl Tupper is the president," the article states, "but, he has given Brownie free rein, and she runs the whole show." Earl Tupper, now nearly invisible as far as the company's high-profile publicity was concerned, dropped further into Wise's long shadow.

What's not clear is whether the Tupperware Home Parties'

new public relations department was feeding the press these stories, or whether it was Wise herself. "It was our idea to promote Brownie because she was so well thought of," said Don Hinton. "The more we did for her, the more the gals thought of her." And according to Jerry, Wise was not a big fan of the demands reporters and photographers put on her personal life, given the considerable demands of her career. But in a history of THP that Wise penned herself, the emphasis is clear: "On magazine stands across the nation appeared more recognition for the success of Tupperware, as shown through the success of Brownie Wise." Even if the articles focused on her rise as THP's charismatic female chief executive, Wise believed the company would benefit. The explosive expansion of Tupperware across America made that strategy hard to dispute.

In January 1955, one hundred distributors and managers from across the country gathered at THP headquarters for another conference. Wise introduced a new Star Demonstrator contest in which dealers could compete for an array of fabulous prizes like diamond rings, diamond wristwatches, and mink stoles. Each distributor was issued a magic slate scorecard on which to judge who gave the best demonstration and was deserving of an award. Seven distributors were inducted as charter members of the Lantern Club for having the highest per-capita sales, including two top Tupperware power brokers from the start: Rose Humphrey and Peter Block.

In Humphrey, Brownie Wise had an obvious ally among the ranks of powerful distributors. But in Peter and Elsie Block, she still did not. They felt that they had thrived with

Tupperware despite their flow of merchandise being cut off by the Hostess Division.

The couple's Poly Sales Company of Pasadena had become so successful that, by 1954, the Blocks were the only distributors in the nation ordering their inventory by the train car load. There's a famous picture of the Blocks posing with dozens of their dealers in front of a huge banner heralding the arrival of that first shipment of Tupperware. "What a relief," Elsie Block wrote. "At the time Tupperware had no major warehousing anywhere in the United States between Massachusetts and us. We were it."

Because of their success, Block claimed Wise often made "urgent" phone calls to her asking if she and Peter had new distributor candidates to take over virgin territories. Despite all the praise Brownie Wise was earning over her training programs and distributor conferences, Elsie Block said new distributors acquired all the tools they needed from the ones who promoted them. "Tupperware Home Parties had nothing to do but sign an agreement to supply them with Tupperware."

From their point of view, distributors such as themselves were the heart and soul of Tupperware's continuing success. However, they also knew Wise wielded plenty of power and used it carefully. Besides training and recognition, it was up to Wise and her staff to motivate and if need be come down on those who were underperforming. Despite the impressive sales of those early years, some distributorships were not renewed.

In 1955, as the positive press kept rolling out—and Brownie Wise was in demand for high-profile public appearances— behind the scenes, the fragile relationships between Wise, the THP staff, and a group of distributors who decided they deserved more power than the company was giving them finally cracked.

According to Wise, a pair of former distributors, Dot and Bill Henry, circulated a letter with "a number of derogatory statements about Tupperware as a product and the policies of Tupperware Home Parties Inc." to many other dealers and distributors.

Tupper sent Wise a confidential memo responding to the Henrys' letter. "It is not good but I see nothing that we can do to stop it now," Tupper advised. "Your dealers are going to at least listen to the offerings of the other side now."

Wise responded with a lengthy note to all Tupperware dealers and distributors. "Every day I receive letters from enthusiastic dealers voicing their gratitude for the good things that have come their way—new cars and homes, education for their children, pianos, surgical and medical treatments, added insurance and savings accounts or security," Wise wrote. "Of the many advantages realized by what we do, all of us feel, I am sure, that the greatest pleasure comes to us and to the distributors from watching the growth and development of people."

A small group of powerful distributors agreed to a meeting in Philadelphia with the idea of forming a distributors' union. If there was one thing the THP staff knew Earl Tupper loathed from the outset, it was unions. And now a handful of his most prosperous distributors were considering the possibility of forming one, carrying another line of product, and moving elsewhere. According to McDonald, when he, Wise, and the rest of the THP management got wind of what was afoot, they knew they needed to act decisively to quell the revolt. After finding out which hotel the distributors planned to use for their clandestine meeting, Jack Marshall went to work.

Through "a friend who had a friend," Marshall managed to get a microphone placed inside the room where the distributors were meeting, allowing the THP management team to find out who the key players were. "When we had that recorder in the hotel room listening to them," McDonald said, "you could hear them vying for position to be the one who was going to be the strength in the organization." According to McDonald, the man jockeying to head up this powerful proposed union was none other than THP's biggest West Coast distributor, Peter Block.

Following up on that information, a group of THP executives flew out to Southern California to confront the "ringleader," Block. In his office, the nation's largest distributor told THP executives that he could do a better job running the company's sales operation than Brownie Wise. In the corner, not saying very much, was Don Hinton, wearing a hidden microphone and recorder that captured the evidence they needed.

Meanwhile, THP executives had to work quickly to build bridges with the other distributors. "You are the organization," Wise and her staff assured them. After letters were sent, THP dispatched representatives to different cities to follow up personally. They argued that no product had the kind of backing or growing national reputation that Tupperware did. In other words, they warned, where you go, Tupperware dealers and dollars may not follow.

In the end, some did choose to leave. But, according to McDonald, they learned the hard way that as distributors they were not bigger than Tupperware. "Fortunately, the product they got involved with was not much in the way of a product," McDonald said. "It wasn't even a knockoff, and it did not succeed, and they did not succeed." Two of the distributors who decided to take part in the revolt were eventually welcomed back into the Tupperware fold without recrimination. The same could not be said for Peter and Elsie Block. At Wise's direction, they were stripped of their distributorship in what Elsie Block referred to as the "Tupperware Raid."

"Seven men from Tupperware Home Parties Inc.," Block wrote, "arrived at our warehouse to finish destroying our business." The two men running the operation, whom Block painted as henchmen for Brownie Wise, were none other than Jack Marshall and Hamer Wilson, whom Elsie and Peter had helped Tupperware recruit in the first place. What wasn't thrown in a truck, Elsie Block said, was heaped in a corner like broken toys. "My grief over the sickening, immoral act perpetrated against our Poly Sales Company," Block wrote, "consumed me more than all else."

In her book *My Tupperware Party Was Over . . . and I Sat Down and Cried,* Elsie Block claimed she and Peter had had no idea why such an act was being perpetrated against their business. "We desperately tried to find out what was going on at headquarters," she reported. "When Peter tried to get information, his calls were not accepted. The General Manager, Brownie Wise, instructed her receptionist to tell the caller that she didn't know anyone by the name of Peter Block." Nowhere in her book does Block make mention of her husband spearheading the drive to unionize Tupperware distributors. Peter, the star distributor awarded a Gold Lantern in 1955, a winner of Cadillacs and other performance-based premiums, and a Tupperware insider who helped grow the ranks of dealers and THP executives, was cut off for good. "He thought he could take the business over," Hinton recalled. "He tried and didn't win."

If indeed Peter Block had made the power play just as Gary

McDonald and Don Hinton described, it cost the Blocks all they had worked for since their days of selling Stanley products in Detroit. "After the Tupperware crew finished with what they were sent to do and left our warehouse," Elsie Block lamented, "Peter and I stood together at the shipping gate as the last truckload pulled away. We turned and stared at the long lines of conveyers that would no longer roll. We went to the back gate, looking at the empty train track, knowing another freight car full of Tupperware would not come. The profound silence was awful."

In a long letter to Tupper, Wise did not acknowledge any "raid" on the Blocks' operation: "I'm not gloating, nor do I tell you this in a spirit of viciousness, but I think you will be interested to know . . . the Blocks have disposed of all their merchandise, hostess premiums and sale merchandise, to the discount houses, and are apparently clearing out the business completely."

While she admitted to Tupper that "the fight got pretty dirty," she did not mention the bugging of the distributors' hotel room or wiring Hinton for the meeting with Block. Deflecting attention to the distributors' discontent with her, Wise instead blamed the revolt on THP's "ultimatum on handling other merchandise along with Tupperware on our party plan."

Whatever the reasons for the revolt of longtime, top-performing distributors like the Blocks, the shock waves of losing a distributor that ordered product by the train-car load were palpable. Because of what Wise referred to as the "holocaust" of 1955, sales figures stood to decline for the first time.

Despite the rocky relationship Wise endured with the distributors, the same did not hold true with the legion of dealers with whom she enjoyed a growing cult of personality and devotion; many felt as if they enjoyed a one-on-one relationship with her. Letters poured in. Always a prolific note writer, often working well into the night with a typewriter on her bed, Brownie Wise made sure the correspondence kept going back in return, with her signature perfectly straight as ever.

"What she was doing was helping people accomplish things beyond their wildest imaginations," McDonald remembered. "They never thought of working, let alone making more money than their husbands."

As another dealer incentive, Wise would give away the clothes she wore to events all across the country. "When she would go out to rallies in the field," McDonald reflected, "people would have thousand-dollar weeks to get the outfits she was wearing. They would lose fifty or sixty pounds in a short time to make it fit." In spite of everything dealers would have had happening in their personal lives, what seemed to haunt many of them most was letting down Brownie.

In a personal letter to Wise, one unit manager from San Diego confessed that, "I'm afraid I've been a disappointment to the company after they've been so good to me." She didn't want her letter to be an "excuse," just an explanation of "the reasons why." After attending one of the Tupperware jubilees, she shared, "my mother suffered a stroke. I returned to find she barely knew me and since she has steadily grown worse. As I write this she is expected to pass at any minute having been in a coma for 6 days." Because of all the adversity she worried that she'd "*barely* been a dealer since."

In another letter, a woman who called herself one of Wise's "Tupperware Children" described holding twenty Tupperware parties in one week: "I had to date 31 parties to have the 20. I had three postponed in one afternoon. But I kept pushing on. I was determined to prove your faith in me if I had to knock on every door in Evansville to date the 20 parties." A mother of four children, one of them an infant, she continued:

So the big week came, the third day I took the flu along with a lot of other people, and my husband had to go out on three parties for me. I broke him in right, he didn't know a thing but hearing me talk around the house. But as always he did a wonderful job. But I had to go out and have my day parties and in the mean time my four sons and Mother (who had come down to stay with my baby while I had the parties) came down with the flu. I would Dr. them up and go on a party, come back and see about them and go on another party. So we had quite a week.

"Thanks to Tupperware," another dealer wrote Wise, "I sent my son a round-trip ticket and he is home for Christmas—first time I've seen him in three years, two months, eight days." She also mentioned that as a prize for having the highest monthly sales, she was awarded a coveted Brownie Wise dress: "It's all over lace with satin ribbon inserts and bow in back, sorta rose shade. It fits me." Letters like these, or, more precisely, the flourishing dealer motivation and drive they convey, were keys to Tupperware's early success, along with the avalanche of press that showed no signs of stopping.

To almost 3 million readers in the March 1955 edition of *Coronet* magazine, travel writer Ludwig Bemelmans recounted experiencing "the true dream of Paris" while accompanying the Tupperware prize winners on that ill-fated trip in September 1954. "Mrs. Wise is a party giver, perhaps the greatest of them," Bemelmans wrote. "At her parties—thousands of them throughout America every day—women demonstrate and sell polyethylene wares. They play parlor games and shop from the same arm chair, an amazing phenomenon."

During this time, Wise scored an admiring cover story written by Charles B. Roth for *Salesman's Opportunity* magazine.

For *Woman's Life,* Roth penned an article about Wise entitled "She Planned Her Way to Success." Also, Wise's forward-thinking attitude about art in the workplace, as displayed in the first annual Tupperware Art Fund, was recognized by *Arts Digest* magazine. "It is all too rare that big business steps out into the arts. When it does, the steps are often cautious and temporary. For this reason," the editors wrote, "we are delighted that Tupperware Home Parties Inc. is continuing and expanding its art program."

In March, the Central Florida Sales Executive Club asked Wise to be one of the headline speakers at a motivational rally held at Orlando's Municipal Auditorium, where, also in 1955, nineteen-year-old-phenomenon Elvis Presley would wow the crowd as a last-minute warm-up act for comedian Andy Griffith. Wise shared the bill with Elmer Wheeler, whose "sizzlemanship" concepts she had used to motivate her early dealers in Michigan, and was thrilled to address a crowd of 2,500 people, having been introduced as one of the three "most outstanding sales authorities in America."

At Tupperware's fourth anniversary, Wise took to the stage once more to give an inspired address capturing the unique, people-helping-people aspect of their business: "The success that we have had and the milestones we've checked off are the achievements of all of us," she told them. "How near we always are to each other in spite of the miles between. Who would be willing to guess the number of new thoughts that will be awakened, the ambitions that will be fired, and the goals of personal achievement that will be reached, as the spirit of this Jubilee. I hope that we may always remember that our interest is common and that any real eminence that we attain as a company will always rest in the personal growth and achievements of our people."

On Tuesday, April 19, 1955, visiting speaker Dr. Norman Vincent Peale underscored the positive thinking at the heart of the Tupperware doctrine. "Fill your mind with positive thoughts," Peale preached. "Think in terms of success and you can achieve whatever you set out to achieve."

The THP team unveiled a new Vanguard shield, crest of the company and "badge of high honor" to the highest-performing managers. Not forgetting distributors, a spring and summer "777" contest would send seven winners to London and Paris and would award seven runner-up winners a trip to the glamorous Mexican Riviera. Wise wrote that there were so many top-performing dealers that, for the first time, runners-up would be added to the list of those who received National Merit Award trophies.

For the four-day 1955 jubilee, the grounds of headquarters were transformed into "Tupperware Gulch." On Wednesday, attendees were treated to a county fair highlighted by a show from the Silver Spurs Riding Club. Each person also received $1,500 in "bogus money" to spend on items inside the line of old western storefronts. At Tupperware jubilees, meetings were always preceded by a recitation of the Lord's Prayer. Drinking and dancing were not allowed. Staff members planned the events with a kind of calculated but professional cheesiness for a very specific reason.

Many of the women who paid their own way to the jubilees came alone; how would it look, in the America of the 1950s, if Midwestern housewives in for training and motivation were seen drinking or even dancing in public? Tupperware Home Parties took great stock in the wholesome image that executives, dealers, and distributors projected. It was also an important recruiting tool when convincing a reticent husband that it was OK for his wife to become a "Tupperware Lady."

After some of his most profitable distributors made clear their discontent, Tupper also made sure to reward and motivate his own workers—though his incentives certainly could not compete with the mink coats and Cadillacs his sales division bestowed on its people. On July 19, 1955, he sent out a notice to his "fellow workers" about a drawing for a trip to tour the Home Party team's Kissimmee headquarters. For a man who avoided social situations, and said little more than "good morning," it is oddly inspirational—a tone intended, undoubtedly, to improve morale:

> Benefits is not the word for us to use. RESULTS is the word we all like—if we do a good job in a good place, we get results.
>
> There are no politics here to hold you back. No one will envy you if you grow and fill a better job—because you will be helping everyone in our plant to do a better job and make more money.
>
> If one of our people is struck by a death in the family, we can't do much to help. We do what we can with such things as flowers and three days off with pay to cope with the problems that arise. Flowers are sent if you are sick so that you know you are missed.
>
> Once in a while, a surprise gift of Tupperware is given to every employee. A summer vacation with pay is standard and then comes Thanksgiving and usually a turkey on the company. After that soon comes Christmas with little gifts and then the second week of vacation with pay.
>
> We are not bragging about all this, but we do think that for a new company in a new place with a lot of problems to solve, and tough competitors to cope with, well we think we have a right to hold our heads up just as we like to see you hold yours up.

If Tupper used his note to rally his troops, Brownie hoped that the August 1955 issue of *Tupperware Sparks* would have the same effect on hers. The front page featured photos of the winning distributors in the "777" contest. And yet, as the distributor revolt smoldered, only the familiar names of Rose Humphrey and Corliss Levitt were among the Europe-bound winners. Underneath all of her usual cheerleading, Wise felt pressured.

"We knew all the other distributors were watching on the sidelines, some of them wavering. That hurt," Wise wrote Tupper. "There was intense pressure for about a year from these renegades, as well as their suppliers who thought, at first, that this motley little crew constituted a gold mine for them." Though that didn't happen, Wise was clearly bothered that cash cows like the Blocks had rebelled against her authority. "It simply didn't make sense," she wrote, "that a bunch of prospering distributors would pull out of a good thing." But in her soul-searching letter to Tupper, Wise never considered that it could have anything to do with her management style or tactics.

This first serious bout of growing pains for Tupperware Home Parties and Brownie Wise manifested itself in the annual sales numbers. Despite triple- and double-digit increases in 1953 and 1954 respectively, and despite the Tupperware dealer numbers at record levels, in 1955 the gross sales of Tupperware to its distributors dropped 8 percent for the year. That shocking turn of events could be tied directly to losing players like Peter and Elsie Block. Either way, it marked the first time during her rapid ascent in the world of direct selling that Brownie Wise experienced failure.

The Tupperware Ladies

While much of the public's attention focused on Brownie Wise in these early years, behind her success story were those of many other women whom she influenced and encouraged to change their own lives. For these self-starters, Wise embodied an alternate path to success—one that sidestepped a corporate ladder they were, for the most part, still not welcome to climb. And it all started at home.

In the warm enclaves where people reared children and shared hard times and true friendship, neighbors were willing to help neighbors with a new business. In return, they made money, too. Wise herself had needed a hand up from a network of friends and relatives after her marriage ended. Now she showed others like her a golden road to a better life paved through suburban America. While Wise steered the ship at headquarters, a legion of new dealers, reminiscent of the business novice she used to be, were sowing the seeds of highly profitable careers.

Sometime near the end of 1955, Pat Jordan became interested in selling Tupperware for the same reason so many others did: money. Jordan had grown up in a poor family where money was always tight. Her husband, Phil, resigned his commission in the navy and had to work two to three jobs to put food on the table. "*That* was motivation," Jordan remembered. "It was money; it was gifts. It was everybody was for everybody. I'm not going to step on you to get ahead; I'm going to take your hand and help you along. It was a big family affair." It was that Tupper feeling, as the song went.

Getting started didn't prove as easy as Jordan had expected, though. Despite having a baby at home and a genuine need for the income Tupperware could provide, her recruiter was cautious. "She said, 'I'm sorry Pat, I don't think this is something for you,'" Jordan remembered. "Time went on, and the more I thought about it the madder I got. I thought to myself, 'I can do anything I want to do.'" She called Rose Humphrey's Orlando distributorship, told them she'd love to sell Tupperware, and finally got the response she'd hoped for. In return for shelling out the $35—a substantial amount in 1955, when the average American household made $4,137 a year, gas was twenty-three cents per gallon, and you could buy a first-class stamp for three cents—a big cardboard box containing a suitcase filled with Tupperware arrived.

In the early days, Jordan knocked on a lot of doors and made countless cold calls hoping to date Tupperware parties. Occasionally, there were nasty dogs to contend with and doors shut in her face, but more times than not, people were receptive. "You know, women were home during that era; there weren't many women working," she said. And there was always encouragement coming from mentors to do more than you thought possible. For Jordan, the person who offered that encouragement was Jean Conlogue.

Conlogue and her husband, Jack, had come out of the Blocks' Poly Sales Company. Having left St. Louis, they took a distributorship in South Florida and developed promising young recruits like Jordan. "Jean was a teacher; she was a motivator," Jordan recalled. "She took my hand and said to me, 'If you want to be successful in this business, you come with me.' And you didn't say no to Jean Conlogue." Together, the distributor and her new dealer headed south to what Con-logue called "the end of the world"—Homestead, Florida. Later famous as ground zero for Hurricane Andrew in 1992, in the mid-1950s Homestead was just another in a string of southern Florida outpost towns full of single-story cinder-block homes within easy reach of U.S. 1.

"I used to do some strange things," Jordan admitted. "I used to knock on the door with bags of lettuce and carrots. This was how we got in the door, asking people to put them in the refrigerator—one in Tupperware, one without. Then, I'd come back in three days. The piece of lettuce not in Tupper-ware would be wilted, the one in Tupperware would not, and that's how we dated parties." It's a method that harkened back to when Wise and McDonald told their Detroit customers to throw away the shower caps. With simple yet effective ex-amples, would-be hostesses could see that the product really worked. It was the same all across America—parties were held, products were sold, businesses were grown, and dealers like Pat Jordan moved up the ranks.

Conlogue promoted Jordan to Tupperware manager. "Then I got pregnant and had another baby," Jordan recalled. "I went to a Tupperware party the night my water broke and went imme-diately to the hospital and had my second child. That's what you did." But Jordan's charmed life as an up-and-coming Tupper-ware sales rep took an unfortunate turn. Her second child, Susan, came down with a serious bout of spinal meningitis. She told Conlogue it was unlikely she could continue. Jordan had a sick baby at home and only one car, which her husband, Phil, needed. Despite the adversity, Conlogue asked her to hold on. Very slowly, Susan started to recover from what could have been a fatal illness. Once she was well enough, Jordan soldiered on.

"I begged a car from everyone I could think of," she said.

"And everybody in my neighborhood knew what was happening and helped me. Sometimes I would put the kids in the car and drive Phil to work in downtown Miami and then drive back. I had a wonderful neighbor who helped watch my children so I could make my parties. Phil did almost all of my bagging and delivering of Tupperware—the latter on his way to and from work—because I was too busy holding parties."

The Jordans were similarly resourceful when looking to recruit new dealers. Pat took the lead, identifying woman after woman to bring into the distributorship. The talkative ones were an easy sell, but Jordan would also go after a wallflower if she saw potential. "I would look at her and say, 'Honey, you need me,'" laughed Jordan. "'You're sweet and darling and all you can talk about is your love of children, which is fine, but there's a big world out there.'" It was that kind of woman who often told Jordan that the idea would never fly with her husband. That's when Pat brought Phil into the game. "I would say to them," Jordan remembered, her tone turning a bit conspiratorial, "'I'd like to bring my husband and talk to your husband.' They'd say, 'It's not going to do any good, but okay.' Phil and I would drive up in our shiny car. Phil would have on his suit and tie and I would have on my five-inch heels. And he would talk about what he did in the early days, how much pride he had in the things I was doing for the family. It was always the family."

After more assurances that they weren't trying to take the man's wife away, that she could do this during the day and wouldn't need a lot of clothes or extras to get started—*and couldn't your family really use the extra money?*—the Jordans gained yet another Tupperware recruit. But that was only the beginning. Often, a shy person would have to be reassured that she was capable of giving demonstrations, not to mention running both a business and a family. "How do you know if you don't try?" was the mantra Jordan said she passed on to her own recruits. "I was on the training team and traveled all over the country. In places like Utah [I would say,] 'What if you could be one of the most successful people in your community and you never tried? What if this would bring so much happiness to your family and you never tried?'"

That kind of motivation came right from the top down; Brownie Wise often spoke to women's dreams to get them to do the kind of things they never thought possible. Once they bought in, people like Pat Jordan began to transform their lives. Within the executive ranks at Orlando headquarters, Elsie Mortland, a once shy and diminutive housewife, was experiencing a similar transition. Credited with helping to instill "a sense of family, loyalty, and leadership" in the company, Mortland was also the director of the experimental kitchen and, by 1955, had become the first person to test any one of Tupper's prototypes. It was all done in his typically clandestine style.

"He had to be very careful about other plastics companies stealing his design," Mortland said. From time to time, a carefully packaged container would arrive at THP headquarters. "He had them sealed with tape, of course, and written on the outside [was] 'To be opened by Elsie Mortland only,'" she recalled. Once, Mortland even made a crucial trip to New York to gain the *Good Housekeeping* Seal of Approval. It was impressive and intimidating.

Elsie Mortland had also become a key member of Brownie's team, and the only other woman with any kind of influence. "If I had any problem, I'd go to Brownie and get it straightened out. She was very willing to help me in any way she could. And if she could push any of her responsibilities on me, she would," said Mortland with a smile.

Wise could provide early dealers with all the motivation in

the world, but in many cases they still had real-world transportation conflicts. To resolve them, Brownie's team came
up with an idea that ranks as one of the great incentive programs in THP history. In the Garden Pavilion, Gary McDonald told the audience that the company had decided on a car
program. That might have caused a stir, but not a big one,
considering how long and often THP had given away cars.
But, McDonald told the audience, it wouldn't be for just the
top ten managers—how about the top sixty? That caused
a great deal more excitement in the crowd. Then, for what
McDonald called "the coup de grâce," he announced that they
had decided to take it another step, and that THP would give a
Ford Fairlane 500 to every Tupperware manager in the world.

Pat Jordan, who was in the audience, attested to the reaction: "You talk about screaming, hysterical women. It was the
biggest thing that anyone could ever imagine: to be able to
get a car free by doing your job that you loved while you were
earning money and earning gifts and earning trips." At least
two women in the crowd fainted at the news.

It earned McDonald the kind of adoration to which Wise
was accustomed, and then some. And it was an idea straight
from her mantra of working hard to make wishes come true.
"They tore the sleeves out of the suit I was wearing," he
laughed. Decades later, TV talk-show hosts like Oprah Winfrey and Ellen DeGeneres would go on to take a similar page
from the Tupperware playbook.

All the Tupperware faithful could take that kind of elec-
tricity back to their own home distributorships and re-create
it there. At Monday morning meetings, they regaled dealers
who didn't make it to Kissimmee with stories of how incredi-
ble the jubilee had been, stoking the competitive fires of those
who promised themselves that they would do what it took to

make it down to Florida the following year. "That's why we kept growing," McDonald said.

Both Tony Ponticelli and Gary McDonald credited Wise and her considerable skills as an executive for bringing those kinds of traits out in the people around her. "It takes an executive to know the talent you have and bring out the best in it. So you gotta give her that," Ponticelli offered. "Then she had a belief in the religion she was trying to teach, which was direct selling and party-plan selling. And I would say that she knew how to work with men where other women did not." Public relations man Don Hinton had done stints with United Press and Pan Am and, before Brownie Wise, had never interviewed for a job with a female executive. "I was impressed because she was sharp, she was intelligent, and asked the right questions," he recalled. "After thirty minutes, she asked me, 'Can you start tomorrow?'"

Beyond the executive offices, Wise toiled late into the night answering dealer letters, fostering a personal one-on-one touch that inspired many to push harder, aim higher, and accomplish more. To the dealers, falling short of sales goals would mean disappointing Wise, and many considered her closer to family than upper management. She was their ideal of who a working woman and mother could be, with or without a man in her life.

That said, as 1955 drew to a close, Wise couldn't escape the increasing difficulty she was having with the most important man in her professional life. In previous years, as profits and new dealers rolled in, she and Earl Tupper had handled most of their business, and their differences, during long one-on-one phone calls. During that time, Tupper had kept a "totally hands-off" approach to Tupperware Home Parties. However, somewhere along the way, Wise's relationship with her boss had become strained, and over the course of 1956, Wise would begin to feel his presence—and scrutiny—like never before.

Best Wishes

On February 27, 1956, *Newsweek* featured a prominent photograph of Wise and a quote from her in an article about the trailblazing women starting to emerge in top corporate jobs. By that time, the magazine reported, three million American women carried union cards. Sixty-five percent of retailer Montgomery Ward's employees were women, and yet every single one of its 568 store managers across America was a man.

"The discovery that women are people is being extended," RCA's chairman David Sarnoff told *Newsweek,* "and opportunity for women should expand with it." However, the article also noted that men often weren't chivalrous toward female colleagues. One former THP secretary at the Kissimmee home

Wise in her office, ca. 1956. Notice her trademark wicker chair.

office during this era put a finer point on the situation: "Men resented Brownie's position and resented working for a woman."

From Earl Tupper on down, the men of Tupperware Home Parties knew that if you took issue with Brownie Wise, you did so at your own peril. When Hamer Wilson ordered some landscaping changed without her consent, she put a stop to it. Then, to emphasize her unhappiness with him, Wise took Wilson for a walk. "She cut him down real bad," Jerry Wise recalled. "When they came back, he didn't look so good." During one of the brainstorming sessions at Water's Edge, a disagreement between Wilson and Wise became so heated that Jack Marshall all but carried him out of the house.

According to her son, Brownie Wise thought Wilson was arrogant, to the point that she didn't even like the way he walked. "Like he had a post lying across his shoulders, like a little prizefighter," Jerry Wise recounted. "Brownie hated that." Those who knew him said Wilson resented Wise because she "started believing her own publicity." The friction could have also come from the fact that Wilson's star was on the rise and that he got on well with distributors, which Wise could have seen as a potential threat to her own position.

As he grew closer in business dealings with Wise, Ponticelli said he tried to warn her not to take all the positive press and ego gratification too seriously. It came after Wise and the public relations men finished courting a writer from *Redbook* magazine. "I'm listening to what I call ego inflation," Ponticelli recalled. "I said, 'You know, Brownie, I hope you don't believe those things that you see. Coming from New York, you have to do that for the public and the press . . . but don't ever believe what you read,' and left it at that." Part of the reason Ponticelli said he was hesitant to go further was the "you're treading on thin ice" look Wise gave him in return.

Her son insisted Wise only put up with the publicity because it was a necessary tool for promoting Tupperware. Because of the great benefits and business the coverage reaped, Gary McDonald said Wise could be forgiven if the attention went to her head: "I'm not sure I know of anybody who would be so selfless that [if] they were subjected to that much adoration, praise, and publicity that they would not start believing it."

For her part, Wise often wrote and spoke of forsaking personal gratification for the good of the whole, and remaining humble even in times of great success. To remind herself of that point, Wise liked to climb into Jerry's small motorboat and steer it over to an undeveloped island in Lake Toho. "I have christened it, *Isla Milagra,* the Miracle Island," she wrote. Local legend had it that hundreds of years ago the Seminole and Calusa tribes had stashed their women and children on the island during times of war. Wise envisioned building a homestead on the 130-acre expanse, planting citrus, and raising cattle and chickens. Strolling alone in the evenings through the untamed flora and fauna, Wise could marvel at the foreboding thunderheads that could roll in quickly over the lake.

She wrote: "Lightning streaks across the great dark bowl of sky ripping it open with a gash . . . then a ponderous roll of thunder will crash against the land and water . . . continuing one roll upon the other. Powerful, echoing notes of nature's wildest music. It does me good to watch a storm on the island. To listen to it. For in the midst of it I am always reminded of God's strength and man's frailty. It is good sometimes for us to be reminded!" And it was in that moment, Wise wrote, that she recognized the limitations of her own existence: "I stand under the great umbrella of night sky, on which a million stars are twinkling, and I stand there long enough to absorb the vastness of the universe. I feel small again . . . and it is good that I do!"

Wise had an abiding faith in God, her son said, but her spiritual nature didn't stop there. According to Jerry, his mother would walk through cemeteries and actually thought she could communicate with the dead, including her grandmother, who'd been so influential molding young Brownie's work ethic, her pragmatism, her fierce independence, and her devotion to giving something back. Wise had big plans for her island paradise—ones that would have made her grandmother proud: "It is my special wishing place that I expect to share with the working wishers of the world." She embarked on an effort to buy the secluded property.

Alongside Brownie's new sense of perspective, the mood among THP brass brightened in April when Florida governor LeRoy Collins agreed to speak at the company's fifth birthday celebration. To mark the important milestone, Wise commissioned what was thought to be the biggest cake ever baked in Florida. Looking like a replica of the headquarters, it measured three-and-a-half feet by ten feet and weighed seven hundred pounds. A special tank made to look like the reflecting pond in front of headquarters served as the punch bowl.

It was a fitting tribute for a guest as honorable as Governor Collins, whom historians credited with being "cool while the rest of Dixie appeared to be burning" after the U.S. Supreme Court struck down segregation in 1954. Like Wise, Governor Collins was also an expert communicator and the first Florida governor to actively court the press. On April 19, 1956, Wise introduced him to a crowd of five hundred invited guests, dignitaries, and Florida Tupperware dealers, managers, and distributors. After posing for photos and cutting the massive cake with a beaming Brownie, Collins congratulated the company for its success. PR man Glen Bump led the crowd in a rousing rendition of "Happy Birthday." Collins then moved to the Garden Pavilion, where his speech was carried live on local radio stations. Despite the honor and validation a visit from the governor brought, Earl Tupper did not attend.

As a companion contest to celebrate the fifth birthday month, Wise encouraged all dealers who held five parties in a day to call collect and let her know. In Silver Springs, Maryland, homemaker Myrtle Scharfenburg accomplished the ambitious goal with six children under twelve at home. If that wasn't frenetic enough, some even managed seven parties a day. THP had come up with another powerful incentive to spur this kind of productivity in their sales force: an invitation to the jubilee.

The 1956 jubilee would be in July, and the company had already secured big-name talent like crooner Rudy Vallee. "Outstanding achievements by dealers and managers will be suitably rewarded by the presentation of awards, trophies and prizes" read an article in *Tupperware Sparks*. "You'll thrill again to a brilliant fireworks display as the sky explodes in beauty. You'll be in the movies too. Yes, there'll be another Jubilee movie made this year. And the highlight of everything will be wish granting! Such excitement, such suspense! There's never been anything like it!"

Back home at Water's Edge, Tupperware's photographer Jack McCollum and Brownie struggled to get a seventeen-year-old Jerry to pose for publicity photos: in a bathrobe shaving, tooling around the lake in a boat with his mother, watching admiringly as she pulled something delicious from the oven, sitting opposite her on horseback. After Wise injured her back, her son says she had to wear a brace and often found such photo sessions painful. "They wanted it to look like she oversaw everything," Jerry remembered.

On horseback with Jerry at Water's Edge, ca. 1956. Jerry said it was not easy for his mother to pose or ride because of her back injury.

By this time, Jerry seemed to take a special pleasure in goading his mother with practical jokes and salty language. Late at night, as his mother sat on her bed typing letters and talking into her Dictaphone in a nightshirt or some other form of undress, Jerry liked to creep in and threaten to snap a photo of his own. "She said, 'Don't you know how to knock?' I said, 'No, I sure don't; can I take the picture now?'" Jerry reminisced.

"Here I am in all my glory," she groused, "and my only child comes sneaking in to my room . . . NO, and that's final!"

Jerry snapped the shutter anyway, prompting his mother to chase him all the way out of the house. She finally caught up to him, retrieved the camera, and popped it open.

"Where's the film?" she demanded.

"There wasn't any in it. I was just kidding," he replied.

"Oh, she was mad," Jerry remembered. "And then she said, 'I want a hot cup of coffee with half and half, and I want it now!'" Perhaps only Brownie Wise could drink coffee late at night as a sedative. She could only get so angry, though; she was a practical joker herself, having once placed a pair of newly dead timber rattlesnakes on the table just to scare the hell out of her dinner guests.

Soon after, Wise added to this sense of domestic bliss by making one of her most special wishes come true. At a law office in downtown Kissimmee, she signed her name to deed papers making the Lake Toho island her own. Unable to hide her elation, she remarked, "You don't just buy an island like you do a bag of groceries or a keg of nails. Bells ought to ring. Flower petals should drift down from somewhere. Banners should unfurl. Something besides signing a paper should open the door to the magic of owning an island!" True to her word, Wise populated the island with a small herd of pure-bred Brahman cattle. Jerry took charge of the animals and the thirty-five acres of citrus already growing there.

Tupper and Wise exchanged ideas about using the island property for Tupperware functions. Instead of giving Wise a raise, they considered the possibility of the company compensating her $10,000 per year to lease the property. That way any improvements she made to the island for possible company use could come out of that pot of money. It's not clear if the two ever came to any formal conclusion; as was their custom up until that point, they often addressed such matters only in their many phone conversations. The same murky business arrangement covered her use of the Water's Edge home and property. Wise would come to regret not getting important business matters between herself and Tupper in writing. For the time being, she had many other ambitious ideas on her agenda.

In 1956, Wise embarked on the idea of writing an inspirational self-help book she could use as another promotional vehicle. She contracted a writer named Robert Froman to help her by ghostwriting a success guide she planned to call *Best Wishes*. Success guru and *The Power of Positive Thinking* author Norman Vincent Peale agreed to write a foreword, and Wise planned to send the book to some of the biggest newsmakers and newsmen of the day.

Few woman in 1956 would have been more qualified to write a book about wishes coming true. Through boundless ambition, tireless work, and endless travel, Brownie Wise had transformed her life into what her alter ego Hibiscus had always written about on those cold Detroit nights. In a decade, she had risen from a government secretary to a tycoon in June Cleaver pearls. And she had done it in what was decidedly a man's world.

Brownie Wise had plenty to say, and with her considerable skills as a writer and communicator, her book could share her secrets with a broader audience, especially women. She had drawn up the blueprints for feminine success on no one's terms but her own. In 1956, the *Houston Post* writer Napoleon Hill wrote this about Wise in his "Science of Success" column: "It has been estimated that Brownie Wise has helped more women to financial success than any other single living person. Moreover, she has proved that no matter what problems face a woman, there is a way to solve them through courage and humor."

Those words may well have been regenerated straight from

a THP press release, but they demonstrate how writers were beginning to see the significant role Wise had already played for women in American business. And *Best Wishes* would be no less ambitious. While writing a book is all but expected of someone who has a significant following in business, media, or entertainment today, in 1956, Brownie Wise would be far ahead of her time.

From a pragmatic standpoint, Wise could use *Best Wishes* to get her motivational wishing mantra into the hands of women outside the Tupperware family who might be willing to become dealers. But more important, she could finally pay forward all the practical advice she'd gotten from her grandmother, her mother, and all the other strong women whom she credited for much of her success.

Wise continued the wishing theme for the 1956 jubilee, calling it "Treasurama." In advance of the event, Tupperware dealers and managers had been sent a questionnaire that asked, "If dreams were for sale, what would you buy?" Seven of the wishes from those questionnaires would be granted. A wishing well would also be dedicated in honor of the six thousand people who reportedly sent back answer cards. At the jubilee, they would be asked to line up and drop their dreams down the well inside tiny Tupperware Midget containers. A young beauty queen, Diane Tauscher, was even hired to play the part of Tupperware's wish fairy

Besides the singing of Rudy Vallee, NBC radio commentator and reporter H. V. Kaltenborn signed on to speak. Both would be carried live on local radio station WORZ. As always, parents and children from all over the Orlando area would pull over alongside the Orange Blossom Trail and watch, in what became a long-standing summer tradition, a spectacular fireworks display.

At 8:30 a.m. on Tuesday, July 3, 1956, Wise blew the trumpet on the opening of Tupperware Home Parties third annual jubilee, the first held in July. Coming from as far away as Hawaii and Canada, twelve hundred dealers and managers had again paid their own way to attend. Greeting the Tupperware pilgrims were twenty-two-foot poles with silk banners, giant tents, pavilions, marquees, and knights on horseback. Jerry and a friend dressed as "costumed gentry astride gallant stallions" in what would be his last jubilee before beginning a six-month stint with the army later that summer.

Eight hundred treasure chests filled with Treasurama prizes—including diamonds, coffeepots, and toasters—would be given out based on the level of sales achievement. "Two women will be crowned queens," Wise announced, "and they'll get their weight in Tupperware." The seven big winners wouldn't know their wishes were coming true until the moment was just right, so the ecstasy of the person chosen could be maximized.

"Tupperware people take a vacation and talk Tupperware," Wise told the audience in her welcome address:

> We *need* work as we need food, human companionship, and divine compassion. Work that is the greatest blessing is that work which we like. Work with people we like, work with things and thoughts and objectives that we like.
>   . . . This work blesses us. It gives us confidence. It points a way to growth. That WORK is food and tonic for our spirit and our bodies.

In a display of camaraderie, hundreds of Tupperware people from across North America recited the company creed:

> In the unity of our ideas and our ambitions lies our greatest strength. No exchange offers so rich a compensation as the exchange of thought. A drop of water contains but an infinitesimal molecule of strength . . . powerless in itself . . . but the merging of billions of drops of water produces the tremendous power of Niagara Falls. There is no process, mechanical or mental, that can measure the power our united effort can create.

As a plane flew overhead, pilot Charles Deck gave the "OK" for a thousand cards to be dropped from directly above Tupperware headquarters. Each one had the name of Tupperware's first lucky wish winner. Dealers and their families raced over to where the cards were still fluttering down. A *Life* magazine photograph showed other dealers raising their hands and pointing to Mabel Best, her mouth wide open in amazement. THP had granted the Kansas City Tupperware dealer's wish: an all-expense-paid, seven-day trip to help her marine son celebrate his twenty-second birthday in Tokyo. Tupperware included enough birthday cake for the young sergeant's entire company to celebrate. An August 1956 *Life* spread detailing the frenzy surrounding Treasurama showed Best and her son having just visited the Buddha at Kamakura—a mother and son unexpectedly reunited through the magic of Tupperware.

There were other wishes granted in similarly creative ways: Doris Stewart of Moline, Illinois, saw her name spelled out in fireworks. Her five-year-old daughter, Susan, had dreamed of their entire family taking an air trip to Disneyland in California; now her fantasy was coming true. San Diego dealer

Kay Tilden watched a Correct Kraft Atom Skier come tearing up the reflecting pond, not knowing it was picking her up. She had wished for an inboard motorboat for her husband. A highway patrolman handed Mary Smorse of Granger, Illinois, a summons carrying the unexpected news that she was about to have two more rooms added to her home. It had gotten too small for her family of five, and she remarked, "I need more room for my Tupperware." Another dealer watched an hour-long fashion show, only to learn that it was all clothing for the new wardrobe she'd requested for her husband. Peggy Allison found out she was getting her wish of a new car, and then the submerged vehicle came floating to the surface of THP's Poly Pond.

All of this razzle-dazzle took long, hard hours to plan and perfect, much of it the handiwork of Tony Ponticelli, Gary McDonald, and George Reynolds. Jerry Wise watched as Reynolds sweated the logistics of submerging an automobile and, after it bubbled to the surface, having it driven up onto a platform. "The pond had to be deepened," Wise remembered, "so the car couldn't be seen."

Then, with a wave of Reynolds's hand, the entire display would happen with flawless timing. Pat Jordan was among the young dealers who experienced the wonder of the 1956 jubilee: "I thought wow, there isn't that much money in the whole world because it was all very impressive. It was all show, it was all glitz, it was all glamour, it was all wonderful."

At the same time, Earl Tupper's product was helping the thousands selling it to achieve success and realize their own dreams, albeit on smaller terms. "I reached my goal, which was owning our own home, in one year, four months," Rae Frank wrote from Rochester, New York. "I think that is wonderful."

Lavon Weber of Wheatheart Sales in Wichita, Kansas, wrote that working in the business with her husband, Bob, had brought them closer together and improved their marriage. More important, with the money they earned, it was possible to adopt two children. "Bobby is 4 and Fran is 2 and saying everything," wrote Lavon. "For them we are so thankful." Both heartwarming and encouraging, Frank's and Weber's success stories perfectly matched the joyful, celebratory tone that characterized the 1956 jubilee.

One fun night, the rain poured down as hundreds of Tupperware people dined on food catered from Morrison's Cafeterias. "You would laugh and slide around in the mud," Jordan reminisced. "We didn't care if we were wet and slimy." Elsie Mortland ran the long training sessions teaching dealers the best ways to demonstrate the product, date parties, and sell multiple Tupperware sets. "I remember taking these copious notes," said Jordan. "I wanted to get everything down because I was anxious to get home and try all of these new wonderful ideas."

With all the Treasurama loot passed out, the inspirational talks given, detailed notes taken, and memories made, what Wise called "their most successful jubilee to date" came to an end. It had been an emotional week for Wise herself: preparing for Jerry's army send-off, dealing with the endless details, and listening to the speech from Reverend James B. Grambling, a Methodist minister who had preached at the church she attended as a young girl. Now it was time to say good-bye to busloads of Tupperware "family." As staff members stood assembled on the front steps of headquarters, the Tupperware chorale sang "Aloha" across sparkling Poly Pond. As *Tupperware Sparks* described, "Tiny lights on masts of sailboats on Tupper Lake blinked a fond 'til we meet again.'" As a final, brilliant piece of recognition for new Tupperware graduates, Don Hinton typed out press releases and sent them to the hometown newspapers of every person who'd graduated from the jubilee training programs.

Eager to maintain the momentum from a successful jubilee, in September, THP kicked off what Wise called "the biggest training program in Tupperware History." The so-called Opp-Hop program would ensure that every dealer could put on the most effective demonstration possible. Tupperware also launched its first national advertising campaign with a full-page color ad in *Woman's Home Companion* and other publications.

Soon after, in a piece so close to the Farnumsville operation that it was sure to catch Tupper's attention, the *Boston Traveler* afternoon newspaper ran a front-page article on Wise. In what was typical of the flattering, but also sexist, articles of the day dealing with women in business, Wise was heralded as "the housewife's dream come true." Perpetuating the notion that any strong woman in business had to be a man-hating shrew, the article's author noted: "Being one of America's top-flight women executives hasn't turned Brownie's pretty head. She has a sunny disposition that makes people like her as much as she likes them." In October, Wise traveled to Boston to accept the Greater Boston Chamber of Commerce award as "the most outstanding salesman of the year, 1956." A crowd of three thousand people watched inside Boston's Symphony Hall as Wise accepted the oversized gold trophy. "Put your wishes to work," Wise told them, "and you will find your passport to happiness."

The honor in Boston became yet another example of how Brownie Wise the sales personality began to overshadow Tupperware, a development that was now testing Earl Tupper's remaining patience. "If [a piece] didn't have the product and the organization as the major element," remembered Gary McDonald, "that was the thing that bothered him," echoing Tupper's 1954 note after the *Business Week* cover story. If she was more interested and intent on promoting herself and her own interests, he worried, would she neglect Tupperware's?

On the contrary, Wise's writings indicate that, despite the accolades, she was passionate about turning around the sales slump caused by the 1955 distributor revolt. In the fall of that year, Wise told Tupper she felt THP and its distributors had experienced a "real settling down" thanks to the company establishing a uniform retail price policy and a program of prepaying the freight for product shipment. "This was perhaps the biggest single step forward THP has ever taken," she wrote Tupper. "You could almost *see* the distributors settling back," she observed, "and saying to themselves, 'Well, now, this is going to work after all.'" Whether Wise actually believed in the importance of these steps, or was simply trying to shore up Tupper's faith in her, is difficult to discern.

Yet behind all of the cheerleading, promotions, and PR, Wise and her staff still had to replace a small but powerful and experienced group of distributors who had left on their own or, like the Blocks, had been kicked out for trying to unionize. That meant trying to squeeze new blood out of the fragile network that remained. "We did everything we could to get the distributors to recommend perspective [*sic*] distributors to us from the manager ranks," Wise recounted. "[We] begged, threatened, cajoled, praised, brow-beat. We got more than we had before, but not as many as we needed."

Looking back, Wise acknowledged that focusing on the dealers and managers, who adored her, at the expense of the distributors so vital to the company's growth, had been wrong. The realization had come during one of the Water's Edge brainstorming sessions. "Through the step-by-step process of retracing our history," Wise wrote to Tupper, "we made a discovery so shockingly stupid it is shameful." The THP team had gotten away from offering any substantive incentive program to the distributors—those on the highest rung of the actual selling food chain. "We were so involved in fighting the runaway distributors, out of disgust, perhaps," she reasoned, "we discounted the personal (and basically human) needs of all distributors. We simply forgot."

In short, as vice president and general manager, Brownie Wise had forgotten where she'd come from. She had forgotten the angst of leaving Detroit on that snowy morning for Florida and an uncertain future. Across America, people like Pat and Phil Jordan, Jean and Jack Conlogue, Peter and Elsie Block, and many others were pulling their children from school, selling their homes, leaving behind a sales network—another family, really—and heading for parts unknown, places like Wichita, Cincinnati, Spokane, and Norfolk, to start all over. Perhaps Wise had been so caught up with the praise, the island, and the book deal that she took her eye off the ball. Regardless, the distributors felt she and THP were leaving them flapping in the breeze, the same feeling that had prompted Brownie to place a furious call to Earl Tupper that very first time.

For someone as detail-oriented and thoroughly devoted to Tupperware Home Parties as Brownie Wise, this was a disturbing revelation. She confessed to Tupper:

> Believe me, we were a shocked little circle that night in my living room. I was so dumb-founded that later I couldn't go to sleep. I walked the floor and the garden paths until almost dawn, wondering how we could have been so stupid.

Inexpressibly stupid. I discovered the next morning that I hadn't been the only one to do that.

While Wise used the word *we,* this was as close as she could come to admitting she was responsible.

However, Wise had not forgotten the distributors; she had made a conscious decision, a serious and expensive tactical mistake, to downplay their importance and concentrate on the dealers. She had confirmed this thinking in a November 1953 memo to Tupper. "Our customers are actually not our distributors at all," Wise wrote, "but the total number of dealers operating in the field." Her acknowledgment of their role in growing the company came only in passing. "It is true that we depend upon our distributors, as other companies depend upon their managers, for general over-all supervision and leadership of the selling, training, and recruiting program," Wise conceded, "but our real stock-in-trade is the dealer force itself."

In typical Brownie Wise fashion, she threw herself into fixing her error by building better relationships with the distributor network: "I made telephone calls, I sent complimentary wires, I followed their goals week-by-week, I kept in close touch."

It's unclear how much Wise's admission may have weakened her position with Tupper. If one thing was certain, Earl Tupper was all business, and the Tupperware distributorships were the heart of that business. The dramatic drop in 1955 sales proved it. In 1956, sales had increased 16.3 percent, but it was clearly not good enough for anyone involved, which set the stage for all of the dramatic developments of 1957.

In the following year, the revelation that kept Wise up all night would not deter her plans to move forward with a book, or the work she wanted done on her island. She would find time to do the interviews, stay in the spotlight, and steer the company back to healthy profitability. But at least one of the executives around her was already starting to see Brownie heading toward professional burnout.

To make matters worse, in 1957 Earl Tupper decided he needed to be more hands-on with the Florida operation. Despite the problems in 1955 and 1956, Wise had enjoyed the freedom to do pretty much as she wished up to this point. When that started to change, she pulled hard at the reins. The informal phone calls between the two morphed into long, contentious memos that would later form the basis of a damning paper trail. Deep fissures started to form in the unorthodox business relationship of the two mismatched personalities. Just as Brownie Wise had forgotten in 1956 what was the heart of the business she loved so passionately, in 1957 she forgot who held the true power in Tupperware.

Soon after, her world started to crumble.

Sunshine Cinderella

At the beginning of 1957, Tupperware had less than half of the 20,000 dealers the company still claimed to have in newspaper and magazine articles. In January, the exact number was 8,816, and by February it had dwindled further to 8,391. The loss of dealers in February resulted in a $60,000 sales deficit for the month compared to the previous year. If Brownie Wise and the Sales Division couldn't find a way to turn the numbers around, expecting sales figures to grow would be a pipe dream.

Yet when Tupper asked Wise what he could expect for 1957, she avowed, "I BELIEVE we WILL do between ten and twelve million, and believe me we're working for twelve or over . . . I realize full well that this is what we should have done, and what we expected to do last year." Gross sales for 1956 had been just over $8 million.

Wise was further risking her credibility with Tupper by forecasting a minimum 25 percent increase in sales for the year. THP hadn't done anything close to that since the record expansion year of 1954. Wise was going to have to dig in and work harder to prove to herself and to Tupper that she could right the ship. She hoped that a particularly brutal stretch of winter weather up north was in large part to blame for canceled parties and dealer drop-off—and that, in conjunction with a thirteen-point incentive plan designed to get distributors back on board, sales figures would blossom along with the spring thaw.

As she struggled to get Tupperware back on course, Wise also suddenly faced battles on many fronts, including high-profile defections within the Tupperware family. Former sales counselors Jack Marshall and Jack McCall left for the more lucrative job of running their own distributorships. By the time he left, Wise felt her former right-hand man, Marshall, had developed "a superiority complex." While "he was making the same salary I am, a distributorship looked awfully good," she noted. Marshall opened Tropical Sales in Miami. Jack McCall started McCall Enterprises in Fresno.

The threat of losing good foot soldiers went beyond the executive team, though. Tupperware employees were also coveted by other businesses putting down roots. Just five miles up the Orange Blossom Trail, the Martin Aircraft Company bought five thousand acres on which to establish a new manufacturing facility. That led to a feeling around THP known as "Martinitis." With the lures of higher pay, a thirty-six-hour workweek, and other attractive, company-paid benefits, there was always a threat THP employees might choose to leave for greener pastures. "We haven't lost anyone to them yet," Wise assured Tupper, "but there are the usual rumblings."

Even Wise's social programs couldn't catch a break. While she had worked hard to expose locals to art and classical music, her efforts had received a mixed reaction. Some initiatives, such as opening up Tupperware's Garden Pavilion to hundreds of schoolchildren for a concert by the sixty-piece Florida Symphony Orchestra—believed to be Osceola County's first concert of its kind—were a success. However, entries in the 1956 Art Fund competition garnered little interest during a one-week stand early the following year at the Tupperware

Museum. The apathy led Kissimmee's newspaper to run the headline CULTURE COMES TO CITY, BUT CITY WON'T COME TO CULTURE. In a time when influential painters like Jackson Pollock were redefining the parameters of modern American abstract art, entries from like-minded artists left the locals a little puzzled. "Some are inspiring," the Kissimmee newspaperman Max Norris wrote, "some are disturbing, some confusing, some pleasing, and at least one, I found downright uncomfortable."

Given the pushback she faced, Brownie Wise turned back to what she knew best: motivation. For yet another incentive campaign, Wise promised to plant a pine seedling on the east end of THP grounds "for each dealer who has opened the new opportunities of Tupperware to a new dealer" during the upcoming April birthday-month celebration. Orlando photographer Fred DeWitt was hired to photograph Wise as she planted the dealer trees. "She talked to some people on the phone with a shovel in her hands," DeWitt remembered. Though Wise was used to putting in marathon days, the long hours were obviously taking their toll. "She seemed very tired," he observed.

Another tried-and-true way Wise and her staff employed to attract dealers was publicity. Even if the dealer and sales numbers were slumping a bit, her profile was as high as ever.

Jon Whitcomb was a writer responsible for one of the most memorable pieces of PR Wise received as head of Tupperware Home Parties. As usual, she charmed him to the point that he appeared to be smitten with her, hence the title of his April 1957 *Cosmopolitan* piece, "Sunshine Cinderella."

"I was expecting to meet a lady tycoon of the type Rosalind Russell used to play in the movies—brusque, clipped, and dominating," Whitcomb noted in the typically male, let's-size-up-this-career-gal way. "She is small and feminine, a 'charm girl' in the words of one of the prosperous-looking, tanned executives who soon strolled in and joined us. Most of Brownie's aides are males, all singularly well adjusted to taking orders from a woman." Or at least that's how it appeared on the surface.

Earl Tupper had to appreciate a photograph of Wise with Tupperware showing Whitcomb how to perform the now-famous Tupperware "burp," as well as a mention of Tupperware's "one hundred different sizes and shapes in several pastel colors." However, when recounting how Wise convinced Tupper to switch to home-based parties, key executives and other home-party distributors like Ann and Tom Damigella—who did business directly with Earl Tupper before Brownie Wise came along—were nowhere to be found. In Whitcomb's rewrite of THP history, when Tupper was sold on the home-party method, he told Wise, "Show us how, you're the boss."

There were also fawning descriptions of Wise's home and work lives: "The boss sits at a king-sized desk in a luxurious office roughly the size of a basketball court. When I walked in, she was taking calls in rotation from three telephones on her desk." And without a quote to support his assertion, Whitcomb concluded that Wise's secretary, Mary Frances Babb, "feels strongly that her boss is a goddess who can do no wrong." Whitcomb reported that Wise had been offered jobs with six-figure incomes by other companies, "but she plans to stick with the company she built from scratch." Whitcomb credited Wise with designing the headquarters that arose out of a vision Wise described to Tupper. "I looked toward the far side and there it stood," Wise told the interviewer. "It was real to me."

At home, the "boss" and "goddess" was still a regular gal who spent free time polishing stones into rings and earrings and raising cattle with her hot-rodding, teenage rancher son, now back from an Army Reserve stint. To go along with the Horatio Alger flavor of the article, in it Wise reportedly got into Tupperware in the first place because Jerry was sickly and Brownie needed money to pay his medical bills, a claim both Jerry Wise and Gary McDonald said wasn't true. Wise also received a nice plug for the soon-to-be-released *Best Wishes* book. "Wishing," the article quoted Wise, "is the art of reacting to the opportunities your ambition uncovers every day."

Wise and her latest writer/promoter even floated over to Isla Milagra on a power barge, taking with them a truck and a station wagon. "We floated into a landing," Whitcomb noted, "beyond which live oaks dripping Spanish moss formed a tall backdrop." Wandering through acres of old citrus groves and below oak limbs wrapped with tangled growth, Wise remarked, "Isn't it still? I feel secure here."

"Sunshine Cinderella," for better or worse, was another milestone in the ascent of Tupperware and the promotion of Brownie Wise as its star sales personality. More important, the month the article was published, THP picked up 840 new dealers, bringing the total to more than 9,400. The sales numbers followed. In April 1957, THP tallied $1,029,271.77 in sales, more than a quarter-million dollars better than the year before, proving, yet again, that puff pieces like the *Cosmo* article reaped high-dollar sales in return.

Soon after, the *Kissimmee Gazette,* which had become a virtual public relations arm for Wise, dutifully noted the *Cosmopolitan* article, lauding Wise as "our most famous citizen." She often made front-page news with civic activities like lighting the Heart Fund torch as publicity chairman for the campaign, and her decision to donate book royalties to the drive brought another article and a glowing quote from Podium

Publishing, which she started. "With a heart as big as the company she heads," said the unnamed publishers, "Brownie Wise has become synonymous with 'sincerity' to her constant desire to contribute good to the world about her."

The paper also ran a review of *Best Wishes,* but the article had no byline identifying its author. The piece cast Brownie Wise as a fairy godmother spreading seeds of Poly-T prosperity across the nation: "Beginning with a handful of dealers, Brownie scattered her stardust into the living rooms of America. Her merchandising methods proved sheer magic for the increasing numbers of dealers who saw fantasy fade from wishing and a bright new business emerge." Wise said she compiled *Best Wishes* "because I wanted to share my thoughts on wishing with everybody, and because a number of people had asked me to put them in writing."

Unfortunately, the finished book didn't live up to Wise's lofty ambitions, and she found the manuscript "disconnected and disappointing." She had hoped to make an inspirational statement with the help of writer Robert Froman, but the two had gotten into a legal dispute about the "interpretation" of their contract. Early in the year, that dispute was the subject of several staff meetings at headquarters. Wise decided to pay Froman $4,000 to make the matter go away. Given that she also cofounded the publishing company under which her book was launched, *Best Wishes* had become a deep money pit. "The book does not have any particular sparkle," Wise confessed to Tupper. "I did not have time to do it myself. It is made up of talks I have given, and therefore it lacks continuity."

Adding to Wise's frustration, Earl Tupper, already irritated by years of reading revisionist history about Tupperware in publicity pieces, bristled at how much time she was spending promoting side projects instead of Tupperware—and how little information she shared about her other endeavors. In an April 29 memo to Wise, he told her he was embarrassed to read about her book in the *Orlando Sentinel* newspaper seeing as he had not received a copy. "Nor have you seen fit to discuss with me how you wish to handle its promotion through T.H.P.," he complained.

Wise shot back, "NO ONE HAD RECEIVED A COPY." Though the *Sentinel* had mentioned the book was near publication, it was late coming out. Wise explained further that she was trying to have a copy sprayed with a fine gold leafing to send to him. "I wanted to have a copy of *Best Wishes* done like that for you," she told him. After two tries, the company she hired to do the job told Wise the binding wouldn't stand up to that kind of treatment. "An hour after that, you were asking Mary Frances to have a book sent to you," Wise recounted. "I'm sorry. It meant a great deal to me to get that special one for you, but it doesn't matter now."

Tupper also quizzed Wise on how she planned to spend time promoting the book. Wise told him she had turned down offers for television interviews in Jacksonville, Miami, St. Petersburg, and Tampa. She did admit signing books for an hour and a half on a Saturday afternoon at an Orlando department store. "THAT CONSTITUTES MY PERSONAL TIME DEVOTED TO THE PROMOTION OF THE BOOK," Wise argued. "Did you have in mind that I was spending a lot of time on the promotion of something personal?" She further quizzed Tupper in her reply memo: "That I was planning to get rich on this book? That I was using the machinery and sales force of THP to increase the book's sales? If so . . . and it sounds that way . . . I'm surprised at you."

Judging from the star-studded list of people to whom Wise wanted complimentary copies of her book sent, she clearly had *something* ambitious in mind for *Best Wishes.* "I appreciate your sending it to me and your kind inscription," Eleanor Roosevelt said in a thank-you note to Wise. Other copies went to Walt Disney, Edward R. Murrow, actress Jane Russell, Dale Evans, Roy Rogers, Steve Allen, Kate Smith, and Billy Graham. If Wise was looking for a way to increase her profile and fame through publication of her book, these were the people who could help her do it. Contrary to her dejected note to Tupper, Wise obviously felt enough pride in her book to send it to a long list of famous, influential people—with good reason.

While the book may not have carried the "sparkle" of Brownie Wise in person, the text does reflect why she was so good at motivating and relating to the everyday dreams and desires of her workforce. "Believe me, there can be no better thing in life than the ability to wish, sincerely, to improve the world about you," Wise wrote. She lamented that "time saving devices" had not made the world easier—just the opposite, in fact: "The key of tension is constantly turning," she empathized, "winding the nervous fibre tighter and tighter, until it frays or snaps completely."

Yet, in *Best Wishes,* Wise testified that she had found her key to happiness: "If you have set a course for yourself and know where you are going—where you should go—you can write your own ticket and find, as I did, that your work is your passport to happiness." She preached patience, determination, and curiosity: "You can salvage success," she assured readers, and get caught in "the quicksand of security." Brownie Wise told the thousands of Tupperware dealers and other women she hoped might be inspired by her words that "a 'working wish' for you is now just the matter of laying out a program. It's simply the practice of taking a goal and breaking it down into the little workable steps of every day, every week, every month, and sometimes even every hour."

One of her motivational mentors, Dr. Norman Vincent Peale, added his endorsement in a foreword to the book: "She loves people and all who work with her share a sense of oneness with her. Having visited Brownie Wise's organization I sensed a pervasive spirit of good will and joy and friendship in that beauty spot in Florida—a business headquarters ostensibly—but in reality an inspirational center as well."

At the time people were reading Dr. Peale's words, the "good will and joy and friendship" Wise had felt toward Tupper and the THP staff had felt toward her was starting to unravel. Wise wrote that she was finding Tupper "edgy and irascible." The once-democratic brainstorming sessions at THP turned autocratic under Wise's tightening grip. "She just considered the whole thing her responsibility," Elsie Mortland observed, "and she could do whatever she wanted."

For the first time, Brownie Wise saw her leadership facing tough questions and close scrutiny. One of her closer associates in the company during that period, Tony Ponticelli, felt Wise was becoming more defensive. For the first time, "doubt was creeping in." Pat Jordan was more blunt. In an interview decades later, she said she thought Wise was less the fairy godmother that she was portrayed to be in adoring publicity and closer to New York hotelier Leona Helmsley, the jailed 1980s tax evader—to many the archetypal female autocrat.

In an attempt to reassure Tupper, and herself perhaps, Wise typed out an impressive thirty-page, double-spaced memo to Tupper entitled "The Business." The epic communiqué dealt with every aspect of her THP duties: her analysis of sales figures, distributor problems and solutions, evaluations of current and former executives, civic activities, and future prospects. It also gave a glimpse into how Wise could adopt a challenging demeanor toward Tupper. Perhaps it was her attempt to prove that she was just as tough as he was. "I should explain first that this is a personal job of typing," Wise told him, "and that I expect to receive the courtesy of having errors over-looked . . . yes, even taken for granted."

Yet her tone softens considerably when bringing up the evolution of the product the two had dedicated their lives to creating and selling:

> I am still amazed every time I go into the consumer's lounge and see the east wall, covered with Tupperware . . . a beautiful sight. . . . I'm still amazed at its beauty, even after a love affair that's eight years old. . . . But I'm still amazed at the richness of our QUANTITY, too, every time I see it. How the line has grown! And to think I used to make a living from 16 or 18 Tupperware items. (I don't want to forget that either.) It's a beautiful array, Mr. Tupper. I have never seen a work of art in any museum with more beautiful lines than some of our bowls here.

She talked about THP's public relations program and some of the press suitors to whom the company said no. "We have had the singular good fortune not to have ever been 'panned' in any story," Wise bragged. "Of course, we've been extremely cagey; we've turned down *Fortune* twice; steered clear of *Time* and *Newsweek,* and turned thumbs-down on some TV tie-ins that were tempting in some ways." THP executives felt that Lucille Ball creating a madcap situation with Tupperware on her wildly popular *I Love Lucy* show had the potential to be demeaning to the product.

Wise told Tupper her ultimate goal was to be in *Reader's*

Digest, a publication of which she had been fond for years. Getting in the magazine had proven more difficult than she'd expected, but she remained hopeful, confident, and perhaps a little falsely modest: "I'm told that we'll probably be ripe for it within the year. We found out two months ago that the *Digest* editorial board had been compiling a file on us, and that the *Cosmopolitan* article was particularly impressive to them. Why, I don't know."

Wise ended her long letter on a note of optimism for their sales prospects, but also sadness that the nature of their own business relationship had changed. "I miss talking with you on the phone occasionally," Wise lamented, "not about a specific something that demands attention, but just to bring you up to date on how things are going."

Despite all of the friction at Tupperware, Wise had a lot to celebrate home at Water's Edge. Sales for 1957 were up 23 percent over the year previous, well within reach of her annual projection. A dozen new distributors had already been appointed, bringing the total number to 117, with plans for 15 more by the end of the year. Jerry had just turned nineteen. "My love for you that cannot be measured or defined," Wise wrote her son, "surely it will surround you and warm you every day of your life. The greatest gift of *my* life is that you call 'mother' the woman others call 'Brownie Wise.'"

The upcoming July jubilee promised to be the most spectacular yet, with an around-the-world theme. Wise decided to move forward on plans to host a Hawaiian-themed luau on Isla Milagra for many of THP's key distributors, managers, and visiting press—a daunting goal.

George Reynolds and his work crews spent many hours clearing land and taming the wild environs enough to make the island inhabitable for the big event. There was no running water, so teams had to dig deep to create thatch-roofed, outdoor latrines. Also, because there were no roads to the island, transportation would be a problem. Everyone would have to be brought there by a so-called power squad of local boat owners. Jerry would take others back and forth on the company barge. Special events man Tony Ponticelli was wary of depending on outside people for transportation and didn't approve of the barges and boats. "You can't take that many people back and forth," he recalled telling Brownie.

Wise should have trusted Ponticelli's instincts. But by that time, he and others were cautious about telling her she might be wrong about anything. This would be her chance to share her miracle island with Tupperware people and the press. In the end, it would also prove to be her Waterloo.

Storm Front

$\mathscr{D}$uring the spring of 1957, Earl Tupper often vented his frustrations about Brownie Wise through conversations with her secretary, Mary Frances Babb. Without the one-on-one phone contact Tupper and Wise once enjoyed, problems between the two worsened. At the end of May, Tupper told Babb he was upset that Wise was taking so long to give him any feedback on a proposed teething and baby spoon. On May 17, the prototype had arrived in Florida with Tupper's instructions for Brownie to give her comments and then return it immediately. "If we move quickly," Tupper had advised, "the mold could be completed in about ten weeks."

"At the time the spoon came in, please believe me," Wise wrote back, "we were involved in things that had to be done— right THEN—and it was two days before we got into an actual discussion about the spoon." If this had been a test of her ability to size up a product's usefulness and marketability, Wise appeared to be very much in control in her memo, providing detailed analysis of the spoon's strengths and weaknesses. But it's clear she found Tupper's impatient inquiry troubling:

> After all this time, why do you get annoyed because we keep the sample spoon for a week, trying to make as good a decision on it as possible? Surely you must realize that while I don't know a great deal about your production picture, I DO realize molds are expensive . . . and that I, in fact all of

us down here, feel a responsibility about advising you to go ahead on a mold without feeling as certain as possible that we can do a good sales job on the product? Don't you want us to look at it that way?

By June, Wise had to put aside these squabbles and turn her attention to readying THP's new "world." For the fast-approaching July jubilee, the theme would be taken from a hit film at the time, *Around the World in 80 Days*. Each Tupperware dealer and manager would be assigned a different destination, depending on the amount of sales achieved. Reynolds and his team produced a footbridge in an ornate Japanese section, windmills to evoke the flavor of Holland, and grass huts found on the road to Zanzibar. Each port of call had corresponding prizes like fine Irish linens and Hong Kong pewter. For the so-called "Around the World Day," attendees would be encouraged to dress in clothes typical of their assigned country. "If any of them come into town in their costumes," the *Kissimmee Gazette* noted, "Kissimmee may take on the appearance of a small United Nations gathering."

The jubilee would be the highlight of the steamy central Florida summer, and the atmosphere promised to be electric. Tupper and Wise had enjoyed a successful year; Tupperware's best of the best across the country were bringing the sales numbers back to where they expected them to be. It was a time for motivation and learning—and a celebration of the unconventional. A new lake and surrounding park would be dedicated at headquarters, along with a plaque commemorating Tupperware's leading Vanguard Club managers. As always, the fireworks would light up the night sky, the bursting colors and wonderment reflected in the children's eyes. It was wholesome, all-American, and spectacular in a way only

Tupperware seemed to know how to do. In many aspects, the nighttime fireworks and around-the-world theme foreshadowed the Magic Kingdom and Epcot, long before Walt Disney put down his own roots on Irlo Bronson's rangeland.

The grand finale of Around the World Day would be kept a secret. Of course, the local newspaper played along: "The Tupperware crowd will be coming into town on that day to embark on a mysterious boat excursion to some foreign land nearby. Full details have not been divulged, but boat clubs throughout central Florida have been alerted and pressed into service to help transport the crowd."

Brownie Wise, with her trim physique flattered by tailored summer dresses, perfectly appointed strands of pearls and matching earrings, coiffed hair, and beaming smile, would again assume the role of fairy godmother to Tupperware wishers. And, of course, the press would be there to capture it all for the local front pages. William Campbell, publisher of *Cosmopolitan,* was high on the guest list, as were *American Salesman* publisher Michael Gore, and Glen Fouche, vice president of *Parade* publications.

On July 1, twelve hundred dealers, managers, and distributors from as far away as Puerto Rico and Alaska streamed into headquarters, where they were greeted by such eclectic, around-the-world attractions as a five-person human totem pole. "Distributors, costumed with the wings, eagle beaks and horns of such totem poles," commented one writer, "mounted the special telephone totem pole and sat on the perches with remarkable stillness."

In the Garden Pavilion, the radiant hostess Brownie Wise engaged in a little horseplay with accountant Herb Young. "Pay me ten bucks," she ordered. "You bet there wouldn't be a man of distinction at this jubilee and there he is." Then she nodded toward sales counselor Jack Mann, who was dressed in a mustache and goatee for an occasion as auspicious as the jubilee's opening day. Forced to acknowledge that this was indeed a man of distinction, Herb Young surrendered a ten spot to the woman who always seemed to come out on top. With that, Mann gave Wise a victorious peck on the cheek. "It tickles," she said and sparkled as her adoring followers laughed and applauded.

Much of the first two days of the jubilee brought a steady stream of motivational speeches and award presentations. William H. Alexander, an Oklahoma City preacher and host of a nationally broadcast radio show, spoke to the Tupperware faithful about his *Life's Quiz Program*. Arthur Motley amazed the crowd with details of hosting the world's largest sales convention ever carried on closed-circuit television. Other speakers hammered home the secrets to sales success, business philosophy, and advertising. Before too many eyes could glaze over, the next important event in the jubilee was the awards program.

After the speeches and awards, on Tuesday afternoon Tupperware guests fanned out into the nine around-the-world stations to marvel at the exotic handiwork created by George Reynolds and crew, and to collect the gifts they'd labored all year to earn. Charlie McBurney assumed the role of cobra-coaxing fakir at the East Indian booth. The human totem pole, in honor of those who had traveled from Alaska, proved to be one of the most popular draws. Amid the joy and merriment, buses rumbled onto Tupperware grounds to take attendees to their mystery trip. The atmosphere was heavy with anticipation and the ever-present humidity of a sultry July day in central Florida.

The long bus procession rolled five miles south down the

Orange Blossom Trail to the Tohopekaliga lakefront, arriving by three in the afternoon. An armada of boats from the Winter Garden Boat Club, the Tohopekaliga Yacht Club, the Orange Boating Club, and other private owners waited to perform transport duty. Dick Makinson, the man who sold Isla Milagra to Brownie Wise, hauled his boat out of retirement. Jerry Wise was also there to take people to and from the island on the Tupperware power barge. All in all, at least fifty rumbling boats were needed to get the large assemblage of Tupperware guests to their secret destination.

Gary McDonald, George Reynolds, and PR man Glen Bump had done a great deal of research into how to transport more than a thousand people on the water. The Coast Guard in South Florida had told them they were too busy to participate. The executives had even looked into whether a landing craft, like those used by the Marines to transport troops, could do the job. That hadn't worked out either. Finally, the Tupperware team had sent invitations to dozens of Kissimmee-area boat owners. In return for participating, the boat owners would get to take part in that evening's mystery gala event.

In the steamy temperatures hovering past ninety degrees, the cool breeze and occasional water spray were welcome relief to the hundreds of guests, many of whom had already been out in the heat for several hours. Hamer Wilson, who had spent ten years as a meteorologist for Eastern Airlines, took note of a bank of thunderheads off in the distance. "The storm was well away from there," Wilson remembered, "considerably so." Isla Milagra sat toward the south end of the 23,000-acre lake. As the island grew closer, revelers could make out stands of bald cypress, Carolina willow, and red maple trees. Shades of deep green from the tropical overgrowth reflected in the water. A line of homegrown, faux-Hawaiian hula girls shook their grass skirts and showed off the dance prowess they had spent weeks perfecting. More girls welcomed each guest with a paper lei and the traditional Hawaiian "aloha" greeting. The night promised to be an over-the-top Tupperware affair.

As guests sipped punch and enjoyed entertainment on a thatched stage, the cooking operation kicked into high gear. For months the people at Morrison's Cafeterias had been planning how to feed a small army in such a remote place. The barge had been used to haul in tons of ice. Eight hundred live, wriggling lobsters were flown in from Maine, and there were just as many baked chickens and fresh pineapples, as well as two thousand ears of roasted corn. The low tables were decorated with bananas, tropical mangoes, and papayas, and in true Polynesian fashion, a suckling pig was prepared in a ground oven. For their meal served under the stars, guests were encouraged to feast in island style, with no spoons, knives, or forks.

Resplendent in an aqua Hawaiian *holomuu* decorated with purple figures, a flowered skirt dusting the ground, and two orchid leis adorning her neck, Brownie Wise was finally living the dream of sharing her island with the Tupperware family. "Isn't it wonderful?" she asked. "Each year is the best and each year is better." Most of the THP top brass were there, too, including Wilson, McDonald, and Mortland. Tony Ponticelli decided he wanted nothing to do with crossing such a big lake on someone else's small boat. Photographers Jack McCollum and Fred DeWitt trudged off boats with their camera equipment. With so many people to feed and the luau already starting late, it would be a challenge to keep the affair on schedule.

The crowd indulged in the food by hand and then mopped themselves up with warm towels. Following the hearty meal, grand prizes were awarded to some of Tupperware's top performers of the year. With the partygoers enjoying the family spirit, good times, and great food, the hours slipped past quickly. "Nobody wanted to go home," remembered McCollum.

This event was unusual because it was not on company grounds per se, and because so many people outside the Tupperware family were included. THP had asked the boat drivers not to drink during the party, but there was no way to enforce that request. As they waited for the party to end and their passengers to return, some drivers in the so-called "power squad" were drinking. McCollum, who had driven his own boat to the luau, felt some of the drivers were drunk. All had been instructed to drive in a large, counterclockwise circle around the island to keep the water route safe and the departure orderly. The THP team handed out maps.

As clouds began to roll in, revelers worried that the increasingly ominous Florida sky could erupt at any second and began heading to their boats more quickly than expected. They knew that when the atmosphere inland was rich with humidity, and the cooler, late-afternoon sea breezes started to blow in off the Atlantic, the meeting of those two forces could quickly produce very large thunderheads. It was a summer phenomenon in central Florida by which you could almost set your watch. If it happened in the middle of the night and you were sitting on an island with no cover, it could be dangerous. That Wise did not realize this and account for this very real possibility in the first place proved to be another major mistake. The people on her island represented the heart of Tupperware's business, and as the possibility of wind, lightning, and rain became more real by the second, she had nowhere to put them.

"At first they were anxious to get off the island,"

remembered Hamer Wilson, "and when we found out they were going to have to wait for the boats, a great number of them sat down on logs and visited." Some, still infused with the spirit of the evening, broke into Tupperware songs. As the night gave way to deep, dark early morning, the number of boats returning from shore grew fewer and fewer. Anxious to get people to safety, McDonald considered a small house and two cabins on the island for cover: "We contemplated the possibility of having them bunk in the three houses over there if things were such that it was impossible to get them back." By several estimates, there were twelve hundred people on the island and not nearly enough boats to get them to dry land.

Jack McCollum put Wise and her secretary on his boat. Passage was so slow and the water so choppy that he was practically idling. Storm clouds had obscured the moon, making the water route almost pitch-black. To help guide the way, McCollum gave another passenger a flashlight and instructions to stand at the front of the boat. Of Wise, McCollum said, "I think she was concerned, but she didn't show it." A long line of guests and Tupperware employees remained on the island, waiting their turn.

Boat owner Bill Boyd had room for four passengers but was taking as many as nine. "The people were crowding in and the boats were way overloaded," Boyd said. "That is one advantage of that bailer on there, it kept the water pumped out; we had quite a bit of water coming over one time with seven people and one time with nine." The effects of the alcohol they had drunk, along with the elements, caused the boat drivers to stray from the longer, circular route they had been instructed to take, making the dark waters more dangerous. "We could see some lights on the water which indicated there was some so-called hot rodders," Glen Bump said, "driving their boats in an irresponsible fashion." Some drivers decided there was too much risk and went home, putting even more pressure on those remaining to help get stranded people off the island.

Gerry Croxton, a forty-four-year-old shop manager, continued to make runs in the darkness. He'd lived on the lake for thirty years, and his wife, Thelma, said Gerry could "run it blind," if need be. The rain came in showers, with flashes of lightning and occasional thunder. Despite the danger, the night was so dark that Croxton insisted on his wife accompanying him back and forth. "I needed her eyes," he recalled.

On the west side of the island, Croxton and his wife picked up two older women and began to depart. He stood to the back of the boat, steering with his left hand, steadying himself on the boat's awning with his right. The three women, including his wife, sat at the front. Gerry Croxton said later he spied another boat headed right for his stern, and there was no time to avoid it: "I tried to go with it is all I could do." The boat plowed into the back of Croxton's craft, tearing the engine to pieces and catapulting him into the water. "I don't remember [the other boat driver] ever hitting the boat," Croxton said later. "I remember him coming and the next thing I knew I was in the water." The women passengers were not thrown from the boat, and Thelma Croxton tried unsuccessfully to throw her husband seat cushions to keep him afloat.

As Bill Boyd drove by, it was only by "a sudden flash of lightning" that he saw Croxton in the water. He jumped in. "I just held him up and he was moaning and groaning," Boyd remembered. "I tried to talk to him but he was out of his head." Another boat came along whose driver helped Boyd

hoist the injured man aboard. It was Kissimmee's chief of police, Bob Best. Boyd treaded water into the reeds, where he
was able to climb back on board his own boat.

When Croxton was brought to the dock in Kissimmee, Dr.
M. L. Jewell treated him. "He had a puncture wound of the
chest and bleeding," the doctor said. Jewell sent the seriously
injured man to the hospital via ambulance. Croxton wasn't
the only person hurt that night. Jewell remembered routing
as many as twenty-one people to the hospital because of accidents and other issues related to the luau.

"You could hear all this crashing, and you knew what it
was," remembered Jerry Wise. "There were some real seriously hurt." As Wise piloted the barge back to the city dock in
Kissimmee, he saw a foreboding sign: two ambulances waiting on shore. One had been there on standby the whole night;
Jewell had ordered the other brought down to deal with the
excess patients. Unaware of what was going on, Wilson and
McDonald had stayed behind to get people off the island.

Inexplicably, as all hell was breaking loose in and around
her miracle island, and the safety of the most dedicated members of her sales force was at risk, Brownie Wise chose to put
her own welfare first and head home.

Boyd finally picked up his wife, Mary, and the last load of
island passengers at three-thirty in the morning. Croxton had
serious internal injuries to the chest and leg. Another man
who worked at a local boat dealership, Rudy Crews, was suf-
fering from internal bleeding. In the wake of the accidents,
both underwent surgery.

Once the shock of the events started to wear off, McDonald realized this could also be a public relations nightmare.
For a teetotaling, family-oriented, all-American company that
prided itself on no negative publicity, the events of Tuesday,

July 2, 1957, could be damaging. How would it look if the local and national press spun the story that several people had been injured after an all-night booze bash on the Tupperware Queen's personal island? "We did everything we could to make it go smoothly," McDonald remembered, "and unlike other times when we had people go into town and it turned out great, this was a disaster." Tony Ponticelli's instincts had been right. "These are individuals with their own boats, and you have no control over them except they're doing you a favor."

Elsie Mortland had been stranded on the island with her sons, John and Larry, until two in the morning. She was furious with Wise and questions angrily ran through her mind. Why did she let the party go on so long? Couldn't she tell a big storm was brewing? With all of the planning and expense that had gone into throwing the elaborate luau, why had she chosen to ignore the weather? And where was she when her leadership was needed most? It seemed as if Brownie Wise had ignored her better instincts. While she rarely delegated within the walls of Tupperware headquarters, she had left to others the job of deciding how to get the rest of her guests off the island and to safety.

According to her son, Wise was wracked with guilt over what had happened. Croxton was an acquaintance with whom she had spoken many times when taking vehicles to the Autrey Ford dealership for service or repairs. She knew his participation in her party had left him seriously injured. "Those were bad times," Jerry remembered.

Her attitude at THP was another matter entirely. Of the luau and the accidents that resulted, Tony Ponticelli said, "She wouldn't admit that was a big mistake." According to Elsie Mortland, "She wanted to sweep it under the rug and let it be gone." Don Hinton said Wise didn't find out about the accidents until the next day. He blamed drinking boat drivers for the accidents rather than the weather or lack of foresight from Wise. But ultimately, her former public relations man and strong ally acknowledged that the buck stopped with Brownie Wise.

For the first time, McDonald and the PR staff would have to attempt to do damage control. George Reynolds, a gregarious and popular personality, went to the Kissimmee newspaper. Don Hinton appealed to editors in Orlando. The time had come to call in some of the bargaining chips Tupperware had earned through all of its goodwill and good deeds in central Florida. According to McDonald, their appeal boiled down to this: "We would appreciate if you don't sensationalize because it was an unfortunate accident. We know it has to be in your paper, but as little space as you can give to it, we'll appreciate it."

The approach worked. The July 4 edition of the *Kissimmee Gazette* read like an issue of *Tupperware Sparks*. Photos splashed on the front page showed the human totem pole, the hula dancers on the island, Charles McBurney and the girls at the East Indian booth, Brownie Wise beaming like a prom queen next to one of the jubilee VIPs, and Dick Makinson's newly unretired boat, *The Venture*.

Coverage of the luau painted it as a smashing success: Guests had feasted on a traditional Hawaiian meal and sipped "non-alcoholic" punch. Buried within the body of the newspaper were the articles making mention of people who'd been hurt in a boat accident. But the incident was in no way connected to Brownie Wise and Tupperware. The one-inch story about Rudy Crews undergoing surgery was dwarfed by an article and photo of local teen Jack Crum headed to a baton-twirling contest in Binghamton, New York.

In a large ad that ran one week after the accidents, while the victims were still recovering from their injuries, Brownie Wise said this about the 1957 jubilee:

TO OUR FRIENDS AND NEIGHBORS IN THE KISSIMMEE AREA: Thank you, most sincerely . . . for helping us make our homecoming Jubilee the most enjoyable and successful ever!

Because of your cooperation, participation and the genuine enthusiasm of our community, we were able to display to the nation the kind of hospitality for which Central Florida has become famous.

Once again . . . the kindness and generosity you continue to show our people has made the members of the Tupperware family feel proud and happy to call this part of Florida their second home.

Thank you each and every one!

Best Wishes,
Brownie Wise

Wise had gotten her own wish; the miracle island blunder hadn't become fodder for the press she was so adept at courting. And the goodwill Tupperware had built in central Florida helped keep the company image intact. "We were good to both cities; I mean, we did all sorts of things," reasoned Gary McDonald. "I ran the first million-dollar United Appeal Orlando ever had. We had people in Kissimmee doing all sorts of things. We were good citizens."

Wise would not get off so easy with Earl Tupper. He came to Florida to assess the impact of the accidents, as well as what insurance coverage might be needed if the company planned to continue transporting people to and from the island. Elsie

Mortland witnessed his fury and disgust over a picture that showed a boat on the way to the luau, overloaded and listing dangerously to one side. "You see the foolish things people do?" he asked Mortland. Tupper pointed to the photograph. "See all those distributors? We could have been out of business."

Brownie Wise had given Earl Tupper another reason to look more closely at the sales operation and to question her decision making and commitment to the business. Their already testy relationship was deteriorating, and after the 1957 jubilee boat accidents, their own collision course was set.

The Breaking Point

After the July boat accidents on Lake Toho, Earl Tupper decided he needed to keep an even closer watch on the Florida operation. "He was very, very suspicious of Brownie," said Tupper's longtime accountant Ed Creiger. "Once she started to divert her attention away from business, he never knew what was coming next." Some of those who were close to Wise felt Tupper's problems with her weren't about business at all but, rather, ego. "He was jealous of her," said Don Hinton, "because she was the queen of Tupperware and he was nothing."

From his Branch River Lab in Woonsocket, Rhode Island, Tupper wrote Wise, "You may feel that all of a sudden I'm asking a lot of questions about a lot of things." He went on to list four reasons: a need to be better informed on the "financial end"; a need to reduce expenses "that do not directly bring in sales"; a general reduction in "all liability risks" in the wake of the boat accidents; and his constant worry about the "probability of increasing income tax rates."

The latter had been in the back of Tupper's mind ever since his tax experts had explained to him that, because he owned all the stock in the Tupper Corporation, the government considered it a "one-man" business. "If I had died," Tupper wrote, "then the government would have arbitrarily valued my estate for at least 20 times earnings and it would have been taxed at 77 and-a-half percent. It would have destroyed my entire estate." Tupper's solution was to quietly start shopping his company to interested suitors.

Unaware of the dealings going on behind her back, Wise believed the source of Tupper's agitation was a newly acquired plastic shoe-heel manufacturing business in Maine, Footwear Plastics Corporation, that was consuming all of his time, effort, and money. However, the business folded in August "after much dissension with the people he had in charge," wrote Wise.

Brownie did not or would not acknowledge that Tupper's problems were also with her. "He was edgy and irascible during the months from April to September or October when I spoke to him on the phone," she recalled, "but not especially about anything concerning the Florida operation." Not coincidentally, that was the same time period in which Tupper had, in fact, been concerned about Wise's ability to bring sales numbers back around and had been infuriated about her book, the luau disaster, and the resulting legal exposure.

In September and October 1957, however, Tupper and Wise seemed to enjoy a relative thaw in their frosty relations. THP continued its push to reach the ambitious sales goals Wise had outlined to Tupper earlier in the year. Thanks to the company's relentless recruiting programs, for the first time all year the number of Tupperware dealers once again surpassed ten thousand. At the end of October, Tupper made a scheduled visit to Florida. "He was not at all unpleasant to me on the occasion," Wise remembered. As it turns out, Tupper made the trip to see if he might be able to recoup out of Brownie's profitable sales side the $85,000 he had lost on the shoe operation. Afterward, Wise and THP no longer enjoyed carte blanche on their own expenses—a change that upset Wise. For all THP did to promote, reward, recruit, train, and advertise, she was known to refer to the amount spent as "hairpins and Kleenex money."

The final rift between Tupper and Wise started to form in November 1957. Tupperware had skirted responsibility for the luau boat accidents in the public eye, but not in courts of law. Gerry Croxton sued Tupper and Tupperware for $150,000, claiming he had suffered permanent injuries to his kidneys, ribs, hip, and lungs. He argued that there had been no lights in the water at the time of the crash, no specific and enforced directions for the boat drivers to take, and no screening to determine if the boat drivers were fit to be entrusted with their passengers' lives in the first place. His suit also claimed that the boat operators operating under the auspices of Tupperware Home Parties Inc. failed to have their boats under control, failed to keep lookout for others in the water, failed to give warning signals of their approach, and failed to follow proper rules of navigation. To make matters worse, during the seven weeks Croxton spent in the hospital, he earned no money. Upon his return, he was so hobbled by his injuries that he was demoted from service manager to mechanic. The suits also alleged that for some unknown reason, prior to the luau, Tupper had canceled the insurance policy intended to provide coverage for the boat excursions.

William Boyd, along with his wife, Mary, filed a similar suit for $151,000. Boyd claimed he suffered back problems and "a great decline in his health" due to his efforts to get Croxton out of the water. The legal action held Tupperware Home Parties responsible for failing "to keep their guests on the said island during the storm, but direct[ing] boat operators to continue to take passengers into a violent rainstorm at night when there was practically no moon, and when they knew, or should have known, that said transfer was very dangerous."

For Tupper, this was a big problem on many fronts, and Wise knew it. For a man so bent on keeping his secrets and his business away from prying eyes, these personal injury suits could bring the kind of scrutiny he could not avoid—and the kind of attention he detested. "Tupper has had, as long as I have known him, an antipathy to any action that would force him to bring his books into court," Wise observed. "He hated being cross-examined. He can be made to blow if he's prodded or needled enough, and when he blows it's an all-out thing; he explodes." Those who had been around Earl Tupper during times of extreme stress could attest to the accuracy of Wise's observations.

After the seemingly uneventful October visit, Tupper told Wise he'd be back in November. When it came time for that Florida trip, he arrived without confirming the exact time and date, and she felt "his attitude was strange during this visit." Inspecting the building and new gardens around headquarters, Tupper seemed to have little to say. "He was not actually disapproving . . . not approving either," Wise wrote of Tupper's demeanor. "It shook morale among some of the executives who were left with the feeling that perhaps he felt they were beneath his dignity, or that he was leaving something unsaid." Wise had a lengthy list of issues she had hoped to discuss with him, including the company's lease of her island, but Tupper was "evasive," instead going on and on about problems on the manufacturing side. Before Wise could get into her list, Tupper informed her he was being called back to Woonsocket, and that he needed her to make arrangements for an earlier flight.

In the ensuing days, a stream of memos started coming from Tupper. Wise found them "cross and unpleasant," and they took "a completely different slant to any mail I had ever received from him before. Several were complete reversals of his previous attitude."

That week, Tupper made another move Wise found curious and unsettling. Seemingly out of the blue, Tupper informed her he was exerting his authority as president of THP on personnel issues. "I believe that all salary changes and discharge of personnel should be done only after we have both agreed as to the proper course of action in each specific case," he told Wise. "I have a deep personal interest in the people at THP whom I know and I expect to become better acquainted with the whole group." For years, Tupper had gone to great lengths to make sure as few people as possible knew who he was when he came to Florida. Now, all of the sudden, he had "a deep personal interest" in them.

On November 16, Wise issued a revised sales estimate for 1957 at $10 million—a 25 percent increase over 1956. Wise sent Tupper a memo explaining that a recent flu outbreak had led to the cancellation or postponement of many parties, and that she thought they were going to fall just short as a result. Not used to coming up short on goals, Wise and her team pushed distributors to finish the year strongly in a "Wind-Up week" promotion for December 2. Sales counselors were in the field doing what they could to motivate dealers. Wise sounded a hopeful note to Tupper: "We're pulling out all the stops in the *hope* that if we can't actually make it, we'll come as close as possible to the projection figure given you."

Tupper's response to the revised numbers stung. He suggested Wise and her team needed to have a "sober re-evaluation" of the "causes of failure to produce." He told Wise he did not feel they were doing a good enough job of sales management. What THP needed, Tupper said, was more "standard operating procedures and planning"—more "controls." The critique seemed harsh since Tupperware dealer numbers had continued to rise in November, past the 10,500 mark. And sales for 1957 still promised to be at least a 20 percent improvement over 1956. Perhaps Tupper had gotten spoiled with years like 1953 and 1954, when he'd enjoyed increases of 102.5 percent and 71.9 percent respectively.

"You spoke of sales *management* as if it were a term we were unfamiliar with in this organization," Wise shot back. "I would like very much to have your ideas on what we should do differently. We have felt all along that we were on the right track . . . we're rather shocked at this point to see that you do not feel we are." In a critique of her own, Wise told Tupper, "We have long felt there should be a closer relationship between what we (from our miles of travel and thousands of contacts in the field) found the consumer wanted and what was developed by Tupper Corporation in the way of new products." Taking an obstinate tone often apparent when her abilities were questioned, Wise wrote, "We wonder what 'controls' you mean. Do you mean something to 'control' sales?"

By that point, the sales numbers were just one of many factors contributing to Earl Tupper's souring attitude toward Wise. Ed Creiger had seen a lot of employees come and go in the Tupper Corporation. "Earl was either high on a person," he said, "or very quickly wanted to pull the rug out from under them."

Suspecting something was at hand due to the change in Earl Tupper's attitude, the five top THP executives—including Wise, Hamer Wilson, and Gary McDonald—signed a letter asking Tupper to come to Florida and meet with them. "What we are greatly concerned with *right now*," Wise complained, "are the bumps between the sales organization and the manufacturer . . . both of whom are presumably interested in the same thing . . . *BUILDING* SALES."

Since he had made two trips to Florida in recent weeks, Tupper told Wise to come to his office in Providence and meet with him on December 9 or 10. Wise wrote back that she was booked solid with long-distance calls from dealers and managers and focused on a sales campaign that was part of a big final push for 1957 called "One to Grow On." Tupper moved the timeline for their meeting to December 19 through 21.

In mid-December, Wise took a fall at her office that resulted in a concussion—the last thing she needed as the pressure was building for a face-to-face meeting with Tupper. She'd once again injured her lower back—this time in the third and fourth vertebrae—and her doctor informed her that she'd be unable to travel for seven to ten days. Tony Ponticelli witnessed George Reynolds carrying her into her office. "I said to myself she must be really ill or having a breakdown," Ponticelli remembered.

The stress of 1957 was taking a serious toll on Wise. In the early days, addressing crowds of adoring dealers used to be a joy for her; now she was canceling meetings and no-showing at out-of-town commitments, which left Gary McDonald and Hamer Wilson to pick up the considerable slack. "We would have to go on without the star," McDonald said, "and that was tough."

The difficult year had also strained her relationship with some of her top deputies, especially Hamer Wilson. The two had an arrangement where they both had to agree on candidates for new distributorships, which had always led to friction. But while others spoke of Wilson's easygoing and friendly demeanor, something about him seemed to spark a deep, visceral dislike and distrust in Wise. In late 1957, Tony Ponticelli was on a flight with Wise coming back from a rally in Chicago when she made it clear to him that his THP star was going to rise in 1958. "She said to me, 'I want more from you than I've asked from you before,'" Ponticelli recalled. Part of the reason for a new opportunity, he said, would be the vacuum created by her plans for Wilson. "She said, 'I'm going to fire him the first of the year.'" Perhaps Tupper had gotten wind of her plans, and that's why he inserted himself in the hiring and firing process. For whatever reason, Wise never had a chance to make good on her intention to fire Wilson.

As 1957 drew to a close, Earl Tupper and Brownie Wise were at a stalemate. Each was resentful toward the other for a lack of accommodation and respect. Together they had built a juggernaut, but when push came to shove, each was so singularly convinced that he or she alone knew the right course of action that any criticism became a deep, personal attack. Both had poured their lives into making the Tupperware machinery work right, but now nothing was as easy as it had been.

Despite the rising tensions, Tupper and Wise entered into an uneasy détente as they celebrated Christmas with their families. At home on the farm, Tupper loved music and made tapes of his family singing and playing musical instruments. He and his wife, Marie, had been married for twenty-six years. Their eldest son, Ronnie, was twenty-five. Myles, who recalled his father's long days of experimentation refining Poly-T, was twenty-three. Glenn and Mark rounded out the four Tupper sons. The breach baby Tupper himself had had to deliver, his daughter, Starr, was nineteen years old. It would be their last Christmas as a family.

At Water's Edge, Brownie and Jerry Wise carried on a

Christmas Eve tradition of leaving the lights off and lighting holiday candles in all the downstairs rooms. She also continued her father's tradition of sprinkling ashes from the old Christmas tree upon the new one. Family legend had it that it could help assure folks of a long life. With Brownie, Jerry, and Rose Humphrey gathered around, they opened all of the Christmas cards they made a practice of saving until Christmas Eve. On Christmas morning, the three always brought their stockings into the dining room at breakfast. After seeing what goodies were inside, and with full stomachs, they took turns opening gifts packed under the tree. It would be their last Christmas at Brownie's dream home.

On New Year's Eve, Earl Tupper made a final attempt to try to get his relations with Wise back on track. His letter came to Wise on the familiar stationery with "Tupperware Home Parties Inc." at the top and the company slogan, "Buyers of Quality Buy Again . . ." below it. Tupper marked it *"PERSONAL"* in bold capital letters and reverted to addressing her with the more familiar "Dear Brownie."

"This is a personal letter that is intended to be friendly and helpful," Tupper began. "First of all, I hope that your concussion difficulties are sufficiently cleared up so that you can wire me an early date after which you will be able to come up here. I'll then give you a date to come." He continued in this cordial tone: "I'm looking forward to seeing you and going over with you the many things that have piled up which you and I alone have to cover." Soon after, Tupper mentioned plans to come to Florida to meet with her lieutenants about their concerns. Then came the gist of why he was writing:

From your recent conduct you seem to resist coming up here. There can be no justification for refusal or unreasonable delay, since I'm the President of the corporation and no business can be conducted unless there is respect for authority. Won't you please recognize that fact? Unless you can give me wholehearted, friendly cooperation, representing my interests fully at THP and in a way to win friends for me there, then you are not doing and cannot do the job that must be done. You are the key person to carry out my wishes and give the organization good tone. If you quarrel with the person above you, then you weaken yourself with those under you.

After signing his full name at the bottom of his air mail letter, Tupper tried to sound a more upbeat and friendly tone, "P.S. Let's go!—For a Happy New Year."

What Tupper received in return was the full-force fury of Brownie Wise in written form, reminiscent of the first time she let him have it over the telephone in 1951. Wise began with full-on, in-your-face insubordination, "This letter is about as 'friendly' as a mad dog, and about as helpful as a first-class case of leprosy. I have read this letter over a dozen times; it is unbelievable. I can't help but wonder if you read it over, even once, before you sent it?" For six double-spaced pages, Wise dissected Tupper's letter and let her own pent-up feelings flow.

"Please look at the facts clearly and tell me where I have failed to respect your authority. Let me make something plain; I have always respected your authority, and I believe my actions for six and a half years speak with a louder voice than either your words on paper or mine," Wise countered. "You have [not] taken a telephone call from me in the last eight weeks. (Even the telephone operators in Winter Park are aware that I cannot get a call placed to you.) Do you consider this good public relations—and how about intercompany relations?"

What upset Wise the most was Tupper's intimation that she was not cooperating with him:

> *Look back over the last six and a half years . . . and bring yourself right up to date . . . give serious consideration to the last eight weeks. It's been quite a picture. Because it's full of action. And action speaks louder than words. The past six and a half—or it's closer to seven—represent a lot of giving, and a lot of giving UP for me. Mr. Tupper, many many people recognize that I have given you much, much more than the "wholehearted, friendly cooperation" you speak of, representing your interests fully as you put it. . . . The fact that you could actually use such words in speaking to me, after the way I have worked for THP and devoted myself so wholly that I have been criticized for it is an absolutely astounding fact.*

Tupperware had been her life—what more, she wondered, could he want from her? "I felt from the very beginning and told you so," Wise declared, "that I was working for something I believed in, and could devote myself to with no reservations. And that's the way it's been. This business has had my time, my thought, whatever creativeness I have, my energy, my plans and my dreams. . . . There's been no time for six years for any outside interests or any social life."

Wise also adopted a personal tone, but only to convey how deeply Tupper's letter had hurt her:

> *I take strong exception to what you say in this letter—because it is not true.*

I HAVE given you one thousand percent of whole-hearted, friendly cooperation—and I have given it to you, without much cooperation in return. I HAVE represented your interests fully at THP (to the sad exclusion of my own) in such a way as to win friends for you. . . . AND THIS HAS BEEN DONE WITHOUT ANY HELP FROM YOU. I don't believe you can be so blind as this letter sounds. So you must have written it to either annoy, anger, or wound me. It has done all three—and much more, because I am not a machine, though I have worked for you. I am a human being.

Earl Tupper must have had one of two motives for writing his December 31 letter. Either he sincerely wanted to try to offer an olive branch and had failed miserably, or he was throwing out a noose and letting Wise put it right around her own neck.

Pictures of Despair

After the two had a chance to blow off some steam, Tupper's response to Wise was brief. "My first concern is your health," he reassured her in a telegram. "Please let me know the earliest date your health will permit you to leave to come up here." In mid-January, Wise made the trip to Providence.

For a day and a half, Tupper and Wise met alone, face-to-face. On the second day, in the presence of Ed Creiger, Tupper told Wise he wanted to cancel the lease on her island due to concerns about the amount of insurance necessary to cover personnel visiting by barge or boat. Only approximately $7,000 in improvements had been made to the island in 1957. Since the agreement was $10,000 a year, Tupper assured Wise they would make up the difference in some way.

At that meeting, the two also discussed the possibility of Wise buying Water's Edge. "He said that it might be awkward for the corporation to let me have it at book value," Wise recalled, "if the actual market value had increased considerably." Certainly, with all the improvements Wise had made to the home, as well as its fame in the Kissimmee area, the value had to have increased a great deal in the five years Wise had lived there. They set aside the discussion for the time being, and no decision was made about ownership of the home.

For the second time, Wise had met with Tupper in person and come away feeling like she had accomplished little. "I tried to bring him back to the list of things I needed to talk about,"

Wise complained. "He was concerned about Russia getting the jump on us with Sputnik, and went into detail about how poorly prepared New England was for a possible invasion. . . . He pulled a map out of his desk drawer, and showed me how a couple of bombs dropped on strategic points in the NY area would paralyze utilities and highway access."

Tupper wasn't just being eccentric or paranoid; he was stalling while he formulated his own answer to her tirade memo. By the end of January 1958, Tupper had gotten wind that Wise and several of her top executives, frustrated with his new hands-on approach, might be plotting some sort of takeover of the sales division or a mass departure to another company. (Two THP supervisory executives, Gary McDonald and Don Hinton, denied any plot ever took place.) How would it look to those interested in buying his company to have such a headstrong woman at the helm of such a crucial division? And worse, how would it look to the public and the press if Wise really was plotting some sort of mutiny? By then she had developed a strong enough cult of personality among the dealers that she just might be able to take a huge chunk of his business with her. Realizing what was at stake, Tupper decided to take back the reins of his live-wire sales division once and for all. Soon after, on a blustery day in late January, Tupper boarded a flight from New England to Orlando and, with Ed Creiger at his side, began his journey to cut ties with Brownie Wise.

Upon arriving in Orlando and checking into the Angebilt Hotel, Earl Tupper and Ed Creiger stayed up most of the night plotting Wise's ouster and debating potential successors. The next day, January 29, 1958, Tupper summoned two familiar faces to his hotel room: Hamer Wilson and Gary McDonald. Wilson, because of his age and varied business experience, would be top man, Tupper announced. Together with McDonald, they would lead THP through the rocky transition from Wise and on to the next phase in its history.

The two had been aware of the friction between Tupper and Wise, but Tupper's plans to get rid of Wise hit Gary McDonald like a hand grenade. Despite his young age, his awe of Earl Tupper, and the risk that he might be thrown out with Wise, McDonald pleaded with him.

"I said, 'You gotta understand, she worked her heart out building this company,'" McDonald recalled. "'You cannot just go out there and summarily say you're done, good-bye. You have to recognize her in some way for all she has put into it. Regardless of how you feel about what she has been doing, what she is doing is building this company, and we all picked her as the person we would publicize. That's what we've done. That's not her fault.'"

McDonald also worried about the dealers, who saw Brownie Wise as not only the First Lady of Tupperware, but also their role model: "I said, 'Their life is built around Tupperware and all those people are our people. To them Brownie is exactly what she was publicized to be. She is the image they're striving for and she is on a pedestal. What you're doing is removing her from that pedestal,'" McDonald argued. "'They're not gonna understand it.'"

"That's what your first job is going to be," Tupper ordered, "enable them to understand it. She's done. Enough of that. She's done."

Knowing that Wise didn't have a contract to protect her, Tupper expressed his intention to fire her with no severance, no golden parachute, no chance to leave with a semblance of dignity. He wanted her expunged from Tupperware as if she had never existed. It would not be that easy.

Later that day, Earl Tupper and other key THP executives met with Brownie Wise. Someone had finally convinced Tupper that firing her immediately was not the way to go. Instead, they presented her with a two-year personal services contract under which she would continue to make $30,000 a year, but take "an inactive part" from that point forward. Like the Queen of England, her new role would be ceremonial, requiring her to attend events like jubilees and seminars but relieving her of day-to-day managerial duties. The contract called for a one-day-per-week commitment—a fifty-two-days-a-year "semi-retirement."

One can only imagine how crushing this scenario had to be for Wise. Not only was she being forced out, Tupper was giving her position and authority to Hamer Wilson, the underling she wanted to fire. And what about Gary McDonald? Was he willing to watch the woman who mentored him for years be forced out and not threaten to walk away with her? This wasn't just a high-profile job Wise was losing; Tupperware was her life. Later that afternoon, Mary Frances Babb saw Wise in her office, stacking papers and crying. "I'm going home to write my resignation," Wise told her.

Babb helped her to the car and Wise drove home to Water's Edge. She summoned her friend and confidant Charles McBurney, her former PR man with whom she had published *Best Wishes*. "Tupper said I'm fired," she told him. "You know, there goes my life. I'm through with life." She told Jerry she'd quit.

The next day, Tupper composed a short letter to Wise, making official what they had informed her of the day before.

"Dear Mrs. Wise," he began, "The following action was taken to clear the way for re-organization of Tupperware Home Parties Inc. operations. A meeting of the Board of Directors was held on January 27th, 1958, and it was voted to cancel the appointment of Brownie Humphrey Wise as Vice-President and General Manager of Tupperware Home Parties Inc. This letter is to serve as notification of same." If Tupper expressed any personal gratitude for all the years of work Wise spent building the sales operation and helping him reap a fortune, it came elsewhere, if at all. It was cold, impersonal, and permanent. "He couldn't get rid of her fast enough," remembered Ed Creiger.

On Friday, Tupper convened a lunch at headquarters with his THP executive staff, including Hamer Wilson, Gary McDonald, Don Hinton, Herb Young, Don Fuhr, George Reynolds, and Dave Seraphine. With the men facing the daunting task of running THP without Brownie Wise assembled, Tupper announced the promotions of Wilson and McDonald. He also made a blunt ultimatum, "You're either with me or with Brownie." Office manager Herb Young, who had been with the company since its early days in the Orlando airport hangar, stood up. "I'm with Brownie," he said, and walked out.

Gary McDonald chose to stay. Ever since his discharge from the military, Tupperware was all he'd known. Now the pressure was on him to take all he'd learned and, along with Hamer Wilson, shepherd the company without the formidable personality of Brownie Wise. Elsie Mortland happened upon McDonald sitting at a table with his head down. "He looked like the absolute picture of despair," Mortland recalled, "and I just went over to him and said, 'Don't worry, Gary, we'll stick by you.'"

Beyond the new pressure to perform, McDonald also struggled with his guilt about choosing to stay rather than following Herb Young's lead. After all, Brownie Wise was far more than just his boss. In Detroit, they had helped bring Earl Tupper's invention out of obscurity. McDonald had also been like a father figure and big brother to young Jerry, and Brownie Wise had been like the mother McDonald had lost at sixteen. Together they'd transformed the lives of thousands of dealers—and their own—but now their seemingly endless journey together had come to an abrupt end.

McDonald did some soul searching: "I felt that she felt that I had betrayed her. And I guess I ask myself, by being willing to stay and run the company, was I?" Judging by his going along with her ouster, Wise would have been justified in believing McDonald, in the end, approved.

In a state of shock, but still believing she might be able to carve out a substantive role for herself at Tupperware moving forward, Wise decided to be a good soldier and compose a face-saving message to the legion of Tupperware dealers, managers, distributors, and all of the staff at headquarters. She diplomatically hid any resentment she might have felt as she dictated a letter that would serve as her official notification of what she had "chosen" to do. It went out as a *Spark-O-Gram* to Tupperware distributors on Saturday, February 1:

> *Well, this is the day . . . the day of glad thoughts and with sad thoughts. I have enjoyed the long hours, the long days and the not-so-long years that I have spent working with all of you, but of course, I have always felt that I would like to spend more time with my son, Jerry. There are many personal creative things that I have often wished for time to do. (Writing, for instance . . . and many of you know*

I'm a "rock hound." . . . I love working with the various stones . . . cutting, polishing, shaping . . . and I certainly appreciate the rocks that you and your dealers and managers have sent me from time to time.)

From now on, I'll be working with Tupperware on a part-time basis. . . . I'll still be part of the Tupperware family . . . and of course, at every Tupperware get together my thoughts will be with you. I'll still be attending some of them in person, too.

I will act as an advisor to the staff . . . though you know the boys . . . sometimes they don't go along with my thoughts and opinions . . . but that's why it's been fun.

You know, I'll miss all of you . . . miss the telephone jangling constantly . . . miss your letters and your wires.

This year will be a great year, as they all have been, but this one greater still . . . and I'll be watching closely . . . watching all of you, because now, as always, you're very close to me.

Best Wishes, Brownie Wise

Wise decided to work with Tupper on the contract offer, rather than rejecting the proposal for what it really was: a cynical attempt to give her false hope, placate the dealers, and minimize bad press and doubts from potential buyers of his company. On Monday, February 3, Tupper had a press release sent out with the heading, "Brownie Wise Goes into Semi-Retirement." Tupper assured those who read it that, "[Mrs. Wise] is still an important member of the Tupperware family." There was no mention of Brownie, the name that had become synonymous with the leader of Tupperware Home Parties.

However, when Wise received the written contract offer, it

little resembled the agreement she thought she had reached with Tupper on January 29. For a ceremonial position at a good salary, Tupper was still requiring the kind of exclusivity and loyalty that Wise had shown when she ran the place. During the proposed two-year period, Wise would have to get Tupper's written permission before pursuing any other sales venture. While the job was supposed to involve only fifty-two days a year, Wise would be required to "render herself available at any time for the performance of such duties."

While Wise was still "an important part of the Tupperware family," the contract required her to turn over "all papers, records and other property of any kind or description, real or personal, in her possession or control, which are the property of the Employer and give the Employer any information which she has relative to the location of any records or papers relating to the Employer's affairs." This open-ended mandate seemed to require Wise to relinquish any and all information she had accumulated over the years to Tupper or his officers at their whim.

The contract also called for an audit of THP's books and records. If Wise didn't agree with the results of that audit, she could, at her own expense, order one done by a CPA of her own choosing. Despite any earlier conversations Wise and Tupper had had about her interest in buying Water's Edge, his position on that had changed, too. "The Employee shall be allowed the use of the Employer's house where she now lives for a period of sixty days," the contract stated. "The Employee shall remove herself and her personal belongings from such property on or before the expiration of said sixty days." It was another devastatingly clear message from Tupper: *Congratulations on your new semi-retired role. You now have sixty days to get out of the house.*

Not only was she required to move, but if Wise failed to live up to any requirements of the contract, it could be revoked immediately. Tupper shrewdly included another proviso that stated that even if the agreement was revoked, "paragraph 3b of this contract shall nevertheless survive." That paragraph effectively banned Wise from getting involved in any other sales activity for two years without Tupper's permission. And he certainly would have no intention of letting her do any such thing if she was no longer on the Tupperware payroll.

On February 25, 1958, Wise wrote her last letter to Earl Tupper, outlining why the agreement was unacceptable. "This contract bears very slight resemblance to the contract outlined at THP on Wednesday, January 29, when you, Herbert Young, Gary McDonald and Hamer Wilson were present," Wise wrote.

> *It was quite specific that ample notice was to be given me about personal appearances. I was to be free to sell real estate, insurance, or any product or service excepting items competitive to Tupperware, on the home party plan. I was not, in any way, to be restricted against using my own ability or my experience except as it conflicted with the specific interests of Tupperware.*

No mention was made of the island lease arrangement on which Wise estimated she was owed $3,000—or of the verbal agreement she thought she had with Tupper on buying Water's Edge. She would not sign the contract without a resolution of these questions.

Dave Seraphine's audit gave Wise another indication that the company was drawing battle lines. The probe questioned her on everything from $49 dresses to 1,880 copies of *Best*

Wishes she had given away to people "not associated with Tupper." Her reply was defensive. "Yes, I bought 6,000 books for THP without any OK," Wise wrote in her answer to the audit. "OK from whom? I also built the pavilion, designed and contracted for the lakes, for the garden wall, wrote purchase orders for $35,000 worth of silver from International Silver etc. without any OK." Wise went on to say the quantity of books had been determined with input and knowledge of other members of the THP staff. A more legitimate company concern about *Best Wishes* came from the fact that Wise had spent $1,261.90 in attorney fees stemming from her failed ghostwriting arrangement with Robert Froman.

But her point in all this was that she rightfully enjoyed a certain amount of privilege as America's Tupperware Lady. Tony Ponticelli agreed: "I would argue any day—I'm drawing from experience out of Madison Avenue—all the executives had unlimited expense money, clothing, vehicles. You want me to be that character. I'm in a movie for you. I need the money to play the part." As Gary McDonald had argued previously about the expenses of putting on jubilees and giving away lavish prizes, the spending didn't matter because the company was making enormous profits in return.

Correspondence between Wise and her "Employer" soon dwindled to letters between their lawyers. The line in the sand had been drawn, and neither Brownie nor Tupperware yielded. After more than a month had gone by, Wise finally received the news that she had been eased out. "The position of Tupperware Home Parties Inc," stated a letter written by a company lawyer and dated March 7, "is that her employment must be considered to have terminated."

"We have to move," Wise informed her son with no explanation.

"Do we have to move this fast?" Jerry asked, bewildered. "I can't get my horses out of here this fast."

"You're going to have to," she told him.

"I left five head of cows at Water's Edge," Jerry recalled. "I kept thinking, why don't we own it?" Wise always thought she'd be given the chance to buy her dream home, but given the tenor of her exit, she now knew that Tupper would never allow her to keep the glamorous trappings of the job from which she had been removed. She very quickly purchased a three-story home on Clyde Avenue in Kissimmee.

However, Brownie Wise would not take her unceremonious ouster without a fight. In response to being terminated, she filed suits totaling $1.6 million, naming Tupper Corporation and THP as defendants along with Tupper, McDonald, Wilson, Seraphine, and Creiger personally. Wise claimed she had been "boycotted and blacklisted" from getting other jobs as well as "accused of embezzlement."

To the newspapers, Earl Tupper said the Brownie Wise lawsuits came from out of the blue. "I was shocked and bewildered after receiving the information by telephone about the suits, because she hasn't had anything but kindness and consideration from us." This was the last thing Tupper needed as he looked toward trying to sell his company and solve his tax worries.

As the legal battle wore on, Wise tried to put on a brave face. She poured out her feelings in private: "This has been the most painful experience of my life. . . . I couldn't begin to describe to you how shattering it's been, and will, I suppose, continue to be for some time." Wise wrote her attorneys:

> *The most serious mistake I have made during my*
> *7-years' association with Tupper and Tupperware, is that of*

being naïve. ("Stupid" is the better word I suppose.) Other-
wise I would have on hand documents to support what I
claim; there would have been contracts and leases and
written "O.K.'s" and I would be in the driver's seat, where
I should be, after these years of blindly putting Tupperware
and its interests ahead of Brownie and her interests.

It was obvious that Tupper and his lawyers also planned
to be ruthless if forced to wage a court battle with Wise. In
the discovery phase of the suit, records show, they demanded
Wise produce evidence of how she had been accused of embezzlement, and how their actions had left her blacklisted.
They also wanted Wise to produce her tax returns dating back
to 1954 for possible scrutiny in open court. Without written
documentation to back up her claims, legal action would be
fruitless. Wise eventually settled everything for $30,000 and
walked away.

After all the years that Brownie Wise had lived in her lakeside mansion, pocketed a handsome salary, taken on a movie
star's persona, and earned the adoration of many, her Hibiscus dreams at Tupperware were coming to an end. For his
part, Earl Tupper never willingly gave her anything in the way
of severance pay, despite all she had done to put money in his
pocket.

At THP, orders were given for a big hole to be dug on company grounds and for the hundreds of copies of *Best Wishes*
still on hand to be dumped in it. "It wasn't until later I found
out about the books being buried. I was kind of pissed," remembered Gary McDonald. He felt the only reason they'd
been disposed of that way was "just because they said 'Brownie
Wise.'"

But books weren't all the company was burying—Earl

Tupper wanted the name "Brownie Wise" erased from the company history. He gave McDonald strict orders on what dates and facts to include when handing out company information to the press. For decades after Brownie Wise departed and filed suit, her name was never associated with the company. "You couldn't mention Brownie anymore," remarked the man who'd gone to such pains to promote her, Don Hinton. "There was never such a person." The annual Tupperware catalogue no longer featured Wise, and in 1958, her name was nowhere in the first post-Brownie, company-generated history, *The Fabulous Tupperware Story*.

To bolster morale and retain employees in Wise's absence, Tupper sent roses to the wives of executives like Tony Ponticelli and took on the role of cheerleader. "I am getting more and more enthusiastic about the future of THP," he wrote in a memo to Wilson and McDonald, "now that B.W. is out." He went on to describe seven products featuring "new type black polyethylene handles which I believe will send the whole housewares industry agog." Tupper anticipated a move by Wise to try to derail his efforts, however. "BW will, of course, be out for any kind of a deal that can be worked with a competitor," Tupper warned. "We can best upset their applecart and store competition by moving fast on a well-planned program with all these new items."

Hard as Tupper tried, however, there was no way he could simply erase Brownie Wise, like markings on a chalkboard, from the hearts and minds of the countless women across the country who still loved her, and who weren't privy to the intrigue behind her ouster. They were still of the mind that Wise was going to continue, though in her semiretired "advisory" capacity. Throughout 1958, she continued to get letters from dealers and distributors everywhere, inviting her to assemblies, wondering if they would still see her, and questioning why she was no longer with Tupperware. "I was quite concerned thinking you were ill or that the company which you had really *made* had given you a dirty deal," wrote one Indiana dealer. "You see, you have been the symbol of things hoped for in my selling career. I think of your life with an ordinary beginning and how you took hold of the things at hand and have truly become a star for any saleswoman to use as a guide."

For her part, Wise was not one to sit on the sidelines for long. She hoped to leverage the devotion of her former workforce and keep her own remarkable career rolling. She had a new home-based selling venture lined up, but she needed the workforce to build it. Brownie Wise was trying to do what Earl Tupper had feared: claim a sizeable chunk of Tupperware dealers. Wise set her sights on the 1958 jubilee, when the loyalty of those dealers would be put to the test in a showdown almost ten years in the making.

Moving On

Even before her departure from Tupperware, Brownie Wise was planning the next phase in her career: capitalizing on her fame in a real estate venture, Brownie Wise Developments. As she told the *Kissimmee Gazette*, "the rivers and lakes at our doorstep are practically untouched as far as real estate development is concerned." On May 2, 1958, Wise was back on the front page of the local paper, celebrating the sale of her first "Hearthside Home" to a former Kentucky coal miner and his wife. The firm already had a half-dozen homes priced at $10,500 going up within the Kissimmee city limits.

Wise also took some time to enjoy personal pursuits, a luxury that her busy role at Tupperware hadn't afforded her. Along with other creative hobbies like writing and working with rocks, Wise became enamored with pottery. She had her own kiln and entered the pieces she made in area competitions. Wise also enjoyed crafts and collected wicker baskets. She even put on a sales seminar and donated the class fees to the Red Cross. Jerry was just happy that his mother would be around more and have time to spend on a "normal" life with him. But even with this newfound freedom, the call of home-based selling was strong, and soon Brownie had more ambitious plans to get back into it.

Once it was clear her career with Tupperware had ended, Wise accepted the post of president of Cinderella International Corporation, a home-selling company with a line of cleaning products and beauty aids for men and women. Some familiar names from the Tupperware days joined her executive staff: Charles McBurney as vice president and Herb Young as administrative director and assistant treasurer. Wise also lured some of her clerical staff away, but was saving her biggest power play for July, when Tupperware was planning to hold its first jubilee without her.

Back at company headquarters, Mary Frances Babb wrote a memo to Earl Tupper assuring him that there would be no replay of the 1957 disaster; most of the jubilee events would take place on company grounds. Scheduled for July 1–4, the 1958 jubilee had a pirate theme, complete with a big, wooden pirate ship. The only off-site activity would be pirate "raids" planned for downtown Kissimmee shops.

To coincide with the opening festivities, Wise took out a large newspaper ad announcing her new venture with Cinderella and inviting Tupperware dealers to pay her a visit. Not only did Wilson and McDonald face the daunting job of putting on their first jubilee without Wise, now she was pulling a pirate raid of her own by coming out as a direct competitor. There was no way they could prevent people from reading the paper or seeing the ad, so they decided to do just the opposite. "We gave copies to people on buses as they arrived," McDonald remembered, "so everybody would see them." Then they announced her plans to the large gathering of visitors. "We know how good Tupperware is, [but] we don't know anything about cosmetics and we don't know anything about Cinderella," McDonald told them. "We do know Brownie Wise and she's terrific. If you want to go see her, we want you to know that it's perfectly fine with us."

No one left.

Wise extended a personal invitation to her friend and

Tupperware's official demonstrator, Elsie Mortland. "I didn't have the belief or the faith in the products that I had in Tupperware. And I told her I just couldn't do it," Mortland recalled. "She said, 'Then we can't be friends anymore,' and I said, 'I'm sorry.'" The two never spoke again. Mortland once ran into Wise near her Cinderella offices in downtown Kissimmee. "I said, 'Hello, Brownie,'" Mortland recalled sadly. In response, Wise turned away and waved to a passing car, ignoring her.

Wise had spent years at Tupperware training dealers to "surrender themselves" to Tupperware, and now she was trying to convince the same people to walk away from it. But they had worked as hard as she had to build up their businesses and livelihoods through the product. Wise's own mother, Rose Humphrey, even continued on as a Tupperware distributor.

For many loyal dealers, Tupperware was more than a product. It was their living, their children's education, their retirement, their family, their future. Perhaps her failure at the jubilee was the moment of clarity for Brownie Wise. If she hoped to catch lightning in a bottle again, she'd be doing it with a novice sales force. The Tupperware family was closing ranks and moving on without her. "I think she had an idea the company would fall apart when she left," Mortland observed, "but it didn't."

Mortland knew something else was afoot when groups of strange men in dark suits started touring the Kissimmee headquarters. "This group of guys looked like they were in the mafia," remembered Gary McDonald. Shortly after, in September 1958, McDonald was called into a meeting room at headquarters. On the table was an annual report belonging to the Rexall Drug Company, the new owners of the Tupper Corporation and Tupperware Home Parties. In a rollercoaster year for McDonald, this was an unquestionable low.

After turning his back on the woman he worked with and admired for years, it was all for this? The company was being sold, which meant he might lose his job. Beyond that, all signs suggested that Tupperware would soon be available in Rexall drugstores. McDonald knew that the distributors would never stand for it. They had worked so hard to keep Tupperware for sale solely through home-based parties, and that exclusivity was key to their success. After he had kept the sales division running for months after Brownie's departure, anger and exhaustion set in.

"I lost it," McDonald remembered.

Tupper and Creiger had signed a $16 million deal with Justin Whitlock Dart, Sr., the former "boy wonder" of the drugstore industry and president of Rexall Drugs—$15 million for the company and another $1 million for potential liability Tupperware faced at the time from the Brownie Wise lawsuit. Dart, an heir to the Walgreen's drugstore chain through his marriage, had taken over the struggling United Drug Company in 1943 and rebranded it Rexall. The purchase of Tupperware was another step in turning the company into a powerhouse conglomerate.

Dart had big plans for Tupperware, which he outlined to THP executives during a meeting at a famous south Orlando restaurant, Gary's Duck Inn. "I want you guys to know something," Dart said in a Tupper-esque tone. "I don't know anything about selling cups and bowls on the party plan. You do that. But these guys will tell you I do tend to make suggestions. But it's like throwing mud against the barn fence. If they stick, fine, if they don't, that's fine, too." But one suggestion on which Dart would not relent was, "You've gotta get overseas." McDonald found his meeting with Dart reassuring because Rexall did not plan to come in and make wholesale changes. To further reassure distributors, at a meeting in St. Louis where the sale was announced, each received a certificate for five shares of Rexall stock.

Tupper signed the sale papers in Worcester, Massachusetts, on September 28, 1958. On the way back, he told the new head of manufacturing, John Ansley: "This thing is going to blow up, it'll never last. Go out and get yourself another job." Two days later, Dart and Tupper made a joint, public announcement of the sale. "In addition to serving as chairman of the Tupper board," Dart said, "Earl Tupper will continue research, designing and development of new materials and products." Tupper confirmed his intention to carry on: "The development program will continue to employ the best polyethylene and polyolefin resins. As in the past, the line will continue to utilize other new materials as they are developed and effectively laboratory tested to meet our exacting requirements." Tupperware also announced that their sales for the first eight months were up 25 percent over 1957.

The old taskmaster was gone, but the company would continue the meticulous standards of perfection he demanded. At every molding machine on every shift, employees sampled the product for color and quality. Every piece had to be as close to perfect as possible. The castoffs were discarded, ground up, melted, and repoured.

Even before the sale, Earl Tupper was a very rich man. "I had 7 million dollars in the bank and was making another 7 and a half million for 1958," Tupper wrote. But his fear of the possibility of a 77 percent government tax on his estate as the sole owner of all Tupperware stock forced him to sell his company at the $16 million "sacrifice price." He also received 175,000 shares of Rexall stock and a seat on the board of directors. Hamer Wilson took over as president of Tupperware

Home Parties, and John Ansley became president of the man-ufacturing division of the Tupperware Corporation. For the first time, the top jobs on the sales and manufacturing sides of Tupperware—positions held by Wise and Tupper since the inception of THP—were occupied by others.

In Kissimmee, Wise continued to make noise about Cin-derella, posing her first eight Florida dealers for newspaper pictures. Holding "Cinderella Hour" demonstrations any time of the morning, noon, or night was her way of trying to re-create the famous Tupperware Party. She announced that the company was experiencing such "rapid growth" that it had to move into larger quarters.

Wise also formed a Kissimmee chapter of the Florida Aero Club and started flying to Cinderella functions in places like Wichita and Cleveland. She adopted a new nickname, "Flori-da's Flying Cinderella." The Cinderella holiday advertisement in the Kissimmee paper was the same size as Tupperware's.

As much as Wise tried to portray Cinderella as a company on the move, the glass slipper never fit. Regardless of how much energy, charisma, publicity, and sales know-how Wise poured into the new venture, the products did not hold the same allure as Tupperware. Time after time, Tupperware dealers would write Wise to tell her how much they missed her. She would write back and talk about a new opportunity with Cinderella. They would politely decline. With little de-tail, on June 5, 1959, the *Kissimmee Gazette* carried the news that Wise and McBurney had resigned their positions. On No-vember 1, the company relocated its headquarters to Orlando, with vice president Herb Young the only executive holdover from the early THP team.

The most devastating blow for Wise came at the end of 1959 with the loss of her mother, Rose. While others were getting ready to ring in the 1960s on New Year's Eve, Wise and her friends and family mourned their loss at the Grissom Chapel in Kissimmee. Throughout the 1950s, Humphrey had played a minor role in shaping Tupperware's history, opening new markets in Florida and Puerto Rico. She was also among the elite early distributors, consistently ranking among the top in sales. With Rose's death, Brownie's last true connection to Tupperware was gone.

After relinquishing his active role in the day-to-day operations of Tupperware, Earl Tupper grew "restless." He divorced his wife, Marie, after almost twenty-eight years of marriage and five children. According to Ed Creiger, Marie received only $50,000, a Ford Thunderbird, and $1,000 per month until she remarried. When Marie found a new husband, Tupper said he had a right to prorate the monthly payment, but he chose not to. Tupper resigned his seat on the Rexall board and sold off his stock, so he could be free to travel and live abroad. Disillusioned with the political direction the country was taking, in 1965 Tupper purchased a home in Nassau, Grand Bahamas. In 1967, he relinquished his American citizenship. "I feel that since I'll never go back to the U.S.A. to live," he wrote, "I want to reorient my whole balance of life to the contented life and place where I now live."

Tupper finally found the paradise he was looking for in San Jose, Costa Rica, settling there for good in 1973. In later life, Tupper became a very generous philanthropist, donating $10 million for the Earl S. Tupper Research Institute at Boston's New England Medical Center. He also gave $4 million to the Smithsonian for a center for tropical disease research in

Panama. From time to time, THP executives like Hamer Wilson and Gary McDonald would communicate with Tupper. When they did, it was memorable.

In the 1970s, while in New York for surgery, Tupper placed a call to Gary McDonald. "They wheeled me down on a gurney and by that time I had a whole bunch of notes because it wasn't nearly what it ought to be," Tupper reported. "A guy gave me gas to put me out, and I said 'Before you do that, is that what you run the blood through?'"

The doctor said, "Yes, it is."

"You have a problem with condensation, don't you?" Tupper asked. "Yes we do," the surprised doctor replied.

"I know how that could be fixed and redesigned," Tupper assured him.

That was typical of Earl Tupper, the farm boy who saw himself as a modern-day Leonardo da Vinci. "A mind like that is looking at everything without exception," McDonald marveled, "everything."

On December 7, 1976, the Society of Plastics Industries inducted Tupper into the Plastics Hall of Fame for initiative and drive in creating useful, high-quality housewares, enhancing the image of the plastics industry. On Friday, October 7, 1983, newspapers worldwide reported Tupper's death from a heart attack. He was seventy-six. "The home parties through which Mr. Tupper sold his goods became a well-known part of American life and made him a millionaire," reported the *New York Times*. There was not one word about the pioneering businesswoman instrumental to his success and riches, a testament to the effectiveness of efforts to eradicate Brownie Wise from the history of Tupperware.

The people whom Tupper entrusted to take Tupperware into the 1960s and beyond did not disappoint. Hamer Wilson spearheaded the company's Cold War–era expansion and became a beloved figure to distributors. "Because the company was so successful," Wilson's wife of fifteen years and former distributor Marylin Mennello remembered, "Justin Dart let Hamer run the business his way." Tupperware became a cash cow for Rexall and later Dart Industries.

Elsie Mortland flew all over the globe giving Tupperware demonstrations in England, Germany, Belgium, Holland, Italy, Costa Rica, and Guatemala, among other new international markets. In 1965, Mortland helped introduce Tupperware in Hong Kong. After the departure of Wise, Mortland became Tupperware's First Lady.

Gary McDonald, "Mister Stanley," outlived everyone else who was there at the beginning of Tupperware Home Parties Inc. Arguably, there was no one closer to Tupperware's journey from the shelves of the J. L. Hudson department store in Detroit—where it sat forgotten and unsold—to the homes of millions of people around the world. Tony Ponticelli reflected: "Gary believed in respecting the public; the customer was always right. The gift of gab came from Brownie to him. He was able to inject his own personality into it and motivate people. I thought we had a good team."

But if all of the people involved with Tupperware's golden era managed to find their footing in the following years, unfortunately the same could not be said for the woman to whom they all, to greater and lesser degrees, owed their success.

After parting ways with Tupperware in 1958, Brownie Wise lived out most of her remaining thirty-four years in a more modest, ranch-style home she had built on the west side of

Lake Toho, with a view of her island off in the distance. Wise lived a quiet country life, feeding her horse carrots or apples right out the kitchen window. She belonged to social groups in Kissimmee, stayed active in her church, and participated in contests and craft fairs through area art associations.

She continued efforts to make a new mark in the business world, and from a distance, the principals from her Tupperware past took notice. In compliance with Tupper's wishes, her name was no longer spoken or even written within the walls of Tupperware. When Wise was replaced after yet another unsuccessful cosmetics venture, her old rival Hamer Wilson reveled in her failure. "For your information," Wilson wrote to Tupper in July 1961, "I heard yesterday that the president of Viviane Woodard Cosmetics was relieved of her duties."

In the 1960s, Jerry said his mother and father attempted a reconciliation of sorts. She was no longer the Tupperware maven and he was in Miami, making a serious go of sobriety and success.

"Yeah, he was kind of neat to be around. And my mother said, 'What do you think of your dad?' I said, 'Well, I've never seen this side of him,'" Jerry recalled. "We went down to see him and Bob was just as sober as could be and looked great." In Miami, Robert Wise was making hydraulic steering wheels for outboard boats and doing quite well. He and Brownie went into business together on a prepaid college tuition idea, a forerunner of a very popular program run by the state of Florida today. But that's as far as the fairy-tale ending went.

"He drank it away," said his son of the business venture. "Brownie was pissed—oh, she was pissed. She said 'We're gonna clean out his building before his creditors show up.'"

Like a broken record, Robert Wise again ended up in trouble with his family and the law. After that last sour experience, Jerry's parents never had any substantive contact. Jerry said his father was around sixty-four years old when he died.

Contrary to reports that painted her as virtually penniless and friendless after the Tupperware days, Brownie owned and developed land and had many hobbies to pass the time. Jerry admitted that his mother was always "a wallflower" when it came to socializing and that she "didn't get out much." After all the problems with her ex, she seemed to be done with men, with a possible exception of one.

Though Wise never talked about her own legacy, she occasionally mentioned significant people and events from her past to trusted friends like her neighbors John and Sharroll Waugh. "Whatever she volunteered I just listened," John reflected, a quality that over the course of his years of friendship with Brownie Wise earned him her trust to confide more personal things. During her years at Tupperware and after, it turns out, Brownie Wise did have someone special in her life.

That man was Adlai Stevenson, the two-time Democratic presidential nominee who lost to Dwight Eisenhower in 1952 and again in '56. In 1960, President John F. Kennedy appointed Stevenson ambassador to the United Nations, and during the Cuban Missile Crisis, his diplomacy helped guide the United States back from the brink of nuclear war with the Soviet Union. Wise referred to him by an endearing nickname, "Addy."

During his years in public life until his sudden death from a heart attack in 1965, Stevenson was divorced and never remarried. Witty and urbane, he had the kind of humor and strength of personality Wise undoubtedly would have found appealing. Her ex-husband's daughter confirmed the relationship, remembering letters Wise showed her bearing Stevenson's signature: "Love always, Adlai."

Though Wise didn't give a lot of detail—and John Waugh wasn't one to press something so personal—he could tell by the loving way she spoke that Stevenson was someone special in her life.

"I'm glad you had that relationship with Addy," he told her.

After a few moments of silence Wise replied, "Why did you tell me you're glad?"

Knowing how things had worked out with her ex-husband and Earl Tupper, Wise's friend replied, "I'm glad you had someone to love."

Later in life, Wise spent a lot of time on creative projects, whiling away the hours in her pottery studio with Sinatra or one of his contemporaries playing in the background. Colored glazes, not unlike what might go into making Tupperware's trademark pastels, lined the walls of her studio so she could add them by hand to her creations. "Clay is joyous," Wise wrote like a mantra for those in her studio to read. "Clay is here to stay!"

As is often the potter's practice, she kept a bowl at her work space containing wet clay—for the next project she was inspired to take on. That was another Brownie Wise mantra: progress, moving on, concentrating on what's around the bend. Besides her beloved pottery, Wise made fabric wall hangings and collected fine wicker baskets. She hand-carved tiles and made tools out of chicken bones.

On the east side of the lake, Water's Edge sat empty after Brownie and Jerry were forced to vacate. For thirty-one years, the stone mansion at the end of Aultman Road absorbed punishment from the unrelenting central Florida summers, shotgun blasts from hunters, and decades of neglect. Trespassers spray-painted graffiti on the bedroom walls Wise had painted pink, left trash in her customized dressing room and the breakfast nook she had constructed over the pool, and defaced the carved fireplace and terrazzo tile floors. The sweeping views of Lake Tohopekaliga out of the home's Roman windows were obscured. The lawn had grown jungle-like, a haven for the alligators that almost drove Wise away before she ever took up occupancy. If Brownie Wise ever had occasion to go by the old place, seeing it in such a state of disrepair had to have hurt.

Brownie and Jerry, in happier
times, at Water's Edge,
ca. 1954.

A spokesman said the company never felt a compelling need to do anything about the place: "It was just one of a group of assets and there was neither a desire to do anything with it nor a need." At the end of 1989, Tupperware finally got around to tearing it down. The same year, Wise was finally invited back to headquarters to give a fifteen- to twenty-minute speech to distributors on "commitment, quality, and goals."

"You think I ought to go out?" Wise asked her son.

"No I don't," Jerry replied. "They didn't want you—say, 'Tough shit.'"

"I don't like that word," she replied, as always.

"Tell them, 'Stick it up their ass.'"

"Oh, I'm not gonna tell 'em *that*."

Brownie Wise may not have been selling Tupperware anymore, but she never relinquished being a *lady*.

Wise refused—reportedly balking at top executives' stipulation that she make pre-approved, scripted comments—and would never have another opportunity to enjoy the homecoming she deserved. From time to time, she gave interviews about the early days, including a 1987 conversation with writer Charles Fishman in which she discussed turning down an *I Love Lucy* producer's plan to have a madcap Tupperware party on the show. "I won't allow it. It won't help us" was her reaction. "I could just see how it would end," Wise recalled, "with Ricky with a Tupperware bowl upside down on his head."

Three decades from the turmoil of her departure, Wise could reflect on the battles with Tupper, often over misguided product ideas like his design for a flour sifter. "I said, 'I will not sell this. It's hard to clean and the holes are too large to do a good job of sifting,'" she remembered. To help make the case, Wise had summoned Elsie Mortland. In front of Tupper and all the other executives, she handed Mortland the sifter. "Elsie, what would you do with this if I give it to you?"

"Whoever made this didn't know about sifting flour, that's for sure," Mortland responded quickly.

Trumped again, Earl Tupper had worn a familiar red face.

When Fishman asked Wise about why she left Tupperware in 1958, her answer was neither bitter nor critical: "Just say the company was changing hands and I decided not to go along."

About her legacy as a trailblazing independent business-woman, Brownie would not put up with being called a feminist or a forerunner of the women's liberation movement. Adopting a tone as if he had repeated this many times, Jerry proclaimed, "Brownie just said, 'I needed the money for me and my kid. So I got out there and made it.'" If talk ever turned to why she left Tupperware, Brownie told her son the patent was about to run out and she wanted to move on to new challenges.

Brownie Wise at a Kissimmee art event, likely 1979.

Her final years were difficult. As cancer weakened her body, Wise took to her bed, depending more and more on prescription painkillers to make it through the day. At the expense of forging a life for himself apart from his mother, Jerry Wise remained at her bedside to take care of her.

When Wise died in 1992 at age seventy-nine, the central Florida newspapers explained just who this mostly long-forgotten woman was. "Some folks thought Brownie was just a sophisticated huckster who psyched up housewives," wrote *Orlando Sentinel* reporter Don Boyett. "They never knew her. She had more business sense than a Harvard MBA. She knew people."

"Most of all though," read the September 29, 1992, obituary, "she demonstrated that success in business, as it is in all other aspects of life, is causing people to do better than they think they can. Yes, sir, she was some lady." It was a fitting—and accurate—final piece of publicity for America's Tupperware Lady, and a tribute that Brownie Wise couldn't have written better herself.

Epilogue

On an unseasonably warm Friday in March 2015, I stopped at a small pioneer graveyard south of Kissimmee to pay my respects to Brownie Wise. A generation after her death, I hoped to get some grasp of her legacy in the place she called home for the last forty years of her life.

If you blinked, you'd miss Pleasant Hill Cemetery—not a particularly apt name given its location. It's a modest plot of sugar sand flatland drenched in sunshine, with only a few scrub trees here and there providing precious little shade. But I recalled Jerry Wise's funeral in 2007 and knew I was in the right place. It's fitting that the mother and son so closely intertwined in life, even sharing the same birthday, are side by side in the hereafter.

I reflected on the day not long before he died, when I convinced Jerry to show me the dusty pottery studio he'd kept like a shrine to his mother. He had lovingly thumbed through her black-and-white publicity photos from the Tupperware days, then showed me a box of ribbons she'd won in art competitions. At her workstation, inside a pot she kept covered, we were astonished to discover that the last pieces of clay Brownie Wise had worked with were still wet, for her son to take and mold himself. Tears ran down his face at the sight of them.

Getting back to thinking about the task at hand, what I had expected to be a quick park and walk in the sticky springtime heat started to get drawn out. After walking in circles for about half an hour, I came to realize something: Nowhere in Pleasant Hill Cemetery is there any clear evidence that this is the final resting place of Brownie Wise, the first woman on the cover of *Business Week* and onetime first lady of Tupperware. Nowhere could I find a proper stone, statue, or epitaph. Something as simple as "pioneering businesswoman" or "build the people and they'll build the business" would have been sufficient to remember her. How could there be nothing? Upon further thought, it seemed apropos given her history.

I ventured on to other places where I might find evidence of her life and career.

North of the cemetery on Harbor Road, Wise's homestead, still overgrown and cluttered, mirrored the messy way life ended for Brownie and Jerry. Friends spoke of tax liens and probate. If you didn't know better, you'd have no idea about the semi-obscured buildings set back from the road under a twisted canopy of trees and vines. It's hard to believe Wise once threw great parties here bringing together disparate groups. Artists mingled with ranchers and church folk. In her living room dozens of candles set a warm mood, and her long dining table featured myriad place settings, none matching. "There are so many beautiful patterns in the world," Wise rationalized. "Why would I limit myself to one?"

On another side of sprawling Lake Toho, down Aultman Road, I drove to a gate with a chain and padlock cutting off the waterfront peninsula where Water's Edge used to stand. Through the magic of Google's satellite photo program, the view from above reveals a couple of remnants near the end of the peninsula. Beyond the cluster of private, pricey homes with a sandy beach fronting Lake Toho, you can still make out the channel Brownie put in to accommodate her son's boat.

Gazing down from the heavens, you can still see the foundation of Water's Edge like a ghostly footprint.

To tourists making the trip down south Orlando's clogged, congested Orange Blossom Trail—past the auto dealerships, strip malls, fast-food restaurants, and the old Florida attraction Gatorland—the site of Tupperware World Headquarters must seem awfully incongruous. The old building Brownie Wise was so instrumental in constructing is long gone; much like the company's early efforts to wipe Wise from its memory, it was torn down years ago. In its place sits a stately complex designed by the same architect who built the Kennedy Center in Washington, D.C. To the north, the land on which Brownie Wise enjoyed some of her greatest success at the early jubilees has been sold off for development. Pat Jordan said it's hard to go by there now without crying.

Nowhere, not in her final resting place or her forgotten homestead—nor in downtown Kissimmee or the Florida Women's Hall of Fame in Tallahassee, as of this writing—is there a lasting memorial to the woman who set Greater Orlando on track to become the tourism Mecca it is today. From the outside, it seemed that only in the hearts of aging friends and neighbors was Brownie Wise still honored and cherished, flaws and all—a thought all the more disturbing because of all I'd learned while writing this book.

To appreciate how ahead of her time Brownie Wise was, consider how many ways she could have parlayed her Tupperware know-how and fame today. She would have been a natural to host her own syndicated talk show, write a national newspaper column, or maintain a popular blog. Wise could have hit the lecture circuit, fetching big money as a motivational speaker, and a New York publishing house likely would have been willing to pay her a handsome advance on a book about her ascent in the home-party sales world. She could have launched an Internet-based consulting and sales business, been the subject of her own reality show, or taken advantage of any number of career opportunities.

Certainly, an executive like Wise would have written into her contract a generous severance package and a Wonder Bowl full of stock options, and any one of a number of competitor companies would have snapped her up. With her personality, communication skills, and proven leadership ability, Brownie Wise could have had a shot at political office if she were so inclined.

And yet, it seems the most powerful memories of Wise remain the vintage black-and-white photos now stored at the Smithsonian in Washington: images of Wise holding oceanside Tupperware parties; bestowing awards upon humble dealers, who may not have had a shred of recognition at any previous time in their lives; and getting the keys to a convertible Cadillac from Earl Tupper himself in Orlando, in her own front yard. Perhaps, I realized, her legacy could live on in other ways.

A concerted—and long overdue—effort to revive Brownie Wise's legacy has begun. One prominent person involved is Rick Goings, CEO since 1992 of the company now known as Tupperware Brands Corporation. "In the 23 years that I've been with Tupperware Brands," Goings wrote me in a 2015 e-mail, "we have consistently been proud of our heritage and of the passionate innovators, like Brownie Wise, who have helped make Tupperware the successful brand it is today."

When Tupperware's financial fortunes slumped in the

United States, Goings mined new territories like Latin America and Asia, employing the same social networking strategies Wise used to coax housewives in post–World War II America.

In Indonesia, Tupperware sales reps identified the potential of a local tradition called an *arisan* (or "gathering"), where homebound women trade local news and gossip, and morphed it into an old-fashioned Tupperware Party. Dealers even took a page out of the Brownie Wise primer, slamming the bright plastic containers on the ground—as she had once bounced Wonder Bowls across terrazzo-tiled Florida family rooms—to prove to doubting women from Jakarta to Bandung that the product is durable and effective.

At the heart of it all is Tupperware's motivating mantra, the Chain of Confidence, meant to improve the lives of women in developing nations like Indonesia, where traditional values of the man as head of the family are institutionalized in the government's 1974 Marriage Law. Their stories mirror those of post–World War II American housewives.

When the restaurant that Rose Amelia ran with her husband barely kept them afloat financially, she struggled to convince him to allow her to become a Tupperware dealer.

"Initially my husband refused to let me sell Tupperware even part time because he thought it might affect the restaurant," Amelia said six years later. "Now he works for me."

According to Goings, that kind of transformative success story could not have happened without the values Wise championed during her years at Tupperware. "She taught women to take ownership of their destinies and she championed the importance of mentorship," he reflected. "These are both key tenets of our business, and of the Chain of Confidence, which we define as our global mission to empower women through confidence by enabling their financial independence and changing their lives through opportunity, support, and relationships."

To continue the conversation, Tupperware Global Brands also invited me to tour the campus, where Brownie Wise's books were once disposed of en masse like garbage—just as she was discarded and forgotten after her ugly ouster. But that was long ago.

My Tupperware Brands tour guide was Elinor Steele, vice president of Global Communications and Women's Initiatives, who showed me to the area known as Tupperware's "Heritage Center." A display on the back of the Tupper memorabilia pays tribute to Wise, a fitting place to celebrate the woman who supercharged Tupper's sales success. The display, built in 2015, includes images of Wise at the height of her glory: the 1954 *Business Week* cover, an event at the edge of Poly Pond, and of course, Brownie holding court at a Tupperware party. One of her dresses adds a three-dimensional touch. More important, the exhibit finally and firmly establishes the legacy of Brownie Wise on par with Tupper to those learning about the ubiquitous product's history for the first time.

Included in the displays are video testimonials of women worldwide, who describe how Tupperware gave them the power to change their lives. At this point in the tour, Elinor Steele confided—in an echo of Brownie's own story—how, as a young mother of three sons, she had escaped an abusive husband to start a new life for herself and her boys. For years, working her way up from a clerical job to management, she did just that.

"Two have master's degrees, the other is now in the military," she said of her sons, beaming with pride. "And I found a wonderful man and married him."

Woven like the strongest steel cables in that oft-mentioned

Chain of Confidence is courage—the courage to change, to set sail on a course for financial and personal independence. In what was decidedly a man's world, with no formal education, no man in her life and a child to raise, Brownie Wise displayed an extreme courage that continues to inspire women worldwide.

Today the company recognizes that it can't possibly tell its own story without including her. "Wise was so successful demonstrating and selling Tupper's plastics," says an item on the Tupperware website, "that he brought Wise into the company in 1951 to build the direct selling system that has made the Tupperware party as famous as the products themselves." The company literature now recognizes her "genius for people and a flair for marketing." And in what is perhaps the ultimate about-face concerning the legacy of Brownie Wise, thirty years after her successors buried Brownie's book on their own campus and at their own expense, a new team at Tupperware decided to distribute paperback copies of it as a gift, to motivate a new legion of dealers.

Wise's legacy also lives on in Tupperware's contribution to popular culture. The product she spent a decade of her life traveling the world to grow and promote has become as commonplace to the American home as Band-Aids, Jell-O, and the Frisbee. People can't seem to resist poking fun at the blend of cornball kitsch and dealer fanaticism that Tupperware evokes. Humorist Dave Barry wrote "The Tupperware Song" and managed to earn an invitation to perform it before one thousand distributors along with his band, the Urban Professionals. "They gave us a standing ovation," Barry boasted, "although in the interest of accuracy, I should tell you that just before we performed, they also gave a standing ovation to a set of ovenware."

Kris Anderson, the actor/writer/female impersonator behind *Dixie's Tupperware Party,* has turned his hilariously campy Brownie Wise homage into a critically acclaimed stage show. If only Wise were alive to bask in the glory, share in the laughter, and make a cameo even, as an over-the-top Sunshine Cinderella.

In Kansas City, a sculptor and part-time demolition derby enthusiast named Mac Maclanahan heard the Tupperware Rock 'N Serve line was bulletproof. Also something of a gun aficionado, he helped put that claim to the test for a newspaper article. On a friend's farm in Lathrop, Missouri, with the help of an XKS sniper rifle, the two men proved that the Rock 'N Serve line should not be substituted for Kevlar. Another artist named Ryan Gale pierced a Rock 'N Serve Medium Shallow with an arrow. Yet not a drop of raspberry Jell-O came out of the container. At the end of the merriment, Gale's grandma inquired, "Did you get all that Tupperware shot?"

In tiny Pearlington, Mississippi, Kathleen Bello raced up to the attic with her eight-month-old baby, Hayden. Hurricane Katrina's storm surge was threatening to carry them both away to certain death. The boy's father, Frank, managed to pull his twelve-foot Boston Whaler up alongside the flooding home. But how could she get the baby down the steep slope of the home's steel roof safely, and into a boat that was rocking madly in the storm? In a flash, she grabbed a Tupperware clothes bin and emptied it. She put her child inside, sealed the top, and slid him down the roof and into Dad's waiting arms.

"I knew we were going to catch him," said one relative who helped steady the boat. "There was no choice."

But for those most responsible for Tupperware's success, its story is simply the stuff of family lore—the memories of moving to new places, setting up an extended family of dealers and customers, and sitting on top of an old station wagon on a steamy Florida July Fourth watching twinkling fireworks reflected in Poly Pond. It's also happy years spent going to sales rallies; hatching promotional gimmicks; and, more than anything, inspiring others to try things they never thought possible, one small piece, one dealer, one order, one customer at a time, each becoming part of an ever-growing mosaic that is Tupperware's American success story.

In 1956, Brownie Wise described Tupperware as "a living drama of success—unequalled success of a product, a plan, an organization." Beginning with Alison Clarke's 1999 book *Tupperware: The Promise of Plastic in 1950s America*, and gaining more momentum with Laurie Kahn-Levitt's 2003 documentary *Tupperware!* Wise's indelible contribution to that living drama can be buried no longer. The early buzz in 2014 revolved around an Oscar-winning screenwriter/director preparing to launch a major motion picture based on her inspiring story.

Brownie could have let the gender stereotypes, poor upbringing, limited education, and abusive spouse resign her to a life of excuses and self-pity. But for Wise—as for many of the so-called Greatest Generation—those limitations simply steeled her ambition.

To say she was a trailblazer is an understatement. Wise was the chief executive of an international sales company when only a handful of women made it any higher on the corporate ladder than secretary. And this was not in progressive New York or Los Angeles; Brownie Wise did it in the Deep South, where racism, sexism, and ignorance could bury the most ambitious of dreams.

Today, hindsight compresses all that happened during the early days of Tupperware. But while she may have been a reticent feminist in her day, today Wise is recognized for helping throw open the doors to executive success through which many women have followed: Sheryl Sandberg at Facebook, Ginni Rometty at IBM, Marissa Mayer at Yahoo!, Mary Barra at General Motors, and more each year.

For decades, the legacy of Brownie Wise has been lost, like a gem buried way down in the marshy central Florida soil and long forgotten. Despite considerable efforts of those who tried to keep that legacy hidden, how fortunate we are to see America's First Lady of Tupperware at long last earn what fuels every salesperson's soul: recognition.

Acknowledgments

This project would not have been possible without the availability of the Brownie Wise and Earl Tupper collections at the Smithsonian Institution's National Museum of American History, Behring Center. Through what in many instances were hundreds of pages of their own writings, it was possible for Wise and Tupper, their families and close associates, to tell their own stories. They were the road map and timeline for this project.

I would also like to thank the many people who were willing to share their time and stories with me: Gary McDonald, Elsie Mortland, Jerry Wise, Tony Ponticelli, Don Hinton, Pat Jordan, Glenn Tupper, Brenda Ansley, Jack McCollum, Esther Dulger, Fred DeWitt, Marilyn Mennello; a special thanks to Melissa Bancroft for helping lay some of the groundwork. Thanks also to the clerks at the Osceola County Courthouse for pulling so many court files. From decades-old depositions came the words of Hamer Wilson, Glen Bump, Dave Seraphine, Gerald and Thelma Croxton, and Bill Boyd. Florida Sunshine Laws have been crucial in helping to tell so much of this history.

Thanks to John and Sharroll Waugh along with Clorinda Sheridan for helping bring this story up to date and adding new details. Thanks to Rick Goings and his staff at Tupperware Brands for welcoming me and acknowledging the vital role Brownie Wise played to make the company the global power it is today.

Thanks to my editor, Matt Inman, and his assistant, Julia Elliott, at Crown for their guidance and passion for this story. Thanks to Kate McKean in New York, and thank you to my attorney Davey Spiciatti-Jay in Orlando. Thanks to Meredith Babb and John Byram at University Press of Florida.

Thanks to my wife, Karen Kealing, and our children, William and Kristen Kealing.

The research for this book is available for scholarly review and study at the Bob Kealing collection, University of Central Florida Libraries, Special Collections.

Notes

PROLOGUE

xiii **$10 million in annual sales:** While exchange rates will vary slightly throughout the book, a good rule-of-thumb to keep in mind is that 1940s and 1950s figures can be multiplied by ten to get a rough estimate of 2016 dollars.

xviii **"That was a bombshell":** Gary McDonald, interview by the author, The Villages, Florida, September 15, 2005 (hereafter cited as McDonald interview). McDonald introduced Tupperware to Brownie Wise and is the last living executive who was involved in the formation of Tupperware Home Parties.

xix **"a pair of geniuses always on the brink":** Charles Fishman, "Is the Party Over?" *Orlando Sentinel,* March 15, 1987. Fishman spoke at length with Wise for this article.

CHAPTER 1

2 **"My grandfather had died":** Brownie Wise, *Best Wishes* (Orlando, FL: Podium Publishing, 1957), p. 37 (hereafter cited as *Best Wishes*).

3 **"Each time that I have seen":** Ibid, p. 58.

4 **"When he was good":** Author's interview with Clorinda Sheridan, daughter of Robert Wise, half-sister of Jerry Wise, March, 2015 (hereafter cited as Sheridan interview).

5 **"Having a child is like being":** Brownie Wise to W. Chandler Marshall letter, July 18, 1946, in Brownie Wise Papers, 1928–1968, Smithsonian Institution, National Museum of American History (hereafter cited as Wise Papers).

5 **Although he missed, the acid hit her:** Jerry Wise, interview by the author, Kissimmee, Florida, December 23, 2005 (hereafter cited as Jerry Wise interview). Wise is the only son of Brownie and Robert Wise.

6 **"DaVinci, Jefferson, Edison and a host of others are proof":** Earl Tupper invention book, Earl S Tupper Papers, Smithsonian National Museum of American History, Kenneth E. Behring Center (hereafter cited as Tupper Papers).

6–7 **the young inventor drew up "No Drip" ice-cream:** McDonald interview.

7 **"That's when my education really began":** "Fascinating Facts About Earl Tupper," www.Ideafinder.com.

7 **"would often stay at the molding machine":** Neil Osterweil, "Tupper Biography," typescript, chapter 6, "A Real Education," Tupper Papers.

9 **"I was searching for a basic premise":** Brownie Wise, undated notebook, Wise Papers.

10 **With "something lovely on the radio awfully late":** Brownie Wise, undated letter written under the pen name Hibiscus, Wise Papers.

10 **"The earth holds its breath when it's snowing":** Ibid.

10 **"I have despaired at each new war bulletin":** Ibid.

11 **"I thought, as I swung open the door":** Ibid.

11 **"Wade Dearest, a waning moon":** Brownie Wise to W. Chandler Marshall letter, July 18, 1946, Wise Papers.

11 **"You'll always be seeking the bit of life":** Ibid.

12 **"I'm going to be making a change in jobs":** Ed Creiger, "Earl Silas Tupper: The Plastic Years 1945 to 1958," typescript, Tupper Papers.

CHAPTER 2

13 **"I could do better":** Jerry Wise interview.

14 **"We have to change":** Biography of Frank Stanley Beveridge, www.Stanley.com.

14 **At first many salesmen:** Ibid.

14 **"The voice exercise":** Elmer Nyberg to Brownie Wise letter, June 13, 1947, Wise Papers.

15 **"Did you go prospecting":** Stanley order form, Wise Papers.

15 **"The man who plods":** Stanley Training Manual, Wise Papers.

15 **"If you and I":** Elmer Nyberg to Brownie Wise letter, October 9, 1948, Wise Papers.

16 **"He is *Genuine*":** Ibid.

16 **"Treat every person":** Ibid.

16 **"reproduce at home":** Elmer Nyberg, "How to Develop Resourcefulness" memorandum, Wise Papers.

16 **"Anybody who works":** Brownie Wise, *Go-Getter*, July 20, 1948, Wise Papers.

17 **"God Gives":** Ibid.

17 **"The secret of education"**: Brownie Wise to Elmer Nyberg letter, September 13, 1948, Wise Papers.

17 **"Ray Arsenault"**: Brownie Wise, *Triangle Unit News*, August 2, 1948, Wise Papers.

17 **"Florence's sales"**: Ibid.

17 **"One half"**: Ibid.

17 **"40 hours a week"**: Ibid.

18 **"Monday morning"**: Ibid.

18 **"Sure . . . but you'll have to book"**: McDonald interview.

18 **"Mister Stanley"**: Ibid.

19 **"As a matter of fact"**: Osterweil, "Tupper Biography," chapter 7.

20 **"With the end of the war"**: Earl Tupper to J. C. Healy memorandum, September 14, 1949, Tupper Papers.

20 **"Poly T: Material of the Future"**: McDonald interview.

21 **"E. S. Tupper Open Mouth"**: "Earl S. Tupper of Upton Granted Valuable Patent," *Milford (Mass.) Daily News*, undated clipping, Tupper Papers.

21 **"Tupperware"**: *Time*, September 8, 1947.

21 **"one-man boom"**: Ibid.

22 **"as good as"**: Alison J. Clarke, *Tupperware: The Promise of Plastics in America* (Washington, D.C.: Smithsonian Institution Press), 42.

22 **As a youngster**: *Time*, September 8, 1947.

22 **"A Massachusetts"**: Ibid.

22 **"We always try"**: Tupper to Healy memorandum, September 14, 1949, Tupper Papers.

23 **"such a thing"**: Ibid.

23 **"think of it"**: Early Tupperware full-page ad, 1948, Tupper Papers.

23 **the tops didn't fit**: McDonald interview.

23 **Twelve thousand employees**: Balch, "How J. L. Hudson Changed the Way We Shop," *Detroit News*, January 26, 2006.

23 **In the days**: Palm, "One Building's Struggle," *Metropolis*, June 1998.

24 **"*That* could be"**: McDonald interview.

24 **"Tommy"**: *Our World*, July 1981.

25 **"Whoever heard"**: McDonald interview.

26 **"You come here"**: *Stanley Pilgrim*, August 22–25, 1948, Wise Papers.

26 **"We Think You're Wonderful"**: Ibid.

26 **"They think this little factory"**: Ibid.

26 **"Remember"**: Brownie Wise, *Go-Getter*, November 25, 1950, Wise Papers.

27 **"I'll show him"**: Jerry Wise interview.

CHAPTER 3

28 **"I'm sure"**: Tupper to Healy memorandum, March 8, 1949, Tupper Papers.

28 **"You have delivered"**: Ibid.

29 **Lone Star State**: McDonald interview.

29 **"Everybody seemed to love"**: Elsie Block, *My Tupperware Party Was Over and I Sat Down and Cried* (Bloomington, IN: Authorhouse, 2004), 56.

29 **"impossible to hold"**: Tupper to Healy memorandum, September 19, 1949, Tupper Papers.

30 **"Turn your leftovers"**: McDonald interview.

30 **she encouraged her dealers**: Ibid.

30 **"We started ordering"**: Ibid.

31 **If she ran short**: Ibid.

31 **"It was the strongest"**: Ibid.

31 **"Nola is making"**: Brownie Wise, *Go-Getter*, August 19, 1949.

32 **"I remember filling"**: Jerry Wise interview.

32 **"You guys have gotta tell me"**: McDonald interview.

33 **"Let's go"**: Jerry Wise interview.

CHAPTER 4

34 **twenty-one hours of driving**: Brownie Wise "Round-Robin" letter to former dealers (hereafter cited as Round-Robin Letter), May 9, 1950, Wise Papers.

34 **"I could never tell you"**: Ibid.

34 **"We oohed and aahed"**: Ibid.

34 **"We gradually began"**: Ibid.

35 **"you KNOW the hens"**: Ibid.

35 **"dripping with Spanish moss"**: Ibid.

35 **"and considered seriously"**: Ibid.

35 **"Our place faced"**: Ibid

36 **"Wise settled on a storefront"**: Ibid.

36 **"There is a little stream"**: Ibid.

37 **"Nothing could be so blue"**: Ibid.

37 **"urgent musts"**: Brownie Wise, *Patio Parties Training Manual*, May 1950. In this early manual Wise started the "feminization" of Stanley dealer training techniques.

37 **"This plan has proved"**: Ibid.

39 **"Suggestions along this line"**: Ibid.

39 **"I AM NOW"**: Wise, Round-Robin Letter.

39 **"My car"**: Ibid.

40 **Her warmth**: Ibid.

40 **"I could go on"**: Ibid.

41 **"In the long run"**: Brownie Wise to Victor Collamore letter, May 30, 1950, Wise Papers.

42 **"I am enclosing the order form"**: Early Tupperware dealer Gwen Lord to Brownie Wise, July 29, 1950, Wise Papers.

42 **on May 25**: Jerry Wise interview.

42 **"The burning point"**: Wise to Collamore letter, May 30, 1950.

43 **"Two of our other"**: Ibid.

43 **"To be perfectly frank"**: Ibid.

43 **"Yes—we know"**: Jayne and Bob Boltz to Brownie Wise letter, June 8, 1950, Wise Papers.

44 **"I have a genuine"**: Brownie Wise to Jayne and Bob Boltz letter, June 10, 1950, Wise Papers.

44 **"I'll try to forget"**: Ibid.

44 **"This thing must be good"**: Wise to Collamore lettter, July 21, 1950, Wise Papers.

44 **"he would continue"**: Wise to Collamore letter, August 1, 1950, Wise Papers.

44 **"I know I CAN"**: Ibid.

45 **"Why in the world"**: Block, *My Tupperware Party*, 60.

45 **"singing off the same"**: Ibid.

46 **"terminate and liquidate"**: Norman Squires to Brownie Wise memorandum, November 3, 1950, Wise Papers.

46 **"Tupperware no longer available"**: Block, *My Tupperware Party*, 65.

46 **"The business was over"**: Ibid, 66.

47 **"He feels sure"**: B. M. Cant to Brownie Wise letter, September 3, 1950. Cant was Norman Squires's secretary at Hostess.

47 **"consistent progress"**: Ibid.

48 **"No other issue"**: Brownie Wise *Go-Getter,* November 25, 1950, Wise Papers.

48 **"We must take *advantage*"**: Ibid.

49 **"I don't know"**: Wise to Squires letter, January 13, 1951, Wise Papers.

CHAPTER 5

50 **"first time in two years"**: Wise to Squires letter, January 13, 1951, Wise Papers.

50 **"Will you please"**: Ibid.

50 **"driven away the sense"**: Wise to Squires letter, February 14, 1951, Wise Papers.

50 **"needle that bit"**: Ibid.

50 **"I don't consider this"**: Wise to Squires letter, March 16, 1951, Wise Papers.

51 **"I have little reason"**: Ibid.

51 **"Most important of all"**: Ibid.

52 **"I *demand*"**: Charles Fishman, "Is the Party Over?" *Orlando Sentinel,* March 15, 1987. Fishman spoke at length with Wise for this article.

52 **"This is Brownie Wise!"**: Ibid.

52 **"anyone, anywhere"**: Ibid.

53 **"$200,000"**: Alison J. Clarke, *Tupperware: The Promise of Plastics in America* (Washington, D.C.: Smithsonian Institution Press), 93.

53 **"unlawfully dismissed him"**: Ibid.

53 **"I'm busy"**: Fishman, "Is the Party Over?"

53 **"Their relationship"**: Ibid.

53 **"On Monday"**: Brownie Wise, "Welcome Speech," Wise Papers. In this speech, Wise recounts her first meeting with Tupper and other early distributors.

54 **"I learned long ago"**: Wise to Squires letter, February 14, 1951, Wise Papers.

54 **"You talk a lot"**: Fishman, "Is the Party Over?"

55 **"Dear Tupperware Dealer"**: Earl Tupper memorandum, May 5, 1951, Tupper Papers.

56 **"hit with asthma"**: McDonald interview.

56 **"I called that doctor"**: Ibid.

57 **"Unpack your sea bag"**: Ibid.

57 **"We trusted his word"**: Block, *My Tupperware Party*, 68.

57 **"I give the man credit"**: Fishman, "Is the Party Over?"

58 **"Walking down the line"**: Brownie Wise, "The Story of Poly," undated typescript, Wise Papers.

58 **"Oh that?"**: Ibid.

58 **"It just stopped me"**: Ibid.

59 **"From this"**: Ibid.

59 **"Just get your fingers"**: Brownie Wise speech to Tupperware dealers in Detroit, 1951, Wise Papers. This is believed to be her first speech to dealers in a managerial role at the new Tupperware Home Parties division.

59 **"Sometime I hope"**: Ibid.

60 **"It's a new day"**: Ibid.

60 **"service representatives"**: Ibid.

60 **"Are you yourself?"**: Ibid.

60 **"When you make"**: Ibid.

60 **"We are not building"**: Ibid.

60 **"Well, 99% perfect"**: Brownie Wise, "This Is the Story of Tupperware," Wise Papers.

61 **"must make"**: Tupperware ad in *Salesman's Opportunity*, November 1951, Wise Papers.

61 **"editor, writer"**: Wise, "Story of Tupperware," Wise Papers.

61 **"First came"**: Brownie Wise, *Tupperware Sparks* 1, no. 1 (November 1951).

61 **"We were urging him"**: McDonald interview.

63 **"It's in what is known"**: Wise to Tupper letter, January 1, 1952, Wise Papers. This letter details the land Wise hoped Tupper would purchase and confirms Orlando was not her first choice of locales.

64 **"Very nice!"**: Ibid.

64 **"If you want"**: Fishman, "Is the Party Over?"

64 **"*PLEASE* don't make a deal"**: Wise to Tupper letter, January 1, 1952, Wise Papers.

66 **"The state is swarming"**: Hal Boyle, "Glowing Picture of Florida Painted by Hal Boyle," *Orlando Sentinel*, January 28, 1952.

66 **"Mrs. Tate was"**: Emily Langer, "Anna Tate, D.C. Area Tupperware Maven . . ." *Washington Post*, March 20, 2013.

67 **"new pioneers"**: Boyle, "Glowing Picture."

67 **"Florida is a land"**: Ibid.

CHAPTER 6

68 **"These distributors"**: Wise to Tupper letter, January 1, 1952, Wise Papers.

68 **"One sour apple"**: Ibid.

69 **"the most complete"**: Wise, "Story of Tupperware," Wise Papers.

69 **"We were riddled"**: Block, *My Tupperware Party*, 73.

69 **"I have been watching"**: Ibid, 75.

69 **"It's not sitting"**: Ibid.

69 **"I could understand"**: Ibid.

70 **"Have a pleasant trip"**: Wise to Tupper letter, January 1, 1952, Wise Papers.

70 MILLION DOLLAR: "Million Dollar Plastic Firm to Come Here," *Orlando Morning Sentinel-Star*, January 2, 1952.

70 **"The organization"**: Ibid.

71 **"I was supervising"**: McDonald interview.

71 **" 'He didn't fire ya?' "**: Ibid.

72 **The judge heard the story**: Ibid.

72 **"We were so relieved"**: Ibid.

73 PLASTIC FIRM OFFICIAL: "Plastic Firm Official Spreads City's Fame," *Orlando Evening Star*, January 24, 1952.

73 **"Like Tupperware Home Parties"**: Ibid.

74 **"I never knew"**: McDonald interview.

74 **"I had the run"**: Jerry Wise interview.

74 **"There was no guard"**: Ibid.

74 TUPPERWARE-ORLANDO!: Wise, *Tupperware Sparks* 1, no. 2 (January 1952).

74 **"So, we started"**: Ibid.

75 **"Tupperware Lady"**: Brownie Wise early Tupperware training manual, Wise Papers.

75 **"She must be willing"**: Ibid.

76 **"outstanding ability"**: Ibid.

77 **"The expense of paying"**: Ibid.

77 **"You aren't looking"**: Ibid

77 **"Pull out that"**: Brownie Wise, "Just between YOU and ME," Memo February 27, 1952, Wise Papers.

78 **"Just a little line"**: Tupper to Wise handwritten note, February 29, 1952, Wise Papers.

78 **"I want to use it"**: Wise to Tupper memorandum, February 27, 1952, Wise Papers.

78 **"the big wheel"**: Wise to Tupper memorandum, March 12, 1952, Wise Papers.

78 **"Believe me"**: Ibid.

80 **"Now the swaddling clothes"**: *Tupperware Sparks* 2, no. 4 (April 1952).

80 **"I've just opened"**: Tupper to Wise handwritten note, April 7, 1952, Wise Papers.

81 **"You will be shown"**: *Tupperware Sparks* 2, no. 5 (May 1952).

82 **"First, I hope"**: Brownie Wise to Russell Bassett, letter, May 2, 1952, Wise Papers. This letter shows how Wise puts the responsibility for an early distributor's struggles entirely on him.

82 **"We have not received"**: Ibid.

82 **"The average home demonstrator"**: Wise to Tupper memorandum, May 9, 1952, Wise Papers. Memo shows Wise's willingness to contradict Tupper edicts especially on sales matters.

83 **"I cannot agree with you"**: Ibid.

83 **"I feel we're just on"**: Ibid.

84 **"feeding or watering"**: Earl Tupper to Brownie Wise sketch, May 4, 1952, Wise Papers.

84 **"The Madness of Genius"**: Tupper to Wise memorandum, May 15, 1952, Wise Papers.

84 **"his holdings"**: Frank Klein, "Bronson Holdings Are the Largest in Osceola," *Orlando Sentinel-Star*, March 12, 1952.

85 **"Tupper, true to his own style"**: McDonald interview.

86 **"The work on headquarters"**: *Tupperware Sparks* 2, no. 6 (June–July 1952).

86 **"To a Star Distributor"**: Ibid.

86 **"We've got millions"**: Block, *My Tupperware Party*, 78.

86 **"When I sat down"**: Ibid.

86 **"It was on that night"**: Ibid.

87 **"The Poly Sales family"**: *Tupperware Sparks* (June–July 1952).

87 **"It is a source of sincere"**: Brownie Wise, "Talk for July Conference," July 1952, Wise Papers.

88 **"for general cooperation"**: *Tupperware Sparks* (June–July 1952).

88 **"Brownie has kept me"**: Earl Tupper to Robert Evans memorandum, August 4, 1952. Important memorandum that shows Tupper's confidence in Wise—particularly to Evans, with whom Wise clashed early on.

88 **"I'm happy"**: Ibid.

88 **"Believe me"**: Ibid.

88 **"The vacant stare"**: Brownie Wise, "Memo to all Distributors and Sub-Distributors," August 15, 1952, Wise Papers.

89 **"It is, shall we say"**: Brownie Wise, "Speech to the Orlando Chamber of Commerce," August 1952, Wise Papers.

89 **"sensational"**: *Tupperware Sparks* 2, no. 9 (September 1952).

89 **"I had the smallest"**: Ibid.

90 **"queen of the week"**: Ibid.

90 **"Hitch your wagon"**: Ibid.

90 **"When we saw"**: Block, *My Tupperware Party,* 86.

90 **"In spite of your absence"**: Thomas Damigella to Earl Tupper, November 10, 1952, Tupper Papers. The Damigellas are a founding Tupperware distributorship and also credited among the first to use home parties.

91 **"hick town"**: McDonald interview.

91 **"it was all you could see"**: Jerry Wise interview.

CHAPTER 7

92 **"like a rifle"**: McDonald interview.

93 **"We now have our roots"**: Brownie Wise, "Opening Talk January Conference," January 1953, Wise Papers.

93 **"eight spacious rooms"**: "Tupperware Purchases House on Lake," *Kissimmee Gazette,* September 14, 1952.

93 **"Gators"**: Jerry Wise interview.

94 **"Good Lord"**: Ibid.

94 **"He studied"**: Wise, "Story of Tupperware," Wise Papers.

95 **"mostly to get rid"**: Elsie Mortland, interview by the author, Kissimmee, Florida, March 8, 2005 (hereafter referred to as Mortland interview). Mortland was the first hostess demonstrator for Tupperware Home Parties.

95 **"they would almost melt"**: Ibid.

95 "that's when": Ibid.

95 "I remember one": Ibid.

95 " 'I want a set' ": Ibid.

95 "No women": Ibid.

96 "How a Typical": "How a Typical Homemaker Learned the Secret That Can DOUBLE Your Family Income," *Salesman's Opportunity,* March 1953.

96 "her top-flight success": Ibid.

96 "[Sterhan] began": Ibid.

97 "sales talk": Ibid.

97 "packed and unpacked": Ibid.

97 "All you have to do": Ibid.

98 "Fellow Workers": Tupper memorandum, February 5, 1953, Tupper Papers.

98 "From what you have seen": Ibid.

98 "That means you": Ibid.

98 "The qualifications": *Tupperware Sparks* (December 1952–January 1953).

98 "I was in heaven!": *Tupperware Sparks* (June 1953).

98 "thundering announcement": Wise, "Story of Tupperware," Wise Papers.

99 "double-in-the-last-half": *Tupperware Sparks* (February 1953).

99 "There are outstanding": Wise, "Opening talk January Conference," January 1953, Wise Papers.

99 "The first step": Ibid.

99 "full blast": *Tupperware Sparks* (March 1953).

99 "ear splitting blasts": Ibid.

99 "specially-designed": Ibid.

100 "giant *cocos*": Ibid.

100 "music to our ears": Ibid.

100 "Upon receipt": Block, *My Tupperware Party,* 71.

101 "Our concern": Ibid.

101 "I'm sorry": Ibid.

101 "Nobody can help you": Ibid, 72.

101 "Tell her": Ibid.

101 "Don't do that": Ibid.

101 **"Is it true"**: Ibid.

102 **"The mural"**: "Tupperware Commissions Huge Mural," *Kissimmee Gazette*, May 15, 1953.

103 **"It's just one of the ways"**: Brownie Wise, Art Fund Questionnaire, January 31, 1953, Wise Papers.

103 **"paying for our room"**: Jerry Wise interview.

104 **"A Verse"**: Tupper to Wise birthday card, May 25, 1953, Wise Papers.

105 **"golden" Palomino**: Jerry Wise interview.

105 **"I don't like"**: Ibid.

105 **"That was the only place"**: Ibid.

106 **"It was interesting"**: Ibid.

106 **"She wanted everyone"**: Ibid.

106 **"And don't throw it"**: Ibid.

106 **"Both symbolic of enduring perfection"**: *Tupperware Sparks* (July–August 1953).

106 **"ideas for dishes"**: Wise, "Story of Tupperware," Wise Papers.

106 **"palatial home"**: "Tupperware Distributors in Conference Here," *Kissimmee Gazette*, June 30, 1953.

107 **"Our Place"**: *Tupperware Sparks* (July–August, 1953).

107 **"100,000 miles"**: Ibid.

107 **"Our ties"**: Wise to Tupper memorandum, November 11, 1953, Wise Papers.

108 **"I have the feeling"**: Ibid.

109 **"My knees"**: Ibid.

109 **"I believe"**: Wise to Tupper memorandum, October 23, 1953, Wise Papers.

110 **"We're having"**: Press Party Invitation, Wise Papers.

110 **"Uncle Fud"**: "Dorothy Shea at the Maisonette," www.Craigsbigbands andbignames.com.

110 **"the Park Avenue Hillbilly"**: Ibid.

110 **"The setting"**: Wise to Tupper memorandum, October 27, 1953, Wise Papers.

111 **"a mere woman"**: Ibid.

111 **"undoubtedly the most"**: Ibid.

112 **"They made a case"**: McDonald interview.

112 **"the *woman* who's the leader"**: Ibid.

112 **"We agreed"**: Ibid.

112 **Earl Tupper himself signed off:** Ibid.

113 **Wise typed:** Wise to Tupper memorandum, November 21, 1953, Wise Papers.

113 **"If this company":** Ibid.

113 **"If you intend":** Ibid.

113 **"This is so serious":** Ibid.

113 **"We have at this time":** Ibid.

113 **"I think it is time":** Ibid.

114 **"And then":** Ibid.

114 **"Not on your life!":** Block, *My Tupperware Party*, 118.

114 **"I stopped":** Wise, "Story of Tupperware," Wise Papers.

114 **"Telegrams":** *Tupperware Sparks* (April-May 1954).

CHAPTER 8

115 **"Dealers and managers":** *Tupperware Sparks* (April-May 1954).

116 **"During those marathons":** Block, *My Tupperware Party*, 118.

116 **"It was an excellent":** Ibid.

116 **"Accredited Tupperware Manager":** Wise, "Story of Tupperware," Wise Papers.

116 **"Organ music":** "Tupperware Ends Homecoming Here," *Kissimmee Gazette*, April 16, 1954.

117 **"Emotion is the high-octane fuel":** *Business Week*, April 17, 1954.

117 **"It is the responsibility":** Brownie Wise to Rose Humphrey letter, January 16, 1954, Wise Papers.

117 **"To make Tupperware":** Wise, "Story of Tupperware," Wise Papers.

117 **"dug their overcoats":** Ibid.

117 **"That's manufacturing":** McDonald interview.

118 **"it was very easy":** Ibid.

119 **"We'd be out there":** Ibid.

119 **"We talked about the 'pilgrimage'":** Ibid.

119 **"freezer units":** "Tupperware Set for Big Celebration" *Kissimmee Gazette*, April 2, 1954.

120 **"Mrs. Wise has led":** Ibid.

121 **"It is a time":** Brownie Wise, "Welcome" speech, 1954, Wise Papers.

121 **"90% of them women":** "Life Goes on a Big Dig," *Life*, May 3, 1954.

122 **"I love everybody":** Ibid.

123 **"They dug the lake"**: McDonald interview.

123 **"raised a crop"**: "Life Goes on a Big Dig."

123 **"Brownie Wise, brilliant chief"**: "Tupperware Makes *Life*," *Kissimmee Gazette*, April 30, 1954.

124 **"If we build"**: *Business Week*, April 17, 1954.

124 **"Prophet in Plastic"**: Ibid.

125 **"She's the greatest"**: Ibid.

125 **"There's an alligator"**: Ibid.

125 **"Everything from a Dale Carnegie"**: Ibid.

125 **"safety valve"**: Ibid.

126 **"I've got that Tupper feeling"**: *Business Week*, April 17, 1954.

126 **"I am glad"**: Brownie Wise, *"Ad Astra,"* Wise Papers.

126 **"reaching to the stars"**: Ibid.

126 **"the stars have always been"**: Ibid.

127 **"*Live* this day"**: Ibid.

127 **"When Brownie Wise"**: *Business Week*, April 17, 1954.

128 **"When she was"**: McDonald interview.

CHAPTER 9

129 **"Nominally"**: *Business Week*, April 17, 1954. The article minimized Tupper's role in his own company.

129 **"hugging his baby"**: McDonald interview.

129 **"Thanks for the pictures"**: Tupper to Wise memorandum, June 1, 1954.

130 **"We were very"**: "5,000 Attend Tupper Open House Sunday," *Kissimmee Gazette*, May 7, 1954.

131 **"She was quite"**: Mortland interview.

131 **"After my mother died"**: Former secretary to Brownie Wise, telephone interview by the author, July 18, 2005 (hereafter cited as Wise former secretary interview). This former employee asked not to be named.

131 **"the most outstanding"**: *Tupperware Sparks* (September 1954).

131 **"I thought it was sensational"**: McDonald interview.

132 **"The article attracted"**: Wise, "Story of Tupperware."

132 **"remind you at all times"**: *Tupperware Sparks* (September 1954).

132 **"Will you have had a part"**: Ibid.

132 **"Would any of these"**: Wise, "Story of Tupperware."

133 **"That was a mess"**: Jerry Wise interview.

133 **"I want the *real*"**: Ibid.

133 **"We're 20,000 strong!"**: *Tupperware Sparks* (October-November 1954). It should be noted the number of Tupperware dealers varied greatly during this time period and claims about dealer numbers were difficult to verify.

134 **"tabulating systems specialist"**: Wise, "Story of Tupperware."

134 **"These magic machines"**: Ibid

135 **"The year 1954"**: *Tupperware Sparks* (December 1954).

135 **"Great things"**: Ibid.

CHAPTER 10

136 **"Mr. Esty"**: Jerry Wise interview.

136 **"in the big front room"**: Ibid.

137 **"She wasn't afraid of him at all"**: Ibid.

137 **"*Woman?*"**: Ibid.

137 **"He loved Jaguars"**: Ibid.

138 **"I always wanted"**: Ibid

138 **"I'm thinking"**: Ibid.

138 **"He met me"**: Tony Ponticelli, early Tupperware special events director, interview by author, Maitland, Florida, September 29, 2005 (hereafter referred to as Ponticelli interview).

139 **"These are way-out"**: Ibid.

139 **"I was converted"**: Ibid.

139 **"In viewing her"**: Ibid

139 **"She struck me"**: Ibid

140 **"You just never knew when"**: Jerry Wise interview.

140 **"Your dad's in jail here"**: Ibid.

140 **"I went through his car"**: Ibid.

140 **"I don't think he belongs"**: Don Hinton interview with the author, Deltona, Florida (hereafter referred to as Hinton interview).

140 **"We assumed"**: Ibid.

141 **"My dad"**: Jerry Wise interview.

142 **"A trim, brown-eyed ex-secretary"**: Obermeyer, "What a Woman!" *Orlando Sentinel Florida* magazine, January 9, 1955.

142 **"Famous people"**: Ibid.

143 **"Brownie's title"**: Ibid.

144 **"It was our idea"**: Hinton interview.

144 **"On magazine stands"**: Wise, "Story of Tupperware."

145 **"What a relief"**: Block, *My Tupperware Party*, 88.

145 **"urgent"**: Ibid.

145 **"Tupperware Home Parties"**: Ibid.

146 **"a number of derogatory statements"**: Brownie Wise, "An Open Letter to Tupperware Distributors and Dealers," August 21, 1955, Wise Papers.

146 **"It is not good"**: Tupper to Wise confidential memorandum, September 21, 1955, Wise Papers.

146 **"Every day"**: Wise, letter to distributors and dealers, August 21, 1955.

147 **"a friend who had a friend"**: McDonald interview.

147 **"When we had that recorder"**: Ibid.

147 **"ringleader"**: Hinton interview. Both Hinton and McDonald confirm the bugging efforts to determine which distributors were trying to unionize.

147 **"You are the organization"**: Wise letter to distributors and dealers, August 21, 1955.

147 **"Fortunately"**: McDonald interview.

148 **"Seven men"**: Ibid.

148 **"My grief"**: Ibid.

148 **"We desperately"**: Ibid.

148 **"He thought he could take"**: Hinton interview.

149 **"After the Tupperware crew"**: Block, *My Tupperware Party*, 26.

149 **"I'm not gloating"**: Wise to Tupper memorandum, May 27, 1957, Wise Papers.

149 **"fight got pretty dirty"**: Ibid.

149 **"ultimatum"**: Ibid.

150 **"What she was doing"**: Ibid.

150 **"When she would go out"**: Ibid.

150 **"I'm afraid"**: Kay Tilden to Brownie Wise letter, March 1, 1958, Wise Papers.

150 **"Tupperware children"**: Notie Baumgardner to Brownie Wise letter, December 2, 1957, Wise Papers.

151 **"So the big week came"**: Ibid.

151 **"Thanks to Tupperware"**: Irene Swan to Brownie Wise letter, December 22 (year unknown), Wise Papers.

151 **"It's all over lace"**: Ibid.

151 **"Mrs. Wise is a party giver"**: "Tupperware Article in March Coronet," *Kissimmee Gazette,* February 25, 1955.

152 **"It is all too rare"**: "Tupperware Plans Larger Museum," *Kissimmee Gazette,* May 20, 1955.

152 **"The success"**: Brownie Wise, "Welcome Address," April 1955, Wise Papers.

152 **"How near we always are"**: Ibid.

153 **"Fill your mind"**: "Dr. Peale Is Speaker at Tupperware Jubilee," *Kissimmee Gazette,* April 12, 1955.

154 **"fellow workers"**: Earl Tupper, "Dear Fellow Workers and Family," memorandum, July 19, 1955, Tupper Papers.

154 **"We are not bragging"**: Ibid.

155 **"We knew all"**: Wise to Tupper memorandum, May 27, 1957, Wise Papers.

155 **"There was intense pressure"**: Ibid.

155 **"It simply didn't make sense"**: Ibid.

CHAPTER 11

156 **"*That* was motivation"**: Pat Jordan, interview by the author, Orlando, Florida, April 4, 2005 (hereafter cited as Jordan interview). Jordan was an early South Florida dealer who went on to distributorships in Norfolk and Orlando.

157 **"She said, 'I'm sorry Pat"**: Ibid.

157 **In return for shelling out**: Ibid.

157 **"You know"**: Ibid.

157 **"Jean was a teacher"**: Ibid.

158 **"I used to do"**: Ibid.

158 **"Then I got pregnant"**: Ibid.

158 **"I begged"**: Ibid.

159 **"I would look at her"**: Ibid.

159 **"I'd like to bring my husband"**: Ibid.

160 **"What if you could be"**: Ibid.

160 **"a sense of family"**: Mortland interview.

160 **"He had to be very careful"**: Ibid.

160 **"He had them sealed"**: Ibid.

160 **"If I had any"**: Ibid.

161 **"the coup de grâce"**: McDonald interview.

161 **"You talk about"**: Jordan interview.

161 **"They tore the sleeves"**: McDonald interview.

162 **"That's why"**: Ibid.

162 **"It takes an executive"**: Ponticelli interview.

162 **"I was impressed"**: Hinton interview.

162 **"totally hands-off"**: McDonald interview.

CHAPTER 12

163 **"The discovery"**: "Women at Work, Business Finds They're People Too," *Newsweek*, February 27, 1956.

164 **"Men resented"**: Wise former secretary interview.

164 **"She cut him down"**: Jerry Wise interview.

164 **"Like he had a post"**: Ibid.

164 **"started believing"**: Marylin Menello, interview by author, Winter Park, Florida, January 27, 2006. (Hereafter cited as Menello interview.) Menello was Hamer Wilson's ex-wife.

164 **"I'm listening"**: Ponticelli interview.

165 **"I'm not sure I know"**: McDonald interview.

165 **"I have christened it"**: Wise, *Best Wishes* (Orlando, FL: Podium, 1957), 169.

165 **"Lightning streaks"**: Ibid.

166 **"It is my special"**: Wise, *Best Wishes*, 169.

166 **"cool while the rest"**: "50 Most Important Floridians of the 20th Century," *Lakeland Ledger*, 1998.

167 **"Outstanding achievements"**: *Tupperware Sparks* (May 1956).

167 **"You'll thrill again"**: Ibid.

168 **"They wanted it to look"**: Jerry Wise interview.

168 **"She said, 'Don't you know'"**: Ibid.

169 **"You don't just buy"**: Wise, *Best Wishes*, 164.

170 **"It has been estimated"**: Hill, "Women Now Coming in to Own in Business World," *Houston Post*, November 6, 1956.

171 **"If dreams were for sale"**: THP questionnaire to dealers, Wise Papers.

172 **"costumed gentry"**: "Mrs. Wise Endorses Reserve Plan: Giving Two Sons to the Army," *Kissimmee Gazette*, June 22, 1956.

172 **"Two women"**: Kauch, "Brownie Creates Magic with Treasurama," *Orlando Sentinel*, July 1, 1956.

172 **"Tupperware people"**: Brownie Wise, "Welcome Home" speech, July 1956, Wise Papers.

172 **"We *need* work"**: Ibid.

173 **"In the Unity"**: Clarke, *Tupperware*, 146.

173 **"I need more room"**: "Kaltenborn, Rudy Vallee Entertain at Tupperware Jubilee," *Kissimmee Gazette*, July 6, 1956.

174 **"The pond had to be deepened"**: Jerry Wise interview.

174 **"I thought wow"**: Jordan interview.

174 **"I reached my goal"**: *Tupperware Sparks* (July 1956).

175 **"Bobby is 4"**: Lavon Weber to Brownie Wise letter, December 6, 1957, Wise Papers.

175 **"You would laugh"**: Jordan interview.

175 **"I remember taking"**: Ibid.

175 **"most successful jubilee"**: *Tupperware Sparks* (July 1956).

175 **"Tiny lights"**: Ibid.

176 **"the biggest training program"**: *Tupperware Sparks* (September 1956).

176 **"the housewife's dream"**: Don Hinton, "Mrs. Wise Is Extended High Honor," *Kissimmee Gazette*, October 26, 1956.

176 **"Being one"**: Ibid.

176 **"Put your wishes"**: Hinton, "Mrs. Brownie Wise Is Extended High Honor."

177 **"If [a piece]"**: McDonald interview.

177 **"real settling down"**: Ibid.

177 **"This was perhaps"**: Ibid.

177 **"You could almost *see*"**: Ibid.

177 **"We did everything"**: Ibid.

178 **"Through the step-by-step"**: Ibid.

178 **"Believe me"**: Ibid.

179 **"Our customers"**: Wise to Tupper memorandum, November 21, 1953, Wise Papers.

179 **"I made telephone calls"**: Wise to Tupper memorandum, May 27, 1957, Wise Papers.

CHAPTER 13

181 **"I BELIEVE"**: Wise to Tupper memorandum, May 27, 1957, Wise Papers.

182 **"a superiority complex"**: Ibid.

182 **"he was making"**: Ibid.

182 **"We haven't lost"**: Ibid.

183 **"Some are inspiring"**: Max Norris, "Culture Comes to the City but the City Won't Come to the Culture," *Kissimmee Gazette*, January 25, 1957.

183 **"for each dealer"**: *Tupperware Sparks* (January 1957).

183 **"She talked to some people"**: Fred DeWitt, interview by author, Winter Park, Florida, August 15, 2005 (hereafter cited as DeWitt interview). DeWitt was a freelance photographer for Wise and Tupperware.

183 **"She seemed very tired"**: Ibid.

183 **"I was expecting"**: Jon Whitcomb, "Sunshine Cinderella," *Cosmopolitan*, April 1957.

184 **"one hundred different sizes"**: Ibid.

184 **"Show us how"**: Ibid.

184 **"The boss sits"**: Ibid.

185 **"Wishing"**: Ibid.

185 **"We floated"**: Ibid.

185 **"our most famous"**: "April Cosmopolitan Has Local Features," *Kissimmee Gazette*, undated clipping, Wise Papers.

186 **"With a heart"**: "Brownie Gives Royalties to Heart Fund," *Kissimmee Gazette*, undated clipping, Wise Papers.

186 **"Beginning with a handful,"**: "Brownie's Book Is Proving Popular," *Kissimmee Gazette*, undated clipping, Wise Papers.

186 **"because I wanted"**: Ibid.

186 **"disconnected and disappointing"**: Wise to Tupper memorandum, May 26, 1957, Wise Papers.

186 **Wise decided to pay Froman**: Legal document outlining Wise settlement with writer Robert Froman, Wise Papers.

186 **"The book does not have"**: Wise to Tupper memorandum, May 26, 1957, Wise Papers.

187 **"Nor have you seen fit"**: Tupper to Wise memorandum, April 29, 1957, Wise Papers.

187 **"NO ONE"**: Wise to Tupper memorandum, May 26, 1957, Wise Papers.

187 **"I wanted to have a copy"**: Ibid.

187 **"THAT CONSTITUTES"**: Ibid.

187 **"Did you have in mind"**: Ibid.

188 **"I appreciate"**: Mrs. Franklin D. Roosevelt to Brownie Wise letter, May 20, 1957.

188 **"Believe me"**: Wise, *Best Wishes*, 17.

188 **"If you have set"**: Ibid.

189 **"She loves people"**: Dr. Norman Vincent Peale, foreword to *Best Wishes*.

189 **"good will and joy"**: Ibid.

189 **"edgy and irascible"**: Brownie Wise letter to attorney Lawrence Rogers, May 30, 1958, Wise Papers.

189 **"She just considered"**: Mortland interview.

189 **"doubt was creeping in"**: Ponticelli interview.

190 **"I should explain first"**: Wise to Tupper memorandum, May 27, 1957, Wise Papers.

190 **"I am still amazed"**: Ibid.

190 **"We have had the singular"**: Ibid.

191 **"I'm told that"**: Ibid.

191 **"I miss talking"**: Ibid.

191 **"My love for you"**: Wise handwritten note to mark her son's nineteenth birthday, Wise Papers.

192 **"You can't take"**: Ponticelli interview.

CHAPTER 14

193 **"If we move quickly"**: Tupper to Wise memorandum, May 17, 1957, Wise Papers.

193 **"At the time"**: Wise to Tupper memorandum, May 27, 1957, Wise Papers.

193 **"After all this time"**: Ibid.

194 **"Around the World"**: "Tupperware Turned in to World in Miniature," *Kissimmee Gazette*, June 28, 1957.

194 **"If any of them"**: Ibid.

195 **"The Tupperware crowd"**: "Hawaiian Luau Is Highlight of Party," *Kissimmee Gazette*, July 4, 1957.

195 **"Distributors, costumed with the wings"**: Ibid.

195 **"Pay me ten bucks"**: Ibid.

197 **"The storm was well away"**: Deposition of Hamer Wilson, September 15, 1959, *Croxton, Boyd, Boyd and Rector v. Tupper, Rexall, Tupper Corp and Tupperware Home Parties Richard Fletcher and William Herrin*, Ninth Judicial Circuit Osceola County, Florida. (Hereafter

depositions in this case will be cited only with the name of person deposed.)

198 **"Isn't it wonderful?"**: "Hawaiian Luau Is Highlight of Party."

199 **"Nobody wanted to go home"**: Jack McCollum, interview by author, Saint Cloud, Florida, July 17, 2005 (hereafter cited as McCollum interview). McCollum was Tupperware's unofficial photographer for years.

199 **"power squad"**: Ibid.

199 **"At first they were anxious"**: Wilson deposition.

200 **"We contemplated"**: Gary McDonald deposition, September 11, 1959.

200 **"I think she was concerned"**: McCollum interview.

200 **"The people were crowding"**: William Boyd deposition, September 11, 1959. Boyd was one of the boat drivers during the luau.

200 **"We could see some lights"**: Glen Bump deposition, September 15, 1959. Bump was a member of the Tupperware Public Relations Department.

201 **"run it blind"**: Thelma Croxton deposition, September 8, 1959. Croxton's husband was a boat driver during a collision on Lake Toho.

201 **"I needed her eyes"**: Gerald Croxton deposition, September 8, 1959. Croxton was a victim of a boat collision.

201 **"I tried to go with it"**: Ibid.

201 **"I remember him"**: Ibid.

201 **"a sudden flash of lightning"**: Boyd deposition.

201 **"I just held him up"**: Ibid.

202 **"He had a puncture wound"**: Dr. M. L. Jewell deposition, October 7, 1960. Jewell triaged boat accident victims and also attended the luau.

202 **"You could hear all this crashing"**: Jerry Wise interview.

203 **"We did everything we could"**: McDonald interview.

203 **"These are individuals"**: Ibid.

203 **"Those were bad times"**: Jerry Wise interview.

203 **"She wouldn't admit"**: Ponticelli interview.

203 **"She wanted to sweep it"**: Mortland interview.

204 **"We would appreciate if"**: McDonald interview.

204 **"non-alcoholic" punch**: "Hawaiian Luau Is Highlight of Party."

205 **"*TO OUR FRIENDS*"**: Advertisment, *Kissimmee Gazette*, July 8, 1957.

205 **"We were good"**: McDonald interview.

206 **"You see the foolish things"**: Mortland interview.

CHAPTER 15

207 **"He was very, very suspicious"**: Ed Crieger handwritten memoir, Tupper Papers.

207 **"He was jealous"**: Hinton interview.

207 **"You may feel"**: Tupper to Wise memorandum, November 23, 1957, Tupper Papers.

207 **"all liability risks"**: Ibid.

207 **"If I had died"**: Earl Tupper, "History of Tupperware," Tupper Papers. This typescript offers Tupper's own account of his company's history. There is no mention of Wise.

208 **"after much dissension"**: Wise to Rogers letter, May 31, 1958.

208 **"He was edgy"**: Ibid.

208 **"He was not at all"**: Ibid.

209 **"hairpins and Kleenex"**: McDonald interview.

209 **The suits also alleged**: *Croxton v. Tupper et al,* Circuit Court of the Ninth Judicial Circuit for Osceola County.

209 **"a great decline"**: *Boyd v. Tupper et al.*

209 **"to keep their guests"**: Ibid.

210 **"Tupper has had"**: Wise to Rogers letter, May 31, 1958.

210 **"his attitude was strange"**: Ibid.

210 **"He was not actually"**: Ibid.

211 **"I believe that"**: Tupper to Wise memorandum, Wise Papers, November 12, 1957.

211 **"a deep personal interest"**: Tupper to Wise memorandum, November 8, 1957, Wise Papers.

211 **going to fall just short**: Wise to Tupper memorandum, Wise Papers, November 16, 1957.

211 **"Wind-Up week"**: Ibid.

211 **"We're pulling out all the stops"**: Ibid.

211 **"sober re-evaluation"**: Wise to Tupper memorandum, December 20, 1957, Wise Papers.

212 **"standard operating procedures"**: Ibid.

212 **"You spoke of sales *management*"**: Ibid.

212 **"We have long felt"**: Ibid.

212 **"Earl was either"**: Creiger, handwritten memoir, Tupper Papers.

213 **"we are greatly concerned"**: Wise to Tupper memorandum, December 20, 1957, Wise Papers.

213 **"I said to myself"**: Ponticelli interview.

213 **"We would have to go on"**: McDonald interview.

214 **"She said to me"**: Ponticelli interview.

214 **"I'm going to fire him"**: Ibid.

215 **"Tupperware Parties Inc."**: Tupper to Wise memorandum, December 31, 1957, Wise Papers.

215 **"This is a personal"**: Ibid.

215 **"I'm looking forward"**: Ibid.

216 **"P.S. Let's go!"**: Ibid.

216 **"This letter is about"**: Wise to Tupper memorandum, Wise Papers, January 5, 1958.

216 **"Please look at the facts"**: Ibid.

217 **"Look back"**: Ibid.

217 **"I felt from the very beginning"**: Ibid.

217 **"I take strong exception"**: Ibid.

CHAPTER 16

219 **"My first concern"**: Tupper to Wise undated telegram (likely early 1958), Wise Papers.

219 **"He said that it might"**: Brownie Wise letter to Rogers, May 31, 1958, Wise Papers.

219 **no decision was made**: Ibid.

219 **"I tried to bring him back"**: Ibid.

220 **Upon arriving**: Creiger, handwritten memoir, Tupper Papers.

221 **"I said, 'You gotta understand'"**: McDonald interview.

221 **"I said, 'Their life is built around Tupperware'"**: Ibid.

221 **"That's what your first job is going to be"**: Ibid.

222 **"an inactive part"**: Wise to Tupper memorandum, February 25, 1958, Wise Papers.

222 **"semi-retirement"**: Ibid.

222 **"I'm going home"**: Neil Osterweil, handwritten notes detailing the timeline of events surrounding Wise's dismissal, Tupper Papers.

222 **"Tupper said I'm fired"**: Laurie Khan-Levitt, *Tupperware! The American Experience*, PBS, 2004.

223 **"Dear Mrs. Wise"**: Tupper to Wise letter, January 30, 1958. This letter, detailing Wise's removal, is believed to be the last correspondence from Tupper to Wise.

223 **"He couldn't"**: Creiger, handwritten memoir, Tupper Papers.

223 **"You're either with me"**: McDonald interview.

223 **"I'm with Brownie"**: Ibid.

223 **"He looked like"**: Mortland interview.

224 **"I felt"**: McDonald interview.

224 **"Well, this is the day"**: Brownie Wise, *Tupperware Spark O Gram*, February 1, 1958, Wise Papers.

225 **"Brownie Wise Goes into Semi-Retirement"**: Tupperware Press Release, February 3, 1958, Wise Papers.

226 **"render herself available"**: "Employment Contract," page 2, section 2, subsection c, Wise Papers (hereafter cited as *Contract*). The dispute over this contract led to Wise being let go from Tupperware.

226 **"an important part"**: Ibid.

226 **"The Employee"**: Ibid.

227 **"paragraph 3b"**: Ibid.

227 **"This contract bears"**: Wise to Tupper memorandum, February 25, 1958, Wise Papers.

227 **"It was quite specific"**: Ibid.

228 **"not associated"**: Brownie Wise, written response to Seraphine audit, Wise Papers.

228 **A more legitimate**: Ibid.

228 **"I would argue"**: Ponticelli interview.

228 **"The position"**: Overstreet to Rogers letter, March 7, 1958, Wise Papers. Letter between attorneys detailing the end of Wise's employment at Tupperware.

228 **"We have to move"**: Jerry Wise interview.

229 **"boycotted and blacklisted"**: *Wise v. Tupper et al*, Circuit Court for the Ninth Judicial Circuit of Florida, Osceola County, Florida (hereafter cited as Wise lawsuit). This was the $1.6 million suit against Tupper and others on THP's executive staff, including Wilson and her one-time protegé Gary McDonald.

229 **"accused of embezzlement"**: Ibid.

229 **"I was shocked"**: Earl Tupper to Don Hinton et al memorandum, June 7, 1958, Tupper Papers.

229 **"This has been"**: Wise to Rogers letter, May 17, 1958, Wise Papers.

229 **"The most serious"**: Ibid.

230 **"It wasn't until later"**: McDonald interview.

231 **"just because"**: Ibid.

231 **"You couldn't mention"**: Hinton interview.

231 **"I am getting"**: Tupper to Wilson and McDonald memorandum, Tupper Papers.

231 **"new type"**: Ibid.

232 **"I was quite concerned"**: Nellie Stewart, Jasonville, Indiana, Tupperware dealer, to Brownie Wise letter, August 21, 1958, Wise Papers.

CHAPTER 17

233 **"the rivers and lakes"**: "Brownie Wise Sees Future Here," *Kissimmee Gazette*, February 3, 1958.

233 **"Hearthside Home"**: "First New Home Is Sold at Brownie Wise Developments," *Kissimmee Gazette*, February 7, 1958.

234 **"We gave copies"**: McDonald interview.

235 **"I didn't have"**: Mortland interview.

235 **"I said, 'Hello, Brownie,'"**: Ibid.

235 **"surrender themselves"**: Brownie Wise, *"Tupperware Is the Way,"* undated speech, Wise Papers.

235 **"I think she had"**: Mortland interview.

235 **"This group"**: McDonald interview.

236 **"I lost it"**: Ibid.

236 **"boy wonder"**: "Justin Whitlock Dart," biography, www.Answers.com.

236 **"I want you guys to know"**: McDonald interview.

236 **"You've gotta get overseas"**: Ibid.

237 **"This thing is going to blow up"**: Fishman, "Is the Party Over?"

237 **"In addition"**: Tupperware press release, September 30, 1958, Tupper Papers.

237 **"The development program"**: Ibid.

237 **"I had 7 million"**: Earl Tupper, "History of Tupperware," Tupper Papers.

237 **"sacrifice price"**: Ibid.

238 **"rapid growth"**: "Cinderella Shows Very Rapid Growth" *Kissimmee Gazette*, November 21, 1958.

238 **"Florida's Flying Cinderella"**: "Executives Fly to Sales Meetings," *Kissimmee Gazette*, August 1, 1958.

239 **"restless"**: Tupper, "History of Tupperware" Tupper Papers.

239 **He divorced his wife**: Creiger, handwritten memoir, Tupper Papers.

239 **"I feel that"**: Earl Tupper, "Renunciation," Tupper Papers.

240 **"They wheeled me down"**: McDonald interview.

240 **"A mind like that"**: Ibid.

240 **"The home parties"**: Treaster, "Earl Tupper, the Father of Home Parties, Dies," *New York Times*, October 7, 1983.

241 **"Because the company"**: Marilyn Mennello interview.

241 **"Gary believed"**: Ponticelli interview.

242 **"For your information"**: Wilson to Tupper memorandum, July 1961, Tupper Papers.

242 **"Yeah, he was kind of neat"**: Jerry Wise interview.

242 **"He drank it away"**: Ibid.

243 **Jerry admitted that**: Ibid.

243 **"Whatever she volunteered"**: John Waugh, interview by author, Kissimmee, Florida, March 2015 (hereafter cited as John Waugh interview). Waugh worked with Jerry Wise and became a friend to Brownie through their mutual love of pottery.

244 **"Love always, Adlai"**: John Waugh interview. Details of Wise's relationship were confirmed by her son's half-sister, Clorinda Sheridan, who saw the letters.

244 **"I'm glad you had"**: Ibid.

244 **"Clay is joyous"**: Sign seen by the author during Jerry Wise interview.

245 **"It was just one of a group"**: "Tupperware Home to Be Demolished," *Orlando Sentinel*, September 16, 1989.

246 **"commitment, quality, and goals,"**: Tupperware to Wise correspondence, September 1989.

246 **"You think I ought to go out?"**: Jerry Wise interview.

246 **"I won't allow it"**: Fishman, "Is the Party Over?"

246 **"I said, 'I will not sell this"**: Ibid.

246 **"Whoever made this"**: Ibid.

247 **"Just say the company"**: Ibid.

247 **"Brownie just said"**: Jerry Wise interview.

248 **"Some folks thought"**: Don Boyett, "The Lady Who Built Tupperware," *Orlando Sentinel*, September 26, 1992.

248 **"Most of all though"**: Ibid.

EPILOGUE

250 **"There are so many"**: John Waugh interview.

252 **"In the 23 years"**: Author's correspondence with Rick Goings, April 8,

2015. (Hereafter cited as Goings correspondence). Goings is CEO of Tupperware Brands Corporation.

253 **"Initially my husband"**: Cochrane, "Tupperware Sweet Spot Shifts to Indonesia," *New York Times*, February 28, 2015.

253 **"She taught women"**: Goings correspondence.

254 **"Two have master's degrees"**: Author's conversation with Elinor Steele, vice president of Global Communications and Women's Initiatives, April 28, 2015.

255 **"Wise was so successful"**: www.Tupperware.com.

255 **"genius for people"**: Ibid.

255 **"They gave us"**: Barry, "Bang the Tupperware Drum Slowly," *Miami Herald*, February 15, 1987.

256 **"Did you get"**: Kaufman, "Appetite for Destruction," *Pitch*, February 7, 2006.

256 **"I knew we were going to catch him"**: "Victims Find Unlikely Survival Tools," Knight-Ridder Newspapers, MyrtleBeachOnline.com, September 12, 2005.

257 **"a living drama"**: Wise, "Story of Tupperware," Wise Papers.

Selected Bibliography

Block, Elsie. *My Tupperware Party Was Over and I Sat Down and Cried.* Bloomington, Ind.: Authorhouse, 2004.

Boyd, Valerie. *Wrapped in Rainbows: The Life of Zora Neale Hurston.* New York: Scribner, 2003.

Clarke, Alison J. *Tupperware: The Promise of Plastic in 1950s America.* Washington, D.C.: Smithsonian Institution Press, 1999.

Dickinson, Joy Wallace. *Orlando, City of Dreams.* Mount Pleasant, S.C.: Arcadia, 2003.

Fishman, Charles. "Is the Party Over?" *Orlando Sentinel,* March 15, 1987.

Green, Ben. *Before His Time: The Untold Story of Harry T. Moore, America's First Civil Rights Martyr.* New York: Free Press, 1999.

Halberstam, David. *The Fifties.* New York: Random House, 1996.

Hetherington, Alma. *The River of the Long Water.* Chuluota, Fla.: Mickler House, 1980.

Kwolek-Folland, Angel. *Incorporating Women: A History of Women and Business in the United States.* New York: Twayne, 1998.

Mormino, Gary. *Land of Sunshine, State of Dreams.* Gainesville: University Press of Florida, 2005.

Wise, Brownie. *Best Wishes.* Orlando: Podium, 1957.

Index

Note: Page references in *italics* refer to photos.

Bob Kealing is a four-time Emmy Award–winning journalist based in Orlando with WESH-TV. He has appeared on national television programs such as *Dateline NBC* and *CBS This Morning* and has been a guest commentator on CNN, MSNBC, NBC, and C-SPAN. He is the author of three books, and his articles have appeared in magazines and newspapers across the country.